Kant and
the Problem
of History

Kant and the Problem of History

William A. Galston

The University of Chicago
Press *Chicago and London*

WILLIAM A. GALSTON is assistant professor of
government at the University of Texas (Austin).
This is his first book.

The University of Chicago Press, Chicago 60637
The University of Chicago Press, Ltd., London

© 1975 by the University of Chicago
All rights reserved. Published 1975
Printed in the United States of America

Library of Congress Cataloging in Publication Data

Galston, William A   1946-
    Kant and the problem of history.

    Bibliography: p.
    Includes index.
    1. History—Philosophy. 2. Kant, Immanuel,
1724-1804. I. Title.
D16.9.G28   901   74-11620
ISBN 0-226-28044-6

To Arthur and Dale Galston, who will see their influence in these pages

Contents

Preface

This study was evoked by the contemporary crisis of liberal democracy. As an immediate practical matter it was important to me to strive for a fair judgment of the contending political forces. More generally, it seemed important to inquire whether what we are now enduring is merely a transitory lapse of confidence or rather the death-throes of an entire mode of political organization and way of life and, if the latter, whether the demise is stemming from uncontrollable external causes or from "internal contradictions." These and related concerns led me to the complex of problems associated with the concept of "history": problems of historical epistemology, expectation, transformation, morality; problems that seemed to me to have found their first recognizably modern expression in the historical essays of Kant. In examining Kant's historical thought I especially wanted to ask whether the concept of history was necessary or fruitful for political analysis or rather (as has often been alleged) the source of vexing theoretical conundrums and dangerous political illusions.

This study began as a dissertation at the University of Chicago. I cannot adequately express my gratitude to my committee chairman, Joseph Cropsey, for his constant devotion to my best interests. His sympathetic understanding coupled with his steadfast conception of and dedication to the highest standards of intellectual rigor left me little to desire. I only hope that I can serve my own students so well.

I must also mention Allan Bloom, now of the University of Toronto, whose vigorous teaching and deep personal concern for his students made such a profound impression on so many who studied with him at Cornell in the 1960s. He has read the manuscript of this study and offered criticisms and suggestions. To his perspicacity I have attempted to respond.

Harvey Mansfield, Jr., Nathan Tarcov, and Susan Shell all gave generously of their time in reading the manuscript with painstaking care; each contributed suggestions that opened up new avenues of thought and enabled me to correct a number of errors.

Note on Citations

In citations to Kant's works, the first reference indicates the page in the best available English translation; the second indicates the volume and page of the standard German edition of Kant's works, that of the Königliche Preussische Akademie der Wissenschaften (Berlin: Reimer, 1902-64). In the case of the *Critique of Judgment,* the paragraph number has been provided as well. The sole exception to this general procedure occurs in the case of references to the *Critique of Pure Reason,* in which the two numbers labeled A and B indicate pages in the first (1781) and second (1787) edition respectively. (The text of the *Critique of Pure Reason* in volume 3 of the Preussische Akademie edition supplies the pagination of the second edition in the margin.)

In citations to Rousseau's works, the first reference indicates the page of the translation (when available); the second, the volume and page of the *Oeuvres complètes* (Paris: Gallimard, 1959-64). The sole exception to this procedure occurs in the case of Rousseau's "Lettre à Mgr. de Beaumont," references to which will indicate the page of *Du Contrat Social* (Paris: Garnier, 1962). Citations to the editors' notes in the *Oeuvres complètes* will provide volume and page references preceded by the abbreviation *O.c.*

In citation to Hegel's works, the first reference indicates the page of the translation; the second indicates either the volume and page of the *Sämtliche Werke* edited by Hermann Glockner (Stuttgart: Frommann, 1927-40), indicated by *S.W.* prefixed to the reference, or volume 8 of the *Sämtliche Werke* edited by Georg

Lasson (Leipzig: Meiner, 1920), indicated by *L.* prefixed to the reference.

Citations to classical works will employ the book and chapter divisions and pagination of the standard editions: e.g., *Ethics* x. 7. 1177b 29.

Citations to all other works, whether primary (e.g., Hobbes, Aquinas) or scholarly, will employ "scientific" style (e.g., Kelly, 1969, p. 96). The year indicates year of publication of the edition used; the bibliography at the end of this volume provides complete facts of publication. Lower-case letters will be used in both citations and the bibliography to distinguish two or more works by an author published in the same year (e.g., Strauss, 1965a, p. 160).

Abbreviations and Translations

KANT

Judgment	*Critique of Judgment.* Translated by J. H. Bernard. Hafner Library of Classics No. 14. New York: Hafner, 1964.
Practical Reason	*Critique of Practical Reason.* Translated by Lewis White Beck. Library of Liberal Arts No. 52. Indianapolis: Bobbs-Merrill, 1956.
Pure Reason	*Critique of Pure Reason.* Translated by Norman Kemp Smith. London: Macmillan, Ltd., 1963.
Education	*Education.* Translated by Annette Churton. Ann Arbor: University of Michigan Press, 1960.
Foundations	*Foundations of the Metaphysics of Morals.* Translated by Lewis White Beck. Library of Liberal Arts No. 113. Indianapolis and New York: Bobbs-Merrill, 1959.
Justice	*Metaphysics of Morals, Part 1: The Metaphysical Elements of Justice.* Translated by John Ladd. Library of

	Liberal Arts No. 72. Indianapolis and New York: Bobbs-Merrill, 1965.
Virtue	*Metaphysics of Morals, Part 2: The Doctrine of Virtue.* Translated by Mary J. Gregor. New York and Evanston: Harper and Row, 1964.
Religion	*Religion within the Limits of Reason Alone.* Translated by Theodore M. Greene and Hoyt H. Hudson. New York and Evanston: Harper and Row, 1960.
"Conjectural Beginning"	"Conjectural Beginning of Human History." Translated by Emil Fackenheim in *On History*, edited by Lewis White Beck. Library of Liberal Arts No. 162. Indianapolis and New York: Bobbs-Merrill, 1963, pp. 53-68.
"Idea"	"Idea for a Universal History from a Cosmopolitan Point of View." Translated by Lewis White Beck in *On History,* pp. 11-26.
"An Old Question"	"An Old Question Raised Again: Is the Human Race Constantly Progressing?" Translated by Robert E. Anchor in *On History,* pp. 137-54.
Perpetual Peace	*Perpetual Peace, A Philosophical Sketch.* Translated by Lewis White Beck in *On History,* pp. 85-135.
"Theory and Practice"	"On the Common Saying: 'This may be True in Theory, but it does not Apply in Practice.' " Translated by H. B. Nisbet in *Kant's Political Writings*, edited by Hans Reiss. Cambridge: Cambridge University Press, 1971, pp. 61-92.

ROUSSEAU

| *C.S.* | *Social Contract.* Translated by Maurice |

	Cranston. Baltimore: Penguin, 1969.
Inequality	*Discourse on the Origin and Foundations of Inequality.* Translated by Roger D. and Judith R. Masters in *The First and Second Discourses,* edited by Roger D. Masters. New York: Saint Martin's Press, 1964, pp. 76–248.
Sciences and Arts	*Discourse on the Sciences and Arts.* Translated by Roger D. and Judith R. Masters in *The First and Second Discourses,* pp. 30–74.
"Beaumont"	"Lettre à Mgr. de Beaumont."
"Philopolis"	"Lettre à M. Philopolis."

HEGEL

| *Phenomenology* | *Phenomenology of Mind.* Translated by J. B. Baillie. New York: Harper and Row, 1967. |
| *Reason in History* | "Introduction" to the *Philosophy of History,* translated by Robert S. Hartman under the title of *Reason in History.* Indianapolis and New York: Bobbs-Merrill, 1953. |

Introduction

The manner of study in ancient times is distinct from that of modern times, in that the former consisted in the veritable training and perfecting of the natural consciousness. Trying its powers at each part of its life severally, and philosophizing about everything it came across, the natural consciousness transformed itself into a universality of abstract understanding that was active in every matter and in every respect. In modern times, however, the individual finds the abstract form ready made [*Phenomenology,* p. 94 (*S.W.* II : 34-35)].

Not only ... is Dasein inclined to fall back upon its world (the world in which it is) and to interpret itself in terms of that world by its reflected light, but also ... Dasein simultaneously falls prey to the tradition of which it has more or less explicitly taken hold. This tradition keeps it from providing its own guidance, whether in inquiring or in choosing.... When tradition thus becomes master, it does so in such a way that what it transmits is made so inaccessible, proximally and for the most part, that it rather becomes concealed. Tradition takes what has come down to us and delivers it over to self-evidence; it blocks our access to those primordial "sources" from which the categories and concepts handed down to us have been in part quite genuinely drawn. Indeed it makes us forget that they have had such an origin and makes us suppose that the necessity of going back to these sources is something which we need not even understand.... Consequently, ... Dasein no longer understands the most elementary conditions which would alone enable it to go back to the past in a positive manner and make it productively its own [Heidegger, 1962, pp. 42-43].

Modern thought is in all its forms, directly or indirectly, determined by the idea of progress. This idea implies that the most elementary questions can be settled once and for all so that future generations can dispense with their further discussion, but can erect on the foundations once laid an ever-growing structure. In this way the foundations are covered up. The only proof necessary to guarantee their solidity seems to be that the structure stands and grows. Since philosophy demands, however, not merely solidity so understood, but lucidity and truth, a special kind of inquiry becomes necessary whose purpose it is to keep alive the recollection, and the problem, of the foundations hidden by progress . . . a special effort is required to transform inherited knowledge into genuine knowledge by revitalizing its original discovery, and to discriminate between the genuine and the spurious elements of what claims to be inherited knowledge. This truly philosophic function is fulfilled by the history of philosophy or of science [Strauss, 1959, p. 75].

Modern history is neither a chronicle of events nor an edifying or moralizing or glorifying report of memorable deeds in the past, but the discovery and the description of man as a specifically historic being, subject to a "development" which transcends any individual life or even the life of peoples or nations. Modern history is not only—as ancient history is—an interpretation and dramatic exposition of "facts," but also an interpretation of the historic "movement" as such. It is, in this respect, the twin brother of mathematical physics. They are both the dominant powers governing our actual life, setting out the horizon of our thinking and determining the scope of our practice [Klein, 1940, p. 149].

We are accustomed to confront nature with history and we do so in consequence of a definite historical situation which arose in the sixteenth century with modern natural science . . . . Two sciences which characterized themselves as new ones gave the first philosophical expression to this distinction: the anti-Aristotelian natural science of Descartes, and Vico's anti-Cartesian *Scienza Nuova* . . . . Only Schelling and Hegel have attempted to reduce the traditional distinction between nature and history, as fixed by Descartes as well as by Vico . . . to a comprehensive notion of nature and mind respectively . . . . Hegel's conception of spirit as comprehending nature and Schelling's spiritual philosophy of nature did not become productive. We are still thinking within the framework of Descartes and Vico. To overcome the dichotomy of Descartes and Vico, it would be necessary that our attitude toward the world, the natural as well as the historical one, be transformed. So-called historicism cannot be overcome without questioning its older counterpart, modern natural science [Löwith, 1966, pp. 17-20].

Since the organization and purpose of this study may appear obscure, it would be appropriate to begin by indicating the central concerns to which it is addressed. These concerns fall into three main groups.

We begin with the *practical* or *political,* in which sphere we are confronted with two massive and familiar problems. The first is the conflict between liberalism and competing doctrines—in large measure a conflict between different conceptions of political morality and of the status of the individual. The attempt to develop a concept of history as distinguished from temporality or historiography seems to be an important element of this conflict. The second is the desire to find some vantage point for the understanding of a world seemingly undergoing increasingly rapid and complex transformations progressively less subject to the will of individuals. The attempt to define a concept of history is one way of asking about the direction or significance of these transformations, and of attempting to account for the individual's sense of domination by external forces (including, of course, his own products).

Having been led through these political phenomena to an interest in the concept of history, our problem is then to understand it. Undoubtedly simple reflection can be productive. But we cannot avoid realizing that we are the inheritors rather than devisers of this concept. It proves useful to undertake a genetic inquiry—the search for the philosophical moments at which the concept of history is most fully and explicitly elaborated. One of the most important of these moments occurs in the thought of Kant. With this discovery the genetic inquiry gives way to the *exegetical*—the task of understanding the structure and intention of Kant's doctrine of history. Exegesis need not be a historical or antiquarian exercise but rather may be a propadeutic to philosophy. No argument can be adequately discussed until it has been expressed in its clearest and most powerful form. In the case of an argument not of one's own devising that employs unfamiliar terms and modes of reasoning, the attempt to state it clearly may require a considerable effort of sympathetic understanding and reconstruction. In the present instance this task leads to the investigation of the relation between Kant's doctrine of history and his general philosophical position, of the relation between that position and the thought of certain of his predecessors, and of the adequacy of certain categories for the understanding of political theory. This investigation issues in the conclusion that Kantian historico-political thought (and modern political thought generally) in part must be understood as a meditation on and reaction to the problems posed by modern natural science. For this reason such thought cannot be fully understood through inquiries that remain entirely within the moral or political sphere.

Finally, we are confronted with the *philosophical* task of evaluating the premises and implications of Kant's doctrine of history.

The Problem of History

The problem of the historical in modern thought manifests itself in three stages: the idea of progress arising from the assumed congruence of intellectual and political advancement or, more generally, belief in the efficacy of conscious human endeavor directed toward universal enlightenment; the idea of history, a force or purpose guiding the totality of human beings toward an end that may not be evident to or intended by any single human being; and historicism—the doctrine that every human situation is circumscribed by a historical fatality that is invisible, unknowable, and arbitrary in the sense that it is not the inevitable or predictable outcome of any preceding situation. The idea of history emerged as a response to the growing realization of the ambiguous moral or political effects of enlightenment and the dubious status of the doctrine of human intellectual equality that underlay it. Historicism emerged as the supposed proofs of the directionality and rationality of the "historical process" began to seem incredible. But the claim of each successive stage to possess superior insight has not been fully accepted historically—that is to say, publicly and politically. The idea of progress was embedded in liberalism; history, in Marxism; and historicism, in doctrines of power-voluntarism or "commitment"; and each is at present a powerful and active political force. It may in fact be most revealing to view modern politics as an internecine struggle among ideological outgrowths of the modern historical consciousness.

The following study is concerned with the complex of problems, moral and theoretical, that led to the emergence of the idea of history in the thought of Kant, and with the political implications of that idea. It is necessarily incomplete, not to say fragmentary; it begins *in medias res* and cannot help looking forward and backward. A truly comprehensive account of the idea of history would require us to trace, in full concreteness, the dialectical necessity of its emergence from the idea of progress, and consequently to understand the genesis and basis of the idea of progress in, e.g., the thought of Galileo, Bacon, Hobbes, and Descartes. It would require us to lay bare the full uniqueness of historical thought taken as a whole, to confront it with nonhistorical thought.

Moreover, if the idea of history achieves its most complete expression in the thought of Hegel, we must say that it cannot be fully understood without assessing the inquiries of Herder, Burke, Schiller, Fichte, and Schelling, all of whom seem to have influenced Hegel to some degree—to say nothing of his complex relation to Christian millenarianism. I will argue, however, that Kant's view of history is very much closer to Hegel's than is commonly supposed and that it is useful to see Hegel's view as resulting from the modification of a few of the principles underlying Kant's. Since the existence of history as a separate dimension of reality or even as a category of analysis is far more problematic for Kant, he lays bare the problems and presuppositions that lead to its emergence more clearly and simply than does Hegel, for whom many of its aspects have ceased to appear questionable and are no longer objects of thematic reflection. The study of Kant enables us to achieve some clarity about the decisive premises and problematic status of the idea of history that, through Hegel, influences both Marxism and existentialism.*

This reasoning is perfectly satisfactory from the standpoint of the intellectual historian. It may be argued, however, that our interest in the idea of history must be purely historical; the idea lacks any philosophical importance, for it has been fully refuted, both in theory and in practice. Its continuing influence on political thought reduces this thought to the status of ideology, myth, or faith. To this there are three types of answers. (1) Whether true or false, the idea of history has had an enormous impact on political

---

*Kant's pivotal position is recognized in Arendt, 1968, pp. 82-85. Gerhard Krüger emphasizes this point more generally: "Kant is our oldest philosophic 'contemporary.' It is he who has 'created' the modern epoch of philosophic activity. But precisely because he was its 'creator,' we still encounter in his work doctrines with which modern thought is no longer concerned" (Krüger, 1961, p. 27; my translation).

practice. The structure of the idea explains in large measure the particular character of its influence. Moreover, the theoretical inquiry into politics now must take into account the undeniable fact that political life is capable of being transformed in this manner. (2) In the thought of Kant, the idea of history is presented as a logical consequence of scientific and moral principles a version of which we still seem intellectually constrained to accept. The question arises whether the idea of history is in fact logically entailed by these principles and, if so, whether the rejection of the Kantian idea of history is consistent with continued adherence to them (see Kelly, 1969, p. 96). (3) The idea of history continues to be a useful way of organizing and explaining certain essential aspects of modern political life.

The remainder of this introduction and chapter 1 are devoted to a discussion of these points. The final two sections of the introduction deal with the relation between the Kantian idea of history and the problems of nihilism and revolutionary idealism that presently confront us. Chapter 1 repeats and extends Kant's effort to indicate the historical phenomena that constitute our everyday life and provide evidence for regarding the idea of rational or directional history as more than an exploded error or hopeful myth.

The following chapters then attempt to define the limits within which Kant's idea of history moves and to examine its premises and implications. Chapter 2 deals with the relation between the idea of history and biblical religion. Its analysis of Kant's "Conjectural Beginning of Human History" shows that the crude view of the philosophy of history as a secularized messianic vision cannot be supported. The idea of history must be understood primarily as a concept that, arising from philosophic premises and problems, deals with questions characteristic of the Judeo-Christian rather than pagan tradition because its own principles lead it to ascribe importance to these questions and give nonbiblical answers to them. (A deeper study, outside the bounds of this work, would show that this situation can arise only on the basis of those aspects that modern philosophy and biblical religion have in common and necessarily unite them in opposition to the classical philosophic tradition. But this union is purely negative: the positive programs of the reluctant allies are fundamentally opposed.) With its status as a philosophic problem secured, the substantive inquiry into the idea of history begins. For Kant, the idea of history arises as a consequence of his doctrines of natural science and morality. These doctrines cannot be understood unless one lays bare the reasons that led Kant to believe that the division of the whole into natural science and morality is both necessary and exhaustive. Chapter 3 lays the foundation for the analysis of Kantian dualism by studying the relation of nature and freedom in the thought of Rousseau, to whom Kant alludes repeatedly in his discussion of history. Chapter 4 begins by exploring the extent to which Kantian morality can be understood as a response to the theoretical weaknesses of classical (Aristotelian) ethics. It then traces Kant's attempt to provide a theoretical foundation for Rousseau's dualism by deducing a new morality that is compatible with (indeed presupposes the validity of) Newtonian science in the entire sphere of sensed or material phenomena. The moral response to Aristotle and the theoretical response to Newton are shown to converge in a new moral orientation. Finally, it turns to the question of the relation between morality and politics—in particular, to Kant's attempt to deduce the principles of public right from morality—in order to study the status of universal and perpetual peace as the allegedly highest and morally required goal of political life and the status of history as the indispensable means for the actualization of peace. Chapter 5 analyzes Kant's systematic presentation of the philosophy of history and concludes with a brief discussion of his relation to Hegel.

In a sense, this study as a whole is intended to elucidate the basis of the astonishing interpenetration of philosophy and political practice in our time that makes it possible (indeed, necessary) to approach modern politics through an analysis of philosophy and its history.

Let me conclude this introductory survey with two remarks on procedure.

(1) The peripheral and tentative character of Kant's historical thought has frequently been noted. Correctly interpreted, this observation provides an important clue for the understanding of Kantian thought, particularly as distinguished from later historical

speculation. But too often tentativeness has been equated with lack of philosophical seriousness and rigor; since the historical essays are so unlike, e.g., the *Critique of Pure Reason* in tone and construction, it has been assumed that they are inferior to it philosophically. Thus, with a few honorable exceptions, interpreters have never confronted these essays with the rigorous analysis to which virtually every line of the *Critique of Pure Reason* has been subjected. But only on the basis of such analysis can we resolve the two philosophical questions of greatest importance: the relation between the premises and implications of Kant's historical doctrine and those of his thought as a whole; and the coherence or incoherence of his historical doctrine considered as an independent argument. I attempt to provide such an analysis, moving from an internal critique of the essays to the broader questions rather than beginning from external premises and scanning the essays for evidence of congruence with or divergence from them.

(2) It may be thought strange by some that a study of Kant's philosophy of history should include detailed examinations of Rousseau and Aristotle and fail to include an equally detailed treatment of the *Critique of Pure Reason*. There are three reasons for this, each of which can only be asserted here and must be justified by the inquiry that follows. First, this study is concerned with Kant's *significance*. Too many studies become ensnared in his terminology and in the myriad technical problems that emerge from particular arguments. These are surely worth studying, but they cannot be fully understood unless they are seen to emerge within the broader Kantian intention or project.* To understand this, it is not enough to note that Kant was a rigorous moralist, fighting against the debasement of morality to utility initiated by the English liberal tradition; for he was also opposed to premodern moral thought that did not conceive of itself as utilitarian. The study of Aristotelian morality reveals something of what is distinctive about Kant and why he felt impelled to embrace his distinctive moral views. And it is not enough to note that Kant was a dualist; we must try to understand why he concluded that dualism was the only possible beginning point for philosophy. The

---

*See the translator's "Foreword" in Kroner, 1956, pp. vii–viii.

exploration of Rousseau's ambiguous relation to dualism clarifies this, for Rousseau was the philosophic guide whose thought Kant pondered most deeply.

Second, this study is not an orthodox essay in Kant scholarship but rather an effort to understand something about modernity *through* Kant. Too often he is treated as *sui generis*; I have attempted to situate him within a tradition, not to dissolve the uniqueness of his thought into a web of borrowings from the past, but rather to reveal his uniqueness more clearly by showing what he did share with other thinkers and how he added to and transformed them. If, as I have argued below, the phenomenon of modernity can be traced to a core of shared principles, then it is necessary to ask what Kant has in common with his predecessors to whom he seems at first glance so dissimilar—if I am correct that Kant constitutes an essential moment of modernity rather than a revolt against it.

Finally, the philosophy of history arises out of the beginning point or structure of Kant's thought rather than the details—i.e., from the general conceptions of morality and natural science that he embraced and from the dualism to which these conceptions led him. To understand his philosophy of history, then, we must understand not only how Kant reasoned *from* these conceptions but also how he was led *to* them; and we cannot do this without elucidating his relation to his immediate predecessors and to the classical tradition, the revolt against which constitutes the beginning, and perhaps the essence, of modernity.

Nihilism

It is widely believed that we are living in the shadow of a grave, even unprecedented, crisis. This view cannot simply be dismissed as historical myopia or the thirst for excitement and significance, though it contains an element of both; for the apparent core of the crisis is neither military-ideological confrontation nor uncontrolled technological innovation but rather nihilism—the systematic denial of the possibility of rational choice among actions and ways of life. At present the explicit nihilism so prevalent a generation ago has been overlaid by a curious combination of sensuality and moralism; but in failing to seek coherent justification, in merely positing or asserting standards, these new attitudes reveal themselves to be within the circle of nihilism. Nihilism has not been overcome; it has merely become boring, or an obstacle to the expression of certain passions and desires. Within the discipline of political science, "value-free" research, itself based on a nihilistic premise, has come to be opposed on the grounds that its procedures are determined by implicit values that favor the maintenance of a particular political system and, more generally, that all research is essentially characterized by a value-orientation. But those maintaining this position for the most part agree with their opponents that the choice among values is irrational or arbitrary; accordingly, there has been little effort to provide a coherent foundation for the new moral orientation that underlies "committed" or "relevant" research or to demonstrate its superiority to the old.

Two arguments may be adduced against the view that nihilism constitutes a crisis. First, it may be argued that while the "crisis" is alleged to encompass the entire political community, it is in fact confined to a small group of intellectuals who are of little political importance. The character of political life is determined by the multitudes of ordinary citizens who are untheoretical and decent, whose opinions are largely formed through unmediated experience of the daily world of common sense and are only marginally affected by changes of intellectual climate. But, to begin with the obvious, political leaders need not be drawn from the ranks of ordinary citizens. They may themselves be intellectuals and in any case are almost certain to rely on the opinions of various "experts" who have been influenced by prevailing theories. Translating these opinions into actions and publicly justifying them, political leaders transmit them to the citizen-body and have a significant effect on common opinion, particularly on beliefs concerning the morally admirable and permissible. Further, in political communities in which the content of culture is not entirely determined by political decisions, there is a constant and enormous influence of "advanced" intellectual trends on the art, literature, drama, and organs of mass communication that shape popular taste.* This

---

*Kant alludes to the connection without describing the mechanism in the preface to the second edition of *Pure Reason,* p. 32, (B xxxiv): it is the duty of critical philosophy "to prevent the scandal which, sooner or later, is sure to break out among the masses, as the result of the disputes in which metaphysicians . . .

phenomenon may be particularly characteristic of our times, although Nietzsche went so far as to blame the decline of Greek civilization on Socratic philosophy, especially as mediated by the collapse of the type of drama that, in his analysis, constituted the core of Greek public life.

Second, it may be argued that "crisis" implies, not an accidental or nonessential difficulty, however widespread it may be, but rather a contradiction arising out of a system of premises the truth and internal consistency of which is seemingly not open to question. In political terms, no merely external threat, however grave, constitutes a crisis; a crisis arises only when the various goals or premises that constitute a regime prove to be mutually incompatible or collectively unsatisfactory, and there appears to be no way of transforming them. According to this argument, contemporary nihilism is important but external; it cannot be deduced from the essential premises of European thought but is merely posited, and gains plausibility only because those who believe in it act to create a body of experience or history that, inevitably, it is well suited to explain. As such, it may be compared to a mass religious delusion. This line of argument is partly valid. The nihilism that spread so rapidly after World War II claimed to be the only honest interpretation of historical experience, but it did not ask to what extent the perpetrators of the horrors and absurdities it interpreted were themselves influenced by the doctrine that everything is permissible.* Further, while it is not the case that ethics must be theistic, nihilism is necessarily atheistic. But from the beginning the death of God was asserted or "announced" rather than proved, supported only by a combination of mockery and moralism. At best the argument was circular: all otherworldliness, belief in transcendence, is moral weakness, the lack of courage to face the abyss, nothingness, or disorder by

---

inevitably become involved to the consequent perversion of their teaching. Criticism alone can sever the root of *materialism, fatalism, atheism, free-thinking, fanaticism,* and *superstition,* which can be injurious universally." See also *Foundations,* p. 21 (IV : 404–5) and Krüger, 1961, pp. 271-72.

    *On this point see Löwith, 1966, p. 10: "Nihilism as the disavowal of existing civilization was the only real belief of all truly educated people at the beginning of the twentieth century. Nihilism is not a result of the Great War but, on the contrary, its cause."

which reality is wholly characterized; but reality reveals itself as the abyss only when God is denied. Nihilism rests on two questionable premises: atheism, and the assertion that all ethics is ultimately based on belief in a revealed God. Understanding the genesis of the latter would require a separate study; I note only that the transmission of classical ethics to modern Europe through Christian theology produced an interpretation, still widely accepted today, that suggests that ethics requires some support beyond the bounds of reason alone. Historically it is of the greatest importance that the revolt against Aristotle was part of a broader polemic against medieval theology and that in the process the tension (which Thomistic theologians had done their best to overcome or obscure) between Aristotelian ethics and the teachings of Christianity was almost completely forgotten.* In short, the decisive premise of modern nihilism was provided by the Christian reinterpretation of classical ethics, an interpretation accepted by the opponents of Christianity.

It would be unwise, however, to conclude that nihilism is merely questionable assertion or bad intellectual history. To be sure, with the exposure of the arbitrary character of modern atheism has come a resurgence of serious theology. In a sense nihilism has been overcome by the very possibility of faith. Yet within philosophy the situation is more complicated. In the past generation, historical studies of the profoundest possible character have succeeded in disentangling classical ethics from its Christian-modern interpretation and exhibiting it more or less as it was understood by its originators.† As a description and analysis of the phenomena, it is subtle and reasonable. Yet more than the accumulation of habit and prejudice or the questionable confidence in the superiority of modernity prevents us from accepting it. It seems that classical ethics ultimately depends on classical physics and metaphysics, which we believe (with good reason) to have been refuted in certain decisive respects by the evident success of modern (post-Galilean) natural science. It may be argued that the priority of physics over ethics is a modern conclusion illegitimately employed in the study

---

*For the basis of these remarks see Jaffa, 1952. The Christian critique of Aristotle is well expressed in Gauthier, 1958.

†See, in particular, Jaffa, 1952; Strauss, 1964, 1965a, 1968, 1969.

of classical thought. Clearly classical thought does not proceed *more geometrico*; there is some evidence that, whatever the rank of man in the cosmos, the classics believed that human things were knowable, objects of a possible science, to a degree that physics and metaphysics were not and that the latter were therefore essentially skeptical and defensive. There are indications of a disagreement between Plato and Aristotle on this point, which moreover is the implicit or explicit theme of a number of important medieval commentaries. But whatever the classics may have thought, the striking successes of modern science, the validity of which does not depend on any external ethical or political principles, must raise serious questions whenever ethics employs concepts that are incompatible with scientific discoveries or principles.

Against this contention, it has been argued that

whatever the significance of modern natural science may be, it cannot affect our understanding of what is human in man. To understand man in the light of the whole means for modern natural science to understand man in the light of the subhuman. But in that light man as man is wholly unintelligible [Strauss, 1959, p. 38].

This argument is valid only if the structure and success of modern science rests necessarily on a claim to describe "the whole." Some interpreters of science have indeed advanced this claim; but others, chief among them Kant, have argued that science itself is intelligible or internally consistent only when it is seen as a description of an aspect or part of the whole. Let us call this part the subhuman. If "human" is to be in any way a term of distinction, it is difficult to see how a change in our view of the bounds or inner structure of the subhuman can fail to affect our understanding of what is human in man. This effect of natural science on the science of man does not presuppose a thoroughgoing materialism or reductionism.

Our view of what is human rests on a view of morality, particularly if, as Aristotle contends, morality most perfectly reflects our "composite nature," situated between beast and god and partaking of both (*Nicomachean Ethics* x. 7. 1177b 29, x. 8. 1178a 20-21; hereafter cited as *Ethics*). Aristotle asserts, in an argument that has been accepted by most subsequent inquiries into ethics, that morality is the sphere of praise and blame and that praise and blame can be assigned only to voluntary actions. The discussion of the nature of the voluntary is perhaps the most dialectical and elusive passage in the entire *Ethics;* but we can say generally that the voluntary act is characterized as that "of which the origin is in the agent himself" *(hou he arche en auto)* as distinguished from a purely external origin—compulsion or violence *(bia) (Ethics* iii. 1. 1111a 22-23). It follows that if an action, however it may appear to an outside observer or even to the agent himself, can be traced back to external compulsion over which the agent in principle has no control, it is removed from the moral sphere altogether and becomes an object of pity, envy, or indifference. The moral impact of modern science rests in large measure on its asserted ability to show that large classes of actions that appear voluntary can better be understood as complex interactions of involuntary forces. For instance, Aristotle's view of the voluntary depends crucially on the premise that the lower animals are capable of voluntary action. Modern science for the most part has never really departed from the Cartesian premise that all lower animals can be understood, so to speak, as pure externality, i.e., as lacking the dimension of inwardness that is the seat of the voluntary (Jonas, 1966, pp. 55-56; see esp. n. 9). If modern science should be correct, then according to Aristotle's own argument all human actions performed by reason of anger or desire are involuntary, a consequence that would destroy the foundation of his analysis of morality.*

It follows that we are no longer free to move within the sphere of "natural consciousness" or common sense; precisely if we begin, as Aristotle recommends, with the phenomena, with what is "first for us," we encounter a triumphant natural science that gradually enters into all disciplines and becomes the standard by which they are judged. It cannot be refuted by bemoaning its consequences, theoretical or practical. If we cannot deny its force, we must determine the sphere within which it is valid and its relation to

---

Ethics iii. 1. 1111a 24-30. The above discussion abstracts from the fact that Aristotle characterizes the violent as the contrary of the natural (see, e.g., *Physics* 215a 2, 254a 10). The way in which Aristotle distinguishes between voluntary and involuntary thus depends on a particular conception of the natural. A thorough discussion of this question would only strengthen the assertion that changes in physics cannot but affect ethics.

other areas of inquiry, for surely it makes sense to move from the more known to the less known.

On the surface this does not appear to pose any real difficulties. If classical ethics makes reference, e.g., to notions of permanence and hierarchy in nature that can no longer be supported, it must be replaced by a modern ethics that does not conflict with accepted scientific views. It may be argued that this change is not only necessary but desirable, that classical ethics supports unjust modes of political organization and fails to give adequate weight to psychological phenomena now thought to be of crucial impor- tance. However, this view is shortsighted. There are good reasons for believing that modern science calls into question, not only classical ethics, but all ethics, that science is in fact that hard core of nihilism.

Ethics is the elaboration of reasonable grounds for distinguish- ing between good and bad choices among actions. Nihilism, the denial of the possibility of ethics, can therefore arise on the basis of three different assertions: (1) that the distinction between good and bad is arbitrary and irrational; (2) that "choice" is illusory or nonexistent; (3) that, whatever the status of choice, actions are determined by causes other than choice. These are embodied in now-familiar doctrines: the distinction between facts and values, or the relativity of all values; the analysis of choice into simpler underlying natural forces whose motion can be understood with- out reference to choice; the division of all things into extension and mind, neither of which can have any influence on the other, from which follows the impotence of mind with reference to bodily action. Science at one time or another has provided grounds for the plausibility of all three doctrines through positivism, mechanistic materialism, and Cartesian dualism. Recently there have been attempts to show that these are not the foundations of or valid inferences from science but rather unwarranted, dogmatic exten- sions or interpretations and that the radical modification of Newtonian physics produced by the quantum and relativity theories requires an entirely new view. Kuhn, Collingwood, Heidegger, and others, in this respect quite properly following the lead of Kant, have emphasized the essentially projective character of science (and of thought generally); "facts" can only come to

light within a structure of categories and hypotheses elaborated in
advance and not fundamentally the outcome of the accumulation
of "data." Northrop, Wiener, and the entire discipline of cybernetics have argued that "teleological causality arises as a special
case of the [quantum] mechanical causality," i.e., that quantum
mechanics provides the theoretical basis for explaining the role of
human purpose and choice without explaining it away (Heisenberg,
1962, pp. 19-20). And, since the traditional subject-object distinction is a reformulation of the mind-body distinction, quantum
mechanics appears to overturn Cartesian dualism by showing that
observer and observed are part of one larger, mutually interacting
system and that it is impossible to consider either abstracted from
the total situation. Heidegger's thought, with its polemic against
Descartes and assertion of the indivisibility of Being-in-the-world,
seems to move toward the same conclusion (Heidegger, 1962, pp.
78-148).

The force and profundity of these efforts notwithstanding,
significant difficulties remain. (1) Kuhn's attack on scientific
positivism results in the inability to determine whether a particular
set of hypotheses or categories is truer than the set it replaces;
science becomes an infinite dialectical movement away from a
situation perceived to be unsatisfactory but toward nothing in
particular (resembling in this regard nothing so much as Hobbes's
account of the origin and purpose of civil society). But if we "have
to relinquish the notion ... that changes of [basic orientation]
carry scientists and those who learn from them closer and closer to
the truth," it becomes impossible to distinguish between scientific
changes and revolutions in artistic or literary style except on
sociological grounds that tend to blur the distinctions between
knowledge and action or belief.* Confronting the problem of
understanding and verifying abstract, mathematical hypotheses,
Werner Heisenberg argues that

the concepts of natural language, vaguely defined as they are, seem to be
more stable in the expansion of knowledge than the precise terms of

---

*Kuhn, 1969, p. 169. Kuhn attempts to respond to this charge in "Reflections
on my Critics" (Lakatos and Musgrave, 1970, pp. 231-78), but he seems to me to
concede the thrust of it. See esp. pp. 264-66.

scientific language, derived as an idealization from only limited groups of phenomena . . . the concepts of natural language are formed by the immediate connection with reality; they represent reality . . . they never lose the immediate connection with reality . . . any understanding must be based finally upon the natural language because it is only there that we can be certain to touch reality, and hence we must be skeptical about any skepticism with regard to this natural language and its essential concepts [Heisenberg, 1962, pp. 200-202].

Science must point beyond itself to the ordering and explanation of those phenomena that are in some sense given immediately. This argument is akin both to the classical view that philosophy must begin from (perhaps even return to) common sense or opinion and to the positivist notion of truth inhering in the individual immediate givens (data) rather than in categories or interpretive constructions (although Heisenberg denies that quantum mechanics is in any way positivistic) (p. 145). The issue is further complicated by Heisenberg's admission that ordinary language is structurally incapable of describing atomic reality in a noncontradictory manner, i.e., that consistency can be achieved only in mathematical formalism. It seems that modern science both requires and rejects the existence of a prescientific world through which its formal hypotheses could receive content and verification.

(2) In a brilliant critique of the Rosenblueth-Wiener-Bigelow paper "Behaviour, Purpose and Teleology," which established the foundation for the cybernetical investigation of human action, Hans Jonas has shown that the proposed uniform, monistic explanation of the alleged continuum running from subatomic particles to individual and political human behavior in fact fails to save the phenomena of purpose and choice as we know them; "the whole cybernetical doctrine of teleological behaviour is reducible to a confusion of 'serving a purpose' with 'having purpose'; and more specifically to the confusion of 'carrying out a purpose' with having purpose" (Jonas, 1966, p. 122). A portion of his argument may be summarized as follows. The cybernetical definition of purposive systems or behavior involves only the presence of receptor and effector elements, the possibility of behavior (i.e., motion) controlled by negative feedback. However, these elements (or—to use the biological analogues—perception

and motility) are necessary but not sufficient conditions for purposive behavior. In machines characterized by negative feedback, all individual parts work toward the equalization of energy levels, i.e., are governed by the law of entropy. Since this motion is obviously not purposive (or could be so considered only if all motion is purposive, in which case teleology ceases to be a term of distinction), cybernetics must contend that purpose resides in the mechanism as a system, i.e., that the machine is a meaningful whole. But consider the example of a self-guiding torpedo. If instead it is manned by a human pilot, the rest of the machinery is a mere tool, no more purposive than an ax. If the pilot leaves, the purpose is removed. The replacement of the pilot by a mechanical link that itself has no purpose cannot lead to the mysterious expansion of purpose over the whole system. The system, judged externally, behaves as if it were purposeful, but we know it is not; it *serves* a purpose but *has* no purpose. Moreover, the human pilot performs certain motions, not merely because he receives a certain sense-message and functions as a feedback mechanism, but primarily because he *wishes* to keep the torpedo on target. In Aristotelian terms, the sense-message is the efficient but not the final cause of the human motion (and, we must note, the input becomes meaningful or relevant, is able to emerge as a message or cause, only in light of a prior purpose that establishes a general structure of significance). Feedback can serve as the ground of purposive action only when it is not merely a feedback mechanism, when receptor and effector are not coupled directly but have interposed between them "will or interest or concern." Further, the particular purpose of the human pilot is linked to an overall or total purposiveness, the general structure of his desire and concern. Each individual act, however insignificant, points beyond itself. If the pilot is drugged or somehow made to behave as an automaton, the mechanism as a whole is purposive only in light of the purpose of the pilot's authority or commander. In short, the question of whether or not a given system is purposive cannot be settled merely by observing its external behavior. The very same motions in space-time may or may not be purposive, depending on whether there is a purpose that guides them. In the case of a man

performing a willed or voluntary action, the intended end constitutes the standard by which the success or failure of the action is
measured. The man differs from a machine in that the end is a
projected idea and that it (as well as the character of the means
employed) is the product not of extrinsic design but of intrinsic
choice. We can derive the notion of choice, intention, or purpose
only from introspecting the character of our own actions and giving
due weight to this immediate experience without the imposition of
any a priori theoretical prejudices as to the limits of "permissible"
objects of experience. No definition of purpose that is purely
external and abstracts from the undeniable element of human
inwardness can do full justice to the phenomena of human action
(Jonas, 1966, pp. 108–34).

Even if we suppose these difficulties to be overcome (although at
present there seems little reason to do so), i.e., if we posit a set of
categories that does violence neither to natural science nor to the
common-sense phenomena of valuation and purpose, a problem
remains that is far more fundamental and intractable. As previously noted, ethics cannot be confined to the elucidation of
rational choice; it must show how such choice can be translated
into action (i.e., bodily motion) or at least demonstrate that the
possibility of this influence of purpose on matter is not undermined by the established principles of other disciplines. In
principle, therefore, Cartesian dualism undermines the very possibility of ethics: human action, the motion of the human body, is
necessarily given over to the realm of *res extensa.* In spite of the
alteration of the subject-object distinction produced by quantum
mechanics, post-Newtonian natural science continues to be fundamentally Cartesian, as emerges very clearly in the authoritative
interpretation that Heisenberg offers. On the one hand, he speaks
critically of the nineteenth-century attempt to create a materialistic
monism. Since quantum theory establishes the necessity and
validity of "natural language," which makes use of such concepts
as mind and soul, science must concede their validity. The attempt
to explain mind as the "mirror of the material world" failed to
ask what mind must be such that this "reflection" is even
possible. All research concerning biological organisms must make

full use of modern physics and at the same time base itself "on concepts referring to those features of organic nature that are not contained in physics. . . ." There can

scarcely be any doubt that the concepts of physics, chemistry, and evolution together will not be sufficient to describe the facts [of psychology] . . . . We would never doubt that the brain acts as a physico-chemical mechanism if treated as such; but for an understanding of psychic phenomena we would start from the fact that the human mind enters as object and subject into the scientific process of psychology [Heisenberg, 1962, pp. 106, 155, 197, 200].

On the other hand, Heisenberg emphasizes that the Cartesian conception, which "excluded all tracing of corporeal phenomena back to spiritual forces" and viewed matter as "a reality of its own independent of the mind" constitutes "by far the strongest component in our present use of the word 'matter' " (p. 148). To be sure, the dualism between matter and energy or force has been overcome, and it no longer seems necessary to view matter as in principle inert or to search for external principles of motion. However, in quantum mechanics mass-energy is con-served and constitutes a closed system in the same sense as did matter in the Newtonian system (pp. 63, 71). Energy is the fundamental substance that can be transformed into all the forms we encounter; it corresponds directly to the Aristotelian concept of matter as "potentia," for it moves to actuality only "when the elementary particle is created" (p. 160). This notion of energy as pure possibility is the ground of the well-known uncertainty or indeterminacy with which quantum mechanics replaces strict determinism. But this weaker notion of causality does not make possible the view that mind enters into a causal relation with either energy or "formed" matter. Even if it is impossible to specify the event that will occur during a particular observation, the range of possible forms that energy can adopt is strictly circumscribed mathematically: "In modern quantum the-ory there can be no doubt that the elementary particles will finally . . . be mathematical forms [that] will be solutions of some eternal law of motion for matter" (pp. 71-72). The complete under-standing of the unity of matter is a genuine possibility and would mean that "the forms of matter in the sense of Aristotelian philosophy would appear as results, as solutions of a closed

mathematical scheme representing the natural laws for matter''
(p. 166). But even if "laws" or "forms" somehow imply the
activity of something like mind, it is an activity fundamentally
different from the ethical causation of human action that is neither
indeterminate nor the random actualization of one of a finite
number of mathematically equal possibilities. There are indeed
times when action diverges from intention in unpredictable ways,
but what must be explained is the nonrandom correlation
between internal purpose or choice and some event in the external
world. From the standpoint both of common opinion and of strict
science, therefore, Heisenberg admits and indeed insists that the
weak causality of quantum mechanics does not in any way explain
the very different (human, intentional) causality, the effects of
which we cannot help seeing in the external world; but since it
seems necessary to say that the human body is subject to both types
of causality, the attempt to explain human action leads to ''various
contradictions'' (p. 201). In particular, the apparently necessary
assertion that the human will moves without being moved leads
to the notion that energy is constantly being created, a consequence that modern natural science cannot accept without
uprooting its most fundamental principles, which, moreover, are
essentially equivalent for Newtonian and post-Newtonian science.
We must conclude, with Heisenberg, that quantum mechanics has
not really overcome Cartesian dualism and that the ground of the
possibility of human (moral) action and of life itself remains
radically mysterious. Heisenberg goes so far as to argue that the
Cartesian denial of "soul" to animals, its interpretation of them as
machines completely determined by material causes, is on its face
mistaken; "the older concept of soul ... in the philosophy of
Thomas Aquinas was more natural and less forced than the
Cartesian concept of the 'res cogitans,' even if we are convinced
that the laws of physics and chemistry are strictly valid in living
organisms'' (p. 80). However, the ontological foundation of
the Thomistic (= Aristotelian) view seems to have been discredited. As Heisenberg himself notes, early modern (and, a
fortiori, classical-medieval) natural science preserves the notion
that the world consists in essentially heterogeneous beings with
different "natures" and moved by different forces. But now we
"know" that it is always the same matter and ultimately the same

forces; all that can be distinguished is "the kind of connection which is primarily important in a certain phenomenon (p. 107). But if the world is merely homogeneous substance (energy) and "connection" (mathematical form), then, setting aside the mysterious character of the spontaneous actualization of form, it seems impossible to deduce or even permit the simultaneous determination of either substance or formed matter by two radically different modes of causality. The problem cannot be solved through analogy to the complementarity or simultaneous codetermination of matter by the "forms" of wave and particle, for these remain on the same causal plane: the notion of indeterminacy or potentiality in no way requires the presence of purpose or choice.

Heisenberg argues that Kant's codification of Newtonian principles as the a priori categories governing our experience is not necessarily refuted by post-Newtonian science; rather there has emerged an unanticipated polarity between the experiential and mathematical components of science, neither of which can be abandoned. Whatever the strength of this argument, which depends on the connection discussed earlier between Newtonianism and "natural language," it is Kant's enduring merit to have given natural science its due and to have perceived a genuine discontinuity between nature and mind. In a sense he restored Cartesian dualism against the dogmatic monism fostered by empiricism. But in so doing he inevitably fell heir to the Cartesian perplexity concerning human action. His clarification of the nature of moral intention and the moral primacy of intention over action could not conceal the need to show how intention can be translated into action:

... even if an unmeasurable gulf is fixed between the sensible realm of the concept of nature and the supersensible realm of the concept of freedom, so that no transition is possible from the first to the second (by means of the theoretical use of reason) [i.e., so that no scientific or materialistic explanation of mind is possible], just as if they were two different worlds of which the first could have no influence upon the second, yet the second is *meant* to have an influence upon the first. The concept of [moral] freedom is meant to actualize in the world of sense the purpose proposed by its laws, and consequently nature must be so thought that the conformity to law of its form at least harmonizes with the possibility of the purposes to be effected in it according to laws of freedom [*Judgment*, p. 12 (V: 175–76)].

There must, Kant concludes, be some ground of unity between the underlying principles of nature and those of morality; but the interpretation of nature that results from this need must be consistent with the principles of natural science. The quest for unity leads to the conception of a teleologically ordered human history. As we shall see, we must constantly be aware of the danger that what purports to be a principled solution is in fact no more than a compromise or restatement of the problem; Kant's most elaborate attempt to provide a theoretical grounding for the concept of history, the "Idea for a Universal History from a Cosmopolitan Point of View," seems to begin by positing the simultaneous influence of mechanical and teleological causation in human affairs. But at the same time we must constantly be aware that in large part "history" comes into being as an attempt to avoid the conclusion that mind (or moral purpose) is impotent to affect bodily action and that the manifold of human affairs is devoid of any purpose, which conclusion unavoidably implies that being human is comical or absurd and eventuates in nihilism.*

Revolutionary Idealism

The crucial political phenomenon of our times is the radical or revolutionary attack on the theory and practice of liberalism. We are required to confront this issue, and in good conscience our stand cannot be conditioned either by what we as citizens are

---

*This is well expressed by Delbos, 1926, pp. 269-70: "la Critique laisse mal défini le rapport de la liberté comme cause à l'impératif comme loi. Il semble que Kant ait été conduit à lier intrinsèquement la liberté et la loi dans un système de morale, précisément par la représentation qu'il s'est faite de la liberté comme fin idéalement nécessaire et par suite comme loi de l'évolution de l'humanité." This suggests the sole critique that might be made of Emil Fackenheim's excellent article, "Kant's Concept of History" (Fackenheim, 1957, pp. 381-98). Fackenheim demonstrates that "Kant's attempt to show a link between nature and morality is in inescapable conflict with his concept of morality itself" (p. 397). But he does not sufficiently emphasize that it is the nonappearance and impotence of morality as Kant strictly defines it that drives him to look for some external ground of moral efficacy. The failure of the attempt to render morality "historical"—i.e., visible and active—leads to a situation characterized by Nietzsche in the following terms: "There is a famous danger in their [i.e., German] 'inwardness': the internal substance cannot be seen from the outside, and so may one day take the opportunity of vanishing, and no one will notice its absence any more than its presence before" (Nietzsche, 1957, p. 26).

taught to believe or by the "class" interests of scholars and thinkers. Whatever some may say, few regimes have ever permitted greater freedom of inquiry and expression than the one under which we now live. But Plato was able to maintain a qualified preference for Sparta as opposed to Athens even though he knew that his own philosophic activity, which he thought to be the noblest and best of all human activities, would have been absolutely impossible in Sparta (Strauss, 1959, p. 126). Justice, after all, is thoughtful concern for the common good, and there is no assurance that some sacrifice will not be required from every man, whatever his rank or dignity. As thinkers we may deplore the limitation and politicization of all inquiry in contemporary China; but this does not settle the question of whether better alternatives are available for China or indeed whether the American regime is superior to that of China. The very existence of a class of inquirers who do not labor presupposes the presence of luxury or surplus (Aristotle *Metaphysics* 981b 23), and in addition to the practical question of whether this surplus exists at a particular time and place, it may be asked from a theoretical point of view whether this surplus is desirable, i.e., whether regimes ought to make a conscious effort to bring it into being.

Clearly the conflict between liberalism and what may loosely be called radicalism is fraught with enormous dangers. If we cannot say, with Hobbes, that strife is the worst of all evils, we may nevertheless say, with Thucydides, that it is a very terrible thing, destructive of all that decent men cherish. Our present peril is hardly novel; Aristotle's *Politics*, the first treatise of political science, indicates that potentially violent controversy is in principle coextensive and coeval with political life. It may plausibly be argued that enduring civil peace founded on widely shared opinions is rare, fragile, and precious; even if the peaceful regime falls far short of perfection, the sacrifices required to bring about sweeping changes will inevitably outweigh whatever improvements may result. It is therefore not only the duty but in the best interest of every citizen to adhere to the fundamental principles on which his regime rests. There are two objections to this argument. First, if civil peace is not the highest good, it may prevail only at the expense of higher goods; tyrannical or despotic regimes may be at peace, may even in some circumstances be required for the maintenance of peace. Perhaps repression or tyranny should be opposed by all possible means even if its overthrow requires bloody strife. Second, although all regimes are characterized by latent fundamental controversies, it is necessary in practice to distinguish between situations in which broad agreement prevails and those in which fundamental conflicts of principle have arisen. In the former case it is usually extremely unwise to contribute to the breakdown of agreement. But in the latter, the insurgent parties cannot be wished out of existence and, even if it were possible to restore the status quo ante by force, the costs of doing so might well exceed those of allowing the new balance of contending principles and interests to result in a certain degree of fundamental change.

Circumstances that are perilous for political practice may be fruitful for political theory. Whatever its merits, if the critique of liberalism has become a significant political force, we would be well advised to consider its arguments carefully. In the first place, we may learn something about the specific character of liberalism or at least about the kinds of human beings whom it leaves unsatisfied. Further, everyone of good will hopes for a restoration of harmony, but this cannot be achieved without knowing what basis for compromise exists—i.e., whether the conflict is primarily over ends or rather means (which is not to suggest that differences of opinion over acceptable means are necessarily less basic than those concerning ends). Finally, it is extremely unlikely that the critique of liberalism is completely misguided. We may be dismayed by the moralism and self-righteousness of the leaders of the critique, the violence of its tactics, and the vengeful destructiveness of the passions that it partly feeds on, partly breeds. But no doctrine is invalidated solely by the character and motives of its proponents. In all those neither blinded by partisanship nor rendered indifferent by thoughtless self-satisfaction the critique of liberalism must somehow, to some extent, strike a responsive chord. This does not mean that liberalism should be abandoned; a sober consideration of the possible alternatives and of our present situation may well lead to the conclusion that concern for the common good as well as self-interest requires us to defend it ardently. Insofar as we defend it with our minds as well as our might, we do so ultimately because of its superiority in justice. Precisely because the radical critique of liberalism reopens the

question of justice and appeals to many of the principles of justice
on which liberalism was founded, principles once explicit but in
recent times reduced to matters of unspoken and unthinking
agreement, the sincere partisan of justice will wish to understand
radicalism, for it may well deepen his awareness of the nature of
justice and the scope of what men desire from political life. What
we believe to be just serves as our guide when the possibility of
salutary change exists, as it always does to some extent.

In seeking to understand the conflict between liberalism and
radicalism, we are struck by the fact that the contending parties
make use almost exclusively of doctrines not of their own devising,
doctrines that they have inherited and of whose origin and
meaning they are largely oblivious. Without entering into debates
concerning the relation of theory and practice, superstructure and
infrastructure, we may say that the doctrines themselves exert an
important influence on political life, as much through the aspects
that have been covered over or forgotten as by the portion whose
meaning is immediately available and present to consciousness.
We must therefore undertake a genealogical or archaeological
investigation of the contending doctrines that leads to their source,
a point at which they are fully elaborated with complete awareness
of their necessary premises. In so doing we are led back to Kant.

We turn to Kant because he stands at a critical crossroad in
modern political thought. He is in an important sense the
completer of liberalism. He provides a philosophic ground for, and
codifies, the doctrine of the rights of man—the inviolable sphere
of freedom and "privacy," secured and guaranteed through
peace. He detaches these rights from their original basis in passion
and self-interested calculation and furnishes them with a kind of
sacred absoluteness and moral dignity. It has been well said that
"[a]nyone who seriously considers the basis of liberalism and
democracy will discover a moral sentiment therein that is absent in
Hobbes and Locke...but given a theoretical support by Kant"
(Hassner, 1972, p. 558). The enormous practical influence of this
moral force may be seen in such diverse phenomena as the
absolutist interpretation of the Bill of Rights and the charter of the
United Nations. Woodrow Wilson's Fourteen Points were a
faithful transcription of both the letter and spirit of Kant's

Perpetual Peace; and even statesmen of the present, presumably chastened by the experience of three major wars since the "war to end all war," hold out the prospect of a "generation of peace" and rekindle hopes that war can be set on the course of ultimate extinction. It seems that Kant has created, or at least expressed in classic form, the deepest and most abiding desires of the liberal soul.

Yet Kant also lays the foundation for the opposition to liberalism that ultimately issues in Marxism. He does so by taking the goals of liberalism more seriously than ever before. In particular, liberal thought argues that the chief aim of civil society is that peace that alone makes possible the individual's self-preservation and pursuit of private advantage. But the safety of the individual is put in jeopardy by two forms of conflict: civil strife and foreign war. It is not enough, therefore, to make provision for unity within each civil society; a consistent liberalism must espouse the aim of universal and perpetual peace. As Kant phrases it, "the problem of establishing a perfect civil constitution is dependent upon the problem of a lawful external relation among states and cannot be solved without a solution of the latter problem ("Idea," p. 18 [VIII: 24]). But while it is a task of incredible difficulty to establish a civil constitution that creates peace by balancing the conflicting aims of individuals and can "maintain itself automatically" (p. 19 [VIII: 25]), it seems impossible in principle to establish through plan or deliberate endeavor a world constitution precisely because there is no universal authority corresponding to the civil sovereign. Universal peace can only be brought about through the actions of civil societies that do not consciously strive to promote it. Kant is compelled to distinguish between the conscious intention of "individuals and even whole peoples," who actively work for their discordant aims, and the "regular movement" of the "human will in the large," which moves individuals and peoples toward peace in spite of themselves (p. 11 [VIII: 17]). This purposive movement or force is what Kant means by "history."

It is obvious that history so conceived tends to restrict the freedom and importance of the individual human will. At the risk of gross oversimplification, we may say that the universality of history, its concern for men as an aggregate or "mass," provides the

basis for Hegelian and Marxian opposition to the radical individualism of liberal theory and thus for the view that the individual is
or can be seen as a "means" toward the universal end. And, since
Kant is famous for defining morality as the uniform treatment of
men as ends and never as means alone, we must suspect that the
mode of operation of history is in Kant's own terms immoral. The
same conclusion is reached through the observation that history is
required to effect certain beneficial political changes that Kant on
strict moral grounds forbids individuals to promote. Thus, the
ends and means of Kantian politics come to stand at some tension
with its morality. To grasp the enormous theoretical and practical
implications of this difficulty, let us take a somewhat broader view.

   Modern political thought, particularly in its radical or revolutionary modes, is characterized by the extraordinary dualism
between an idealism of ends and a Machiavellianism of means; the
alleged goodness of universal ends has formed the basis for the
most appalling callousness and brutality in the course of attempts
to actualize them. To a certain extent, the problem stems from a
failure to determine whether the proposed ends are practicable or
even to inquire into their possibility, on the grounds that past
experience cannot circumscribe our hopes for the future. If our
profoundest hopes are within our power, then the failure to realize
them must be traced to avoidable human shortcomings. It is no
accident that modern revolutionary politics issues in extremes of
public self-criticism and of scapegoating. If we have not yet
attained our goals, we must redouble our efforts, for the fault lies
within ourselves or others rather than in the nature of things. If the
"others," whoever they may be, cannot be reformed and reeducated, they must be removed by whatever means necessary. More
fundamentally, the distinction between permissible and forbidden
means virtually has been obliterated. Goodness is thought to
inhere in the ends of activities (peace, equality, etc.) and not in
activities themselves; lying and killing, far from being reprehensible, are enjoined as sacred duties if the ends require them.

   It may appear that this Machiavellianism of means is opposed by
the whole of Kantian thought; after all, Kant surely teaches that
virtue inheres in the activities themselves rather than in any end or
effect. Nevertheless, he cannot help affirming that political life is

oriented toward certain ends or hopes; in fact, he clarifies these hopes and presents them with an unequaled intransigence. The difficulty is that their actualization requires means that are morally forbidden; in particular, there is an absolute prohibition against revolution even when it is directed toward the overthrow of a brutal tyranny. The disjunction between noble hopes and impermissible means appears unbridgeable (see Hassner, 1972, pp. 567–69). It is in part to resolve this difficulty that the concept of history as a cause or moving principle is elaborated. History is beyond good or evil, or rather it performs evil in order to bring about the good, without forcing men to the extremes of despair or immorality; it lifts the moral burden of political action from their shoulders. Yet, although history is an external force, it is immanent in human actions and is in a sense only the sum of them. As individual moral actors, revolutionaries are blameworthy, as agents of history, praiseworthy.

This ambiguity (or, one might say, dilemma) comes out most clearly in Kant's discussion of the French Revolution. He sees in it "an event of our time which demonstrates [the] moral tendency of the human race" ("An Old Question," p. 143 [VII: 85]). Yet it is filled with "misery and atrocities"; even though the revolutionary movement is directed toward philosophically justified ends of freedom and right, the right is "still only an Idea of which the realization is restricted to the condition of the accord of its means with the morality which the nation may not transgress; and this may not come to pass through revolution which is always unjust" (p. 146 n. [VII: 87 n.]). The moral tendency of mankind is therefore exemplified only by the "spectators" of the revolution; their passionate desire for its success is motivated by abstract principles of right rather than by any self-interest whatsoever, and they have not dirtied their hands with atrocities. Yet Kant implies that the revolutionaries themselves were "idealistic," actuated by principles of right rather than self-interest; the sole distinction between spectator and actor is that the actor commits immoral acts in the service of right. The moral tendency of the spectator manifests itself in enthusiasm for immorality, for acts that he himself as a moral man would not commit. In addition, it may be observed that the moral man does not always have the luxury of being a spectator. If he lives under a tyrannical regime, it is more than likely that some revolution will eventually seek to overthrow it. He will then be faced with the choice between lawful (i.e., moral) acts, enjoined by the tyranny, directed toward the defeat of the revolution that embodies his profoundest hopes, and the immorality of striving to realize the principles of right in a revolutionary manner.

The extraordinary tension between ends and means in Kant's political thought is exacerbated by the concept of idealistic or selfless action that he applies to the description of political life. In a sense this concept is not new: according to the classics, the distinction between the goodness of kingship and the badness of tyranny is that while the tyrant rules only with an eye to his own immediate advantage, the king is guided by the common good. Yet while classical thought had no difficulty in identifying and describing tyranny, the problem appears much more obscure, both theoretically and practically, in modern times. For present purposes we may disregard the distinction between facts and values that, if valid, obviously makes condemnation of tyranny impossible. Within the sphere of modern political thought that seeks to preserve at least a portion of those judgments that citizens cannot help making, it is much more difficult now than formerly to distinguish between self-aggrandizing acts and those directed to the common good. The root of the difficulty is the phenomenon of ideology. Each ideology claims to be universal, to embody a correct description of justice or of the best regime. This is tremendously advantageous to ambitious men, for they no longer need to possess unusual rhetorical inventiveness but can cloak themselves in ready-made ideological mantles and claim devotion to the common good. Once in power, tyrannical regimes can continue to justify repressive measures and obscure their real purposes through constant use of ideological explanations.* Yet one may wonder

*This peculiarity of modern politics was already perceived by Hegel. See *Reason in History*, p. 46 (*S.W.* XI:66): "At no time as much as in our own have such general principles and notions been advanced with so much pretentiousness. At other times history seems to present itself as a struggle of passions. In our time, however, though passions are not wanting, history exhibits partly and predominantly a struggle of justifiable ideas and partly a struggle of passions and subjective interests under the mask of such higher pretensions. These pretensions, regarded as legitimate in the name of the supposed destiny of reason, are thereby validated as absolute ends. . . ."

whether the abuse of ideology by ambition is universal or inevitable. In Kant's terms, ideologies are principles, and selfless acts are those acts in accordance with and for the sake of principles. The status of ideology rests on the existence of selfless political acts.

To explore this question, it is useful to allude briefly to the controversy between Alexandre Kojève and Leo Strauss on the nature of tyranny. Writing from an Hegelian perspective, Kojève considers the classical argument (which he labels "pagan" or "aristocratic") that the desire for tyranny stems from the desire to be honored or "recognized" by every member of one's political community (or perhaps even universally, by all men) and comments:

> It would be false to say . . . that only the "desire to be honored" and the "joy which comes from honor" makes one "endure any labor and brave any danger." The *joy* that comes from labor itself and the desire to *succeed* in an undertaking can, by themselves, prompt a man to undertake painful and dangerous labors. . . . A man can work hard, risking his life, for no other reason that to experience the joy which he always has in the execution of his plans or, what it the same thing, in the transformation of his "idea," or his "ideal," into a *reality* conditioned by his own *efforts*. . . . Thus—though it is an extreme case—a man can aspire to tyranny in the same way that a "conscientious" and "enthusiastic" workman can aspire to adequate conditions for his labor [Strauss, 1968, p. 148].

Strauss comments as follows:

> Kojève seems to think that a man may aspire to tyrannical power chiefly because he is attracted by "objective" tasks of the highest order, by tasks whose performance requires tyrannical power, and that this motive will radically transform his desire for honor or recognition. The classics denied that this is possible. They were struck by the similarity between Kojève's tyrant and the man who is more attracted to safecracking by its exciting problems than by its rewards. One cannot become a tyrant and remain a tyrant without stooping to do base things; hence, a self-respecting man will not aspire to tyrannical power. But, Kojève might object, this still does not prove that the tyrant is motivated chiefly or exclusively by a desire for honor or prestige. He may be motivated, e.g., by a misguided desire to benefit his fellow men. This defense would hold good if error in such matters were difficult to avoid. But it is easy to know that tyranny is base; we all learn as children that one must not give others bad examples and that one must not do base things for the sake of the good that may come out of them. The potential or actual tyrant does not know what every reasonably well-bred child knows, because he is blinded by passion. By what passion? The most charitable answer is that he is blinded by desire for honor or prestige [pp. 204–5].

We cannot enter fully into this controversy. However, some remarks are necessary for our purposes. In the first place, the crucial phenomenon to be explained is modern revolutionary (and post-revolutionary) tyranny. No observer can fail to be impressed by the extraordinary asceticism of many modern revolutionary leaders, their complete dedication to a "cause." To be sure, some jettison their alleged principles after attaining power; others, preserving a revolutionary shell or façade, make only those minimal changes required to perpetuate their personal authority. But in the most interesting and significant cases, authority is principally a vehicle for effecting sweeping political changes. The revolutionary is a founder but, unlike the founder of a wholly new political community, he is a usurper whose success depends on uprooting all important aspects of the *ancien régime*. The victory of the revolution over the old order usually requires brutal, even criminal means. The essential question is whether these extreme measures, resulting not infrequently in misery and death for millions, can be viewed simply as the outcome of the revolutionary leader's desire for honor or prestige, or as responses to threats against his authority. One is tempted to say that extreme measures result from a collision between cherished ends on the one hand, and the recalcitrance of nature and human will on the other, when it is believed that the ends justify any and all means. The leader is deeply convinced both that his ends are practicable and that they are the highest, best, and most needful things in the world, before which all else, even human happiness and life itself, must give way. He may be wrong on both counts. But there is surely a distinction between ambition and delusion. Delusion may arise from a moral disgust at existing institutions so strong that a man is unable to believe that imperfections are ineradicable. The worse the world is perceived to be, the less one has to lose from even a destructive and unsuccessful attempt to alter it. At his height, the revolutionary usurps the position of God; he destroys in order to create again *ex nihilo*, for any "matter" that does not receive its "form" from him might counteract the perfect justice of his intention. Yet God does not create in order to be honored, but rather from the fullness of His Being.

Second, it is not at all clear that "one must not do base things

for the sake of the good that may come out of them." In fact it
seems (as Strauss has elsewhere argued) that every act that is rightly
considered base in the course of normal political life may become
necessary, hence just, in certain extreme situations. There is,
moreover, no rule that enables us to decide whether a situation is
normal or extreme, although the decision is not arbitrary. Generally speaking, a situation is extreme when an end that the
political community cannot but cherish is in imminent danger of
destruction. It may then be ruinous to shrink fastidiously from
doing the base things that the good requires (Strauss, 1965a, pp.
160-61). But this is precisely the justification that every revolutionary regime provides: if a certain class is not deprived of
influence, expropriated, "reeducated," the efforts of the regime
to bring about justice will be frustrated. Now it may well be that
modern revolutionary thought and practice is characterized by a
blurring of the distinction between normal and extreme situations
or (what amounts to the same thing) a forgetfulness of the awe,
caution, and regret that ought to attend and restrain every breach
of ordinary morality. But if the revolution is correct in believing
that it knows what justice is and that the actualization of justice
can only be brought about by the temporary employment of
criminal means, then one is hard pressed to find grounds on which
to oppose their use; one can only regret the inscrutability of the
providence that appears to link justice and injustice so indissolubly. The critique of modern tyranny cannot simply be a critique
of means but must confront the extremity of its goals; there is
surely nothing worse than blood shed in a cause that can be known
beforehand to be either unjust or impracticable. But, to repeat,
unless the extremity of the goals, however illusory they may be,
can be shown to stem from a blameworthy desire for honor, then
(at least within the confines of the argument Strauss offers) the
baseness of the means cannot be reduced to an avoidable moral
lapse. In short, it is not clear that messianic political idealism is
simply immoral, even assuming that it is unwise.

Finally, it must be noted that the problem of idealism, of action
out of devotion to a cause and purely for the sake of a cause,
transcends the problem of tyranny or, more generally, the distinction between good and bad rulers. Kojève does not hesitate to

apply his description of the tyrant as idealistic artisan to legitimate monarchs and all "bourgeois" statesmen. Strauss transforms the discussion of tyranny into a comparison between the philosopher and the "ruler," arguing that "the political man is characterized by the concern with being loved by all human beings regardless of their quality." We must remark that this erotic possession is according to Strauss a form of blindness and that it thus becomes extremely difficult to distinguish in principle between the good ruler and the tyrant; rather, their ends are identical, they differ only as to the means. The tyrant will do anything, whereas the desires of the good ruler are counteracted by attachment to a certain quality of means. Let us call this moderating disposition "moral virtue." It can easily be shown that virtue in this classical (Aristotelian) sense is unerotic or "idealistic"; it prescribes a certain range of acts and states of character as choiceworthy for their own sake without direct reference to any desire or higher end (see below, pp. 152-59). At least on the political level, the conflict between Strauss and Kojève is not over the existence of idealism but rather over its nature and scope. Strauss comments:

What Kojève calls the pleasure deriving from doing one's work well or from realizing one's projects or one's ideals was called by the classics the pleasure deriving from virtuous or noble activity. The classical interpretation would seem to be truer to the facts. Kojève refers to the pleasure which a solitary child or a solitary painter may derive from executing his projects well. But one can easily imagine a solitary safecracker deriving pleasure from executing his project well, and without a thought of the external rewards (wealth or admiration of his competence) which he reaps. There are artists in all walks of life. It does make a difference what kind of a "job" is the source of disinterested pleasure: whether the job is criminal or innocent, whether it is mere play or serious . . . [Strauss, 1968, p. 204].

Strauss appears to agree with Kojève that a large range of activities may have in common the quality of "disinterestedness"; but he argues that the moral or hierarchical distinctions among these activities are more significant in determining their character and render the initial or apparent similarity in fact a fundamental heterogeneity. I am not convinced that Kojève would contest this point in its entirety. But the essential question concerns the status of the political criminal. It is not clear that the tyrant is lower in rank than the moderate, just, disinterested shoemaker. Nor is it self-evident that the ruler who attempts to improve his political community through a series of extreme measures is lower than the ruler who is content to sustain an unsatisfactory situation. Surely if it can be known with certainty that the unsatisfactory situation is the best possible under the circumstances, then extreme measures will be worse than useless. But it may be that this knowledge is not available. Or it may well be that in some cases there is a genuine choice between significant improvements achieved at the cost of atrocities and the maintenance of the status quo within the framework of ordinary morality. The ruler who chooses to commit atrocities has surely rejected ordinary morality, but it is not self-evident that he has been "blinded" to its demands; is it not possible that oligarchs must be destroyed so that more of the young in future generations can be raised in such circumstances as to actualize their potential for virtue? More generally, if the actualization of virtue or justice requires the employment of immoral or unjust means, can a founder or ruler not choose these means "idealistically," with a view not to honor or glory but to the good? The ruler who chooses to tolerate injustice will almost certainly be gentler; he may even be loved by many men. But is he "higher" than the idealistic criminal? And, to repeat, even in the extreme case in which the attempt to bring justice into being can be known to be impossible, the ignorance or delusion may stem from sincere, misguided abhorrence of injustice rather than the desire to be recognized and honored as the greatest founder.

The peculiar character of modern revolutionary idealism may be traced in large measure to Kant's moral and political doctrines. As we have seen, Kant is compelled to approve of revolutionary ends while abhorring revolutionary means. This is not an accidental difficulty; it will be shown later that the revolutionary ends are deduced, at least in part, from the character of Kantian morality and that they therefore possess a measure of that sacred absoluteness with which his morality is invested. The possibility of political idealism, the selfless dedication to revolutionary ends, is akin to and grounded in the selflessness of moral action. It may be said that the exalted status of political idealism in modern times and its principled obliviousness to the "subjective" desires of rulers and victims, its asceticism and its brutality, are traceable to the radical emancipation of Kantian morality from any tutelage to desire or nature, and to the assertion that morality is the highest and most divine thing in man. Whatever the difficulties of classical political thought, grounded as it was in an analysis of morality that Kant rejects, by advancing the possibility of a philosophical way of life that is both radically individualistic and higher than political life, it circumscribed or provided a horizon for politics as a whole, mitigating that total and deadly serious immersion in political action that all too often allows idealism to shade over into dangerous and fanatical delusion.

The core of the movement from idealism to fanaticism is a forgetting of the question whether actualization of noble ends is possible in given circumstances (or indeed, in any possible circumstances). This forgetting is decisively mediated by the Kantian doctrine of history. For instance, it may well appear that Kant merely posits history as a means of achieving universal peace after all the more obvious means prove ineffectual. What, one may ask, is the justification for reasoning from the goodness of peace to its possibility (let alone inevitable actualization), especially since every honest man must admit that past experience gives us no ground for hope? Kant's response is twofold. First, he denies that experience that can serve as a guide.

For whereas, so far as nature is concerned, experience supplies the rules and is the source of truth, in respect of the moral laws it is, alas, the mother of illusion! Nothing is more reprehensible than to derive the laws prescribing what *ought to be done* from what *is done,* or to impose upon them the limits by which the latter is circumscribed [*Pure Reason,* p. 313 (A 319, B 376)].

If universal peace is a strict moral command, it would follow from Kant's premise that experience is wholly irrelevant to the question of its actualization. More positively, Kant argues that since the possibility of peace can be neither proved nor disproved on the basis of experience, the possibility of peace may at least be affirmed without contradiction as a moral imperative (*Justice,* pp. 127–28 [VI: 354–55]). We may note that such arguments have proved enormously influential in discrediting the limiting or "conservative" implications of the appeal to experience and hence in decisively broadening the scope of modern utopian thought. The practical consequence has been to widen, in an unprecedented manner, the range of hopes and expectations from political life.

To grasp the novelty of Kant's procedure, it suffices to glance at the character of classical Greek utopian thought. Classical thought had formulated its view of the best political order through a rigorous purification of and deduction from aspects of past political practice and experience. As Aristotle remarked, "almost everything has been discovered already, though some of the things discovered have not been coordinated . . . (*Politics* ii. 5. 1264a 3-4). The construction of the idea of the best regime thus consisted in the thoughtful combination or rearrangement of previously known elements. Even though the total vision that emerged from this process had never come into being in any existing regime, the simultaneous occurrence of a number of unlikely but possible contingencies would make its actualization possible. The demonstrated impossibility of a given utopia would delimit or illuminate the inherent bounds of public policy, of politics itself. In Kant's view, the possibility of the emergence of political "elements" different in kind from any seen heretofore could not be ruled out on theoretical grounds. The path was thus cleared for the emergence of political "ideals" that presupposed qualitative or revolutionary alterations in the basic character of political life.

But it appears that Kant was not wholly satisfied with this reply to those skeptical of the possibility of peace and of the reality of history. We suggest that his doubt or hesitation may be traced back to the equivocal status of the domain of politics taken as a whole. If political right is coextensive with or deducible from morality, then the systematic exclusion of all experiential considerations from political right follows validly from Kant's characterization of morality as a purely a priori doctrine. But if political right necessarily refers to, and incorporates an admixture of, empirical elements, it then becomes legitimate to question the feasibility of any particular political goal on the basis of what can and has been observed. Thus, Kant comes to address himself to the problem of whether the course of human events yields us "an intimation, an historical sign" of hope; he concludes that "there must be some experience in the human race which, as an event, points to the disposition and capacity of the human race to be the cause of its own advance toward the better. . . ."*

We began by observing that Kant both completes and points beyond liberalism. The completion is achieved through morality, the transcendence through history. But history emerges or is posited as the necessary preparation for the actualization of universal peace that, as the essential premise of public right, is allegedly deduced from the demands of morality itself. The tension between liberalism and the historical aspects of Hegelian or Marxian thought might then be traceable to a contradiction within Kantian morality stemming from its genesis and inherent in the very attempt to make it applicable to politics.

* "An Old Question," pp. 142-43 (VII: 84). For a discussion of this question see below, pp. 246-49, and Hassner, 1972, pp. 571-72.

1

The Present Status of the Idea of History

If we could first know *where* we are, and *whither* we are tending, we could better judge *what* to do, and *how* to do it.

Abraham Lincoln

Introduction

It is as difficult as it is necessary to find a vantage point from which to view and weigh the succession of events. Repeatedly we see the profoundest significance attributed to occurrences or opinions that soon reveal themselves as trivial and transitory. "Crises" and "turning points" follow hard upon one another, but things do not seem to change. Our attention is dominated by a rapid and bewildering succession of issues and fads that streak brightly across the horizon and fade away. Yet we cannot allow ourselves to become complacent or wholly cynical; the past furnishes examples of genuine discontinuities and catastrophes, many of which were decisively prepared for by an accumulation of minor events whose tendency or significance was grasped only in retrospect and might have been mitigated or prevented by clearsighted, resolute acts. It is of course possible that univocal significance is spuriously attributed to these events in light of an outcome the character of which they did not in fact crucially determine; but we must nevertheless attempt to find grounds on which the meaningful and enduring can be distinguished from the trivial both theoretically and in specific instances. This requires a comprehensive description of our present situation that fully exhibits its particularity—i.e., what distinguishes it from previous (indeed, from all other possible) situations.

For some this procedure will appear invalid on its face; there is no "present situation," no "modernity," but only an endless variety of phenomena that must be understood individually. To speak of modernity is necessarily to suggest that the thoughts, beliefs, institutions, and practices that now confront us have a common core that sets them apart from those of other epochs, which possessed either a different principle of unity or no unity at all. For instance, it has always been acknowledged that differing modes of political organization created unities within the various political communities—but *partial* unities that did and always would stand opposed to one another. Regardless of time and place, democracies would create democratic men and democratic culture, aristocracies, aristocrats and aristocratic culture; the oppositions engendered by differences of *form* were fundamental. The idea of modernity implies that the political communities of our time are unified by a force more fundamental than the oppositions of formal organization.

The question of modernity is not merely theoretical. Those who doubt that the present world is a distinctive and unified phenomenon will tend to emphasize links and correspondences with the past and to believe that the various problems that confront us can be dealt with individually. They may feel concern; they will not fear a cataclysm. But those who view modernity as a unity will be led to wonder whether it is not vulnerable to attack at a few crucial points—the pillars of questionable premises and unfulfillable hopes that if undermined would bring the entire edifice crashing down. They will inquire whether the shattering events of our century are the birth pangs of a new world struggling to be born or rather a collision of modernity with unyielding nature and with itself. Within political analysis, and thought generally, the most fundamental split is between those who argue that "modernity has progressed to the point where it has visibly become a problem" (Strauss, 1959, p. 172) and those who believe that our present theoretical principles or practical wisdom are sufficient to minister to any ills we may inadvertently have generated. Until very recently, this split corresponded to the quarrel between continental and Anglo-American thought.

In considering the question of the unity of modernity, let us begin with the obvious. The idea of progress is a force that has deeply shaped the American situation and, increasingly, the world situation. For generations no statesman could publicly maintain, and perhaps none even privately believed, that the most pressing human problems were insoluble. It was thought that poverty, ignorance, disease, and war itself would ultimately be eradicated through technology and growth. If new problems were generated by this progress, they too would be solved through subsequent application of the new resources it had generated. Progress was produced, partly through human decision and effort, partly through an irresistible and directional flow of events that came to be called history. Politics consisted in a conflict between the "progressives" who worked to further the movement of history and the "reactionaries" whose opposition was ultimately fated to be vain.

The Attack on the Idea of History

It is evident that the faith in progress or history has been considerably weakened in recent times. Influential thinkers have ridiculed the doctrine of a directional historical process; and they have argued that the traditional notion of progress is radically insufficient because it stems from an incomplete awareness of the deepest human longings and needs. Progress itself has shown signs of inherent self-limitation; it might appear that specific further gains must be balanced by retrogressions in other aspects of human life. The growing uncertainty has not yet affected our political institutions and practices, which arose and grew under the influence of the idea of progress; but, clearly, the collapse of this idea as an active faith would produce incalculable changes in the world political order.

However, here as elsewhere, we are in danger of misconstruing as a long-term "trend" what may be in fact only a temporary disruption, soon to be overcome through redoubled effort and strength of purpose or momentous improvements not even the outlines of which can now be perceived. Not only is the effort to predict fraught with difficulties; it may well divert us from our more fundamental task—the attempt to understand the basis and genesis of the ideas of progress and history, as they have come to affect political practice. Our final judgment concerning the truth or falsity of these ideas will prove nothing about their fate, unless one believes that truth will necessarily embody itself in political practice—that is, unless one begins by accepting a certain version of the progressive doctrine. But at least we cannot help believing that these ideas are unlikely to be completely erroneous or merely self-fulfilling prophecies; their enormous impact on political practice reflects an analysis of political possibilities that cannot be lightly dismissed.

We must begin, however, from what is perhaps the crucial political phenomenon of our times—the growing disjunction between the most powerful ideologies and the most advanced scientific or philosophical belief, which has tended to deprive these ideologies of their original scientific claims and to reduce them to the status of faith or myth. In particular, philosophy of history, considered as the attempt to discover meaning, an order, or a unifying principle in the sequence of human deeds, seems to be thoroughly discredited. To the extent that it constitutes a theodicy, it is rendered unnecessary or refuted by atheism, or even by the rigorous separation of philosophy and faith. The belief in the inexorable movement from worse to better has been undermined by the distinction between facts and values and by the intellectual and moral reaction to shattering political events of this century. Confidence in science or technology as the vehicle of progress has been superseded by the conviction that it is at best instrumental, serving an invariant matrix of passions and desires, or by the fear that it has emancipated the basest and most dangerous of them. A sober observer can speak of the "impossibility . . . of imposing on history a reasoned order or of drawing out the working of God . . ." and flatly state that "to the critical mind, neither a providential design nor a natural law of progressive development is discernible in the tragic human comedy of all times" (Löwith, 1962, p. v). It is argued that the idea of reason in history was naïve, unhistorical, and inauthentic—a last desperate effort to create order and meaning, to shield Western man from the nihilistic consequences of his progressive destruction of the Christian and philosophic traditions

—and that this evasion is now forbidden by our superior clarity, honesty, and courage (see Nietzsche, 1964, p. 308).

Yet it would be unwise to dismiss without investigation the philosophy of history or join the popular revolt against the idea of progress. One may well wonder whether contemporary atheism is more than a prejudice, or at best a conclusion drawn from dubious premises. In addition, it is possible to argue that the philosophy of history arises or becomes necessary on the basis of purely secular philosophic problems. The fact-value distinction presupposes that the definition of "fact" has been conclusively elucidated or that it is intuitively clear. The bloody wars and tyrannies of our century do not render all optimism impossible; for the philosophy of history is distinguished from the doctrine of the Enlightenment precisely by the teaching that war and misery are the vehicles of the progressive realization of the good. For this reason science cannot be discredited by the (rather belated) discovery that it renders warfare more deadly and destroys the desirable as well as ugly aspects of prescientific or primitive existence. Finally, it is not self-evident that the sequence of human acts is patternless or chaotic. For instance, it might be argued that modern politics is on a global scale progressively dominated by the doctrines of universal freedom and equality, to the exclusion of all other principles of legitimacy or right, and that the ultimate consequence or meaning of all contemporary political practice, whatever its conscious intention, can only be understood in light of the progress of these ideas.

In an influential book written to justify interest in the philosophy of history to an audience of dubious British positivists, W. H. Walsh argues that the term "philosophy of history" is ambiguous because the term "history" is ambiguous. "History" covers "(a) the totality of past human actions, and (b) the narrative or account we construct of them now." Philosophy of history, then, can concern itself either with "the actual course of historical events" or with "the processes of historical thinking." The former is a "speculative," the latter a "critical," philosophy of history. This distinction may be clarified by noting a similar ambiguity in the relation of philosophy to scientific inquiry. "Philosophy of nature" is concerned "to study the actual course of natural events, with a view to

the construction of a cosmology or account of nature as a whole.''
"Philosophy of science," on the other hand, consists in "reflection
on the whole process of scientific thinking [and] examination of the
basic concepts used by scientists...." These distinctions show that
the rejection of a "speculative" philosophy of history, the attempt
to find pattern, direction, or meaning in the overall course of
human events, does not entail the rejection of the more modest
"critical" endeavor (W. H. Walsh, 1966, pp. 14-15).

Walsh's conclusion and the distinction that underlies it rest on
the assumption that there exists a form of inquiry into thought or
language that does not itself rest on "speculative" or metaphysical
principles and is not directed toward obtaining them. He clearly
implies that contemporary philosophy of science is an example of
such nonmetaphysical inquiry. But this is most questionable. There
would seem to be only two possibilities: either philosophy of science
is descriptive, i.e., a set of inductive generalizations from the
behavior exhibited by practicing scientists; or it is an attempt to
prescribe a priori a set of principles or procedures that scientists
ought to follow and that alone would guarantee the validity of their
findings. If the former is the case, the philosophy of science would
have to face the fact that the scientific behavior it describes reflects
the seventeenth-century revolt against teleological physics, a revolt
that until the present has never been repudiated but only deepened
and itself rests on speculative or metaphysical principles. But if
the latter is the case (if philosophy of science is "prescriptive"), then
once again there are two possibilities: either it is simply equivalent
to formal logic, or it is distinguished from it by the presence of
substantive principles that at the very least are intended to
characterize the relation between the "logical" and the "empirical." In the first case, it is possible to ask whether logic itself does
not rest on certain metaphysical presuppositions (a question asked
in various ways by thinkers such as Hegel and Heidegger). Even if
this were determined not to be the case, the identification of the
philosophy of science with formal logic would mean either (a) that
the philosophy of history = philosophy of science = logic or (b)
that philosophy of history makes use of substantive principles in a
way that philosophy of science does not. Point (a) is not absurd, but
Walsh rejects it. He argues that since scientific and historical inquiry
are directed toward different *domains*—nature on the one hand,

human action on the other—the inquiries differ in character in ways
that reflection on them (philosophy of science and of history)
necessarily reflects. This argument leads inexorably to the rejection
of (b) as well, for to the extent that the philosophy of science reflects
the character of its particular domain it departs from formal logic,
strictly understood. We are led then to the second possibility, that
philosophy of science (and, a fortiori, philosophy of history) is
distinguished from logic by the presence of substantive principles.
Ex hypothesi, these principles are not inductive or empirical
generalizations (though they may have been suggested by certain
observations). At the very least, then, they must be a priori
principles of the form or possibility of experience, i.e., must belong
to what Kant calls "transcendental" as opposed to formal logic. But
if this is the case, it becomes very hard to argue that "philosophy of
science" is distinguished from "philosophy of nature" by the
absence of metaphysics.

That Walsh's distinction necessarily breaks down can be shown
even more directly. (1) Walsh's argument for the existence of the
philosophy of history rests on the assumed distinction between the
natural and the human. History is "the past of human beings" or
the totality of "human experiences and actions." The historian "is
not concerned, at any point of his work, with nature for its own
sake; only with nature as a background to human activities" (p. 30;
see also p. 65). But the distinction between the natural and the
human rests on substantive metaphysical principles. For many
scientists, and in particular the more ardent materialists, the
distinction is purely provisional, to be dissolved eventually by
satisfactory brain models or computer simulations of human mental
activity.

(2) Walsh emphasizes that "critical" philosophy of history must
concern itself with the problem of *explanation*: since historical
inquiry aims not at collecting "facts" but rather at creating an
intelligible or significant picture, the philosophic examination of
that inquiry must ask about the nature of historical explanation,
that is, about what qualifies as a "cause" or as an answer to the
question "Why?" But there are many different doctrines of causality, the decision among which is necessarily substantive or metaphysical. The decision cannot be made by looking at the characteristics of historical inquiry but, as Walsh makes clear, requires investi-

gation of the field of action itself, i.e., the domain of supposedly "speculative" philosophy of history. For instance, Walsh argues that the problem of historical explanation necessarily leads to that of human nature. The historian's knowledge of human nature, "the characteristic responses human beings make to the various challenges set them in the course of their lives, whether by the natural conditions in which they live or by their fellow human beings," is the "fundamental set of judgments on which all his thinking rests." It is "in the light of his conception of human nature that the historian must finally decide both what to accept as fact and how to understand what he does accept. What he takes to be credible depends on what he conceives to be humanly possible.... The science of human nature is thus the discipline which is basic for every branch of history"(p. 65). But, Walsh concedes, the implied assumption that human nature remains unchanged through time is not easy to demonstrate. "Speculative" philosophy of history may be described as the attempt to preserve the philosophical character of historical inquiry within the context created by the conclusion that human nature is changeable—a conclusion that Walsh admits is possible. In short, speculative and critical philosophy of history would seem to be, not different species of inquiry, but rather different answers to the same sorts of questions. The fact that "critical" philosophy of history does not discuss the meaning or purpose of human events taken as a whole does not mean that it is indifferent to this issue; rather, the decision that it is possible to proceed without reference to it has definite substantive consequences for every "epistemological" issue to which critical philosophy of history subsequently turns its attention. Conversely, "speculative" philosophy of history argues that the demand that human events be described as "intelligible" (a demand conceded to be reasonable by the critical camp) necessarily leads to questions about the meaning or purpose of human events taken as a whole—i.e., that "intelligibility" has a moral or cosmological dimension or that at the very least the question "What is intelligibility?" is inherently metaphysical.

At best, these arguments can make us aware of a *question*. Let us return to the surface and proceed more systematically.

The Defense of the Idea of History*

The Case for History

We wish, in the first instance, to view the political things freshly, clearly, and without mediation, not to act or choose, but to understand. Yet we can hardly begin without becoming aware that our vision is clouded and restricted by our opinions—by hopes and expectations, by notions of justice, by implicit answers to the question "What is the political?" This is not a new difficulty. The political thought of Plato may be said to have taken as its starting point the omnipresence of opinion and the difficulties of transcending it in even a qualified way. Platonic thought therefore begins by attempting to compare and understand the various opinions concerning political things.

If we begin in the same manner, we discover that the opinions we encounter in ourselves and in others derive for the most part from organized systems of political thought—e.g., liberalism, communism, anarchism—which we have come to call ideologies. Ideologies characteristically serve as the core of mass political movements or of regimes; at the same time, they claim to be rational or scientific, to constitute a comprehensive analysis of the whole of politics. Each ideology originates in the doctrines of one or more outstanding political thinkers. But when we compare the ideologies to the original doctrines, we are struck, not only by the dogmatizing and trivialization that occurs, but also by the fact that the doctrines attempt to resolve profound difficulties whose very existence is subsequently forgotten or obscured. To understand our everyday opinions, we are compelled to return to their source, i.e., to study their genealogy.

In doing so, however, we are in danger of taking for granted what is most remarkable—the enormous impact of political philosophy on the formation of opinion. In fact, the existence and force of ideologies seems perfectly natural to us, and we can hardly imagine a world that lacks this thorough interpenetration of systematic

---

*It should be made clear that I do not wholly subscribe to the arguments that follow. Rather, I am attempting to construct the strongest possible *case* for taking "history" seriously as a descriptive category.

thought and popular opinion. But if we consider the political philosophy of classical antiquity, we discover that it is never transformed into ideology.* The phenomenon (and concept) of ideology, far from being coeval with politics, emerges historically, and its significance and purpose can only be understood through historical inquiries. Further, classical thought does not speak of ideology or appear to conceive of its possibility. It seems that the passage of time has unfolded a wholly new political phenomenon, and therefore that the content of political thought, and politics itself, is intrinsically historical.

This analysis is misleading insofar as it assumes that ideology is the only means by which political thought achieves a practical effect. The most superficial glance at the origins of political philosophy in classical Greece exposes this error. From the very beginning it was apparent that political philosophy was not related to politics in the way that, for instance, astronomy was related to celestial bodies. Although Socratic thought proceeded in private conversation, it could not avoid having political consequences, whether intended or not. Almost its first effect was to weaken the authority of previously existing sources of opinion. Further, it became a new source of opinion, particularly when transformed into extreme skepticism or dogmatism, or when affecting those with the intellectual but not the moral prerequisites for profiting from it. Not only did political philosophy investigate political problems; it was itself a political problem. The practice of politics was fundamentally transformed by the emergence of political philosophy, which both brought into being a crucial political phenomenon and claimed to supply a basis for transcending the entire political domain; since the time of Socrates it has been clear that philosophy is in its intention universal and incompatible with restriction by any kind of regime.

For these and other reasons the relation between political philosophy and the political order was at first controversial; the suppression or destruction of philosophy appeared to some public-

*Even if Nietzsche's questionable assertion that Christianity is vulgarized Platonism were to be accepted, the fact remains that ideology claims to be purely rational or philosophic whereas Christianity originally claims to be pure faith and to stand in opposition to all philosophy.

spirited men necessary to preserve the integrity and authority of the political order. The emergence of philosophy, far from marking the completion or even the progress of political life, was viewed by them as a corruption or decline. In defending itself before the political tribunal, political philosophy emphasized the respects in which it supported and improved existing political practice and sought to obscure those aspects that challenged or transcended practice. But this defense was far from completely successful, as illustrated by the fate of Socrates, the flight of Aristotle from Athens, and the protests of Cato the Elder against the introduction of Greek philosophy into Rome.

More recently, however, political communities ceased to fear philosophy, came to think it beneficial and to believe its claim to universality to be fully compatible with the community's particularity. Philosophy ceased to be marginal and became central to the political order. It did not thereby lose its universality. Rather, a transpolitical force was placed within politics—a force the motion of which is largely self-generated and the direction of motion self-determined. In accepting philosophy, political communities were compelled to accept the autonomy of its motion. As is well known, this new relation between philosophy and politics was made possible by the great transformation of philosophy into "natural philosophy" or science associated with the names of Galileo, Bacon, Hobbes, and Descartes.

As a result of these and related developments, the relation between political thought and political practice in our times has ceased to be viewed as problematic. We do not wonder at the enormous effect of Locke and Marx on our political institutions; if we oppose one ideology as false, dangerous, or immoral, it is usually on the basis of another ideology. The interpenetration of philosophy and politics has not gone unquestioned, as evidenced by the passionate assertions of Rousseau and Nietzsche that politics is thereby corrupted. Yet significantly, the thought of these two men was itself transformed into enormously influential ideologies. Nietzsche's fate is particularly striking. He attempted to reestablish the legitimacy of aristocratic rule, the dominance of the few extraordinary men, in the face of what he saw as a leveling and dehumanizing democratization of political life. But his thought prepared the way for the ideology of a political movement that was every bit as "mass" or "popular" as those it opposed. We are compelled to wonder whether an aristocratic ideology is possible, whether, once widely promulgated, there is not an inevitable contradiction between the intention of aristocratic thought and its fate.

If we look more closely, we realize that the impact of Rousseau and Nietzsche on political practice and opinion was not accidental, even if the character of that impact was somewhat unintended. Both men intended to revolutionize politics by establishing new standards for judging the sickness or health of political life. They agreed, then, with their adversaries that political philosophy can and must have a public, political role; if erroneous or debased philosophy has corrupted political life, it is the task of clear-sighted and noble philosophy to purify it. On this basis, it remains a question whether Rousseau and Nietzsche would have chosen to proceed in this public and polemical manner if they had not been confronted with the ravages wrought by previous public thought. But, at the very least, their procedure implies that thought can only be overcome by thought, that the transformation of political life through thought brings about a novel and perhaps irreversible historical situation. If anything, they have strengthened the opinion that thought should serve as a public guide to action and that the tension between philosophy and practice that existed in former times, far from being intrinsic, was the product of the particular inferiorities of both, which now have been overcome. This opinion underlies all ideologies and all political communities organized in accordance with them; we must at least consider the possibility that it is the horizon within which all modern politics moves, a principle that gives modern political communities a kinship more fundamental than the irreconcilable differences that divide them.

We have been repeatedly compelled to speak of "modern politics" and of "historical situations." Let us summarize the respects in which ideology necessarily leads us to consider historical phenomena. (1) The critique of our common opinions reveals their source, not in unmediated reactions to political affairs, but in the doctrines of political philosophers. Since these opinions are frag-

mentary decay-products of unified systems of thought whose
genesis has been covered over, we are compelled to engage in
genealogical studies to recover their full significance. (2) Ideology
seems to have contributed to a massive transformation of politics
that makes it meaningful to talk of "modern" politics. It is a new
and unforeseen political phenomenon that demonstrates the
essentially mutable or historical character of political things. (3)
Each ideology claims to be a fundamental forward movement that
lays the basis for genuine political progress. It is the discovery of
the principles of true public right—of the just distribution of
property, offices, and honors and of the real ends of politics. It can
be promulgated to and understood by all men, who have thereby
been improved to the extent that they are freed from the
exploitation that ignorance permits. Finally, since the ordering of
political society is determined by men's beliefs or "consciousness,"
not only is the transformation of society through ideology possible,
but society will necessarily come to reflect the accuracy of the
analysis embodied in ideology. Society can and will progress to the
point of becoming "rational." (4) The study of ideology makes us
aware of its historical emergence, and therewith of the distinction
between the general category of political belief and ideology, a
particular instance of it. Ideology, far from being coeval with
political life, is a novel phenomenon with specific and questionable premises. The difficulty of imagining nonideological politics
reveals that ideology is one of the invisible walls circumscribing our
particular historical situation.

    The existence of ideology suggests that political science must
concern itself with great movements or changes, with what has
come to be called history. A brief consideration of political science
as a discipline supports this conclusion. Political science must, in
the first place, seek to enumerate, describe, and classify the various
forms of government. But governments are to a certain extent the
product of human plan, desire, and imagination. The possibility
exists that human endeavor can produce new governments radically
different from all preceding forms, in the same way that new
modes of poetry come into being. An enumeration of regimes is
either purely inductive and therefore provisional, or it must seek to
prove that it is exhaustive. Any such proof must be based on the

isolation of a limited number of general principles or variables asserted to be of highest importance in determining the character of regimes, from the permutation of which the forms of all regimes may be deduced. But the important variables appear to change through time in number, character, and relative rank.

Second, political science must concern itself with the human and material preconditions or "givens" that circumscribe in each instance the alternatives of the political planner. But these are subject to change or human manipulation; our wealth, power, and control over the natural world increase steadily and seemingly limitlessly. Our forefathers could hardly dream of our feats, and we can as little imagine the achievements of those who will come after us.

Finally, political science is inescapably practical; at the very least it describes and seeks to provide guidance for political decisions or statesmanship. Such decisions are, to the extent that they are rational, the product of deliberation; and, as Aristotle demonstrates, we do not deliberate about matters that are outside our powers or impossible to change (*Ethics* vi. 4. 1140a 32-34). Political science must then attempt to determine the limits of the possible, to provide the standard whereby the sober reformer can be distinguished from the conservative for whom the possible is circumscribed by the past and from the utopian for whom everything is possible. But although in particular situations the possible may be roughly perceived, it seems extraordinarily difficult to establish general principles; our past experience seems to show the frequent emergence of the "impossible," and we have no right to assume that the same process will not be repeated indefinitely. In this sense our history seems to favor the utopian over the conservative.

For these reasons the status of political science seems analogous to that of biology: it can assume neither that the species with which it deals are eternal nor that all possible species (and in particular the highest possible) are presently in existence, or even imaginable. Biology responded to this problem in two ways: by searching for principles or modes of existence that all species share, an underlying and persisting homogeneity in light of which the apparent diversity of the existing species can be understood or even

deduced; and by seeking laws or rational principles regulating the
temporal emergence and evolution of the species.

Similarly, it might be argued, political science ought to proceed
along the first path, i.e., turn away from the transitory and
epiphenomenal forms of government to the study of the abiding
unit of all politics—the individual human being. "Human nature"
provides the horizon within which all political activity moves.

But, even setting aside the problem of whether human beings
can be fully understood as prepolitical "individuals," the question
necessarily arises whether the notion of a permanent nature or
essence of man is not dogmatic or, at the very least, an unwarranted
absolutization of necessarily limited experience. Man's beliefs, it
may be argued, are decisively shaped by his education, his desires
by his expectations; if he is "creative," he creates not only artifacts
and effects in the external world, but also himself. In particular,
this line of argument suggests, the assertion that man is unalter-
ably greedy, fearful, and selfish is grounded on the observation of
a transitory and extraordinary condition; or, far from being scientific, it is the basis of a program that has brought into being political
institutions that make men selfish, becoming thereby the sole
ground of its own verification. We have no right to assume that
revolutions will not issue in "revolutionary consciousness," the
"new man" who is fully devoted to the common good.

If it were the case that political science could not safely employ
any particular concept of human nature as a premise, it would, it
seems, be compelled to follow the second path, i.e., to attempt to
discover principles governing the transition from one form of
government and human consciousness to the next. Within the
horizon of this task, the series of transitions that constitutes human
history would cease to be merely an epiphenomenal sequence of
events and would become rather the arena in which the various
possibilities of human self-transformation are successively actualized. Political science would seek order in history in the attempt
to justify its claim to be a science and because history would hold
out the possibility of revealing the most important human phenomena.

"History" is an attempt to find order and meaning in sequences
of events that otherwise appear chaotic. It is a sort of force or cause

distinguished from the purposeful deeds of individual human
actors; it reflects the belief that the human world, the realm of
"common sense," cannot be fully comprehended through an
analysis of human intentions. Evidence for this belief arises in part
from the organization of political life into giant nation-states that
exceed the comprehension of any individual. The life of the
individual is largely determined by men who are fellow-citizens
and yet complete strangers. The sense of individual efficacy, of an
immediate relation between intention and political effect, is lost
for citizens both as ruled and as rulers. Every act is mediated,
filtered, opposed; if it happens to achieve its end, it is with the
momentary collaboration of thousands or millions of others whose
temporary agreement vanishes as quickly and mysteriously as it
arises. The actions of a town meeting or small assembly can be
encompassed and comprehended by an educated observer in a
way that the acts of a nation-state cannot. Yet the town meeting
lacks power over the full range of political concerns; it is both
affected by and subordinate to the larger political community. Its
intelligibility depends largely on accepting the effects of the larger
community as unquestioned premises of action. But these effects
change over time; they form a sequence. The subordination of the
intelligible political part to the unintelligible political whole is
perceived as submission to fate—over time, as submission to
history. But men believe that they ought to control their political
destiny, if not fully, at least to a greater extent; the alternative to
submission is a revolt that, when ineffectual, eventuates in blind
anger. Anger may be viewed as a force that leads men to treat other
men as though they were objects, or objects as though they were
men. The idea of history unites these tendencies. Fellow-citizens,
who are yet strangers, are objectified as the They, then Other,
finally as fate or history perceived as a wholly alien and external
force; the revolt against history, the general constraining conditions
of life, is then translated back into a hatred of men, but
abstractly—the "oppressors," the "Establishment," the Jews.

    The sense of domination by the alien or external is exacerbated
by the development of politics into world politics and the
accompanying disruption of the relation between foreign and
domestic policy. There is at present no significant event within a

political community that is not immediately perceived, analyzed, and used as a basis for action by all other communities (see Strauss, 1971, p. 1). Although most citizens are strangers in large communities, there is a tenuous bond uniting them—the presumed adherence to the fundamental principles or beliefs constituting the community, and the implicit conviction (whether well founded or not) that there does exist a public interest or common good that is distinguished from the mere sum of the desires of individual citizens. Relations among nations do not possess even this fragile unity. There is no agreement on fundamental principles, no all-encompassing community of which nations are members. Nations are more or less closed with respect to one another; it is to their advantage to obscure their acts, and the intentions and reflections that underlie them. If internal policy must be evaluated in light of its effect on external policy, it is subjected to a domain that is necessarily strange, obscure, and disordered, uncontrolled not only by citizens but by nations. Yet, over time, changes occur in world politics that are nonrandom, even if unintended by any single nation.

Moreover, domestic policy is more essential to the very idea of political community than is foreign policy. It is possible at least to conceive of a community so isolated that it has relations with no other community; even in such a case, the essential problems of public policy would retain their full urgency, complexity, and controversial character. The emphasis on foreign policy, its partial absorption of domestic policy, constitutes a movement from the politically essential, the realm at least partially subject to order and principle, to the accidental. This assertion is not contradicted by the fact that the conduct of foreign policy is frequently a nation's most urgent task.

To be sure, domestic policy must frequently minister to problems of mere life, of preservation, which may be forced upon it—natural catastrophes or insurrections by a discontented few. But it is never wholly unconcerned with the problems of living well, which transcend, at least potentially, the realm of the purely bodily and are at least partially subject to considerations of principle. Foreign policy is almost exclusively concerned with war and the avoidance of war. It deals with force, the irrational and unexpected, and all too often is compelled to subordinate the principled to the necessary, for there is no limit to the ugly means whose use can be legitimated by a sufficiently unscrupulous and determined enemy (see Strauss, 1965a, p. 160). It compels us to harm those who do not deserve to be harmed, men whose only "fault" is membership in a political community that momentarily happens to oppose ours. Far more than domestic policy, foreign policy is essentially unjust. It thereby contributes both to the idea of fate or history as an alien force that estranges us from our deepest desires by dividing the world into warring communities, and to the desire to find within history, the sequence of crimes and wars, the explanation or justification for a condition that appears so needlessly evil.

Thus, the most striking features of modern life combine to suggest the existence of a previously unknown force, which has come to be called history. But the movement from one "historical situation" to the next remains mysterious. We turn to a consideration of the evidence that this movement is ordered or rational.

The Case for Rational History

Every regime must attempt to provide for national defense, the crucial requirements of which are (as they have always been) courage, weaponry, and skill. In our times, the relation or balance among these has been radically altered by the progress of military technology. Napoleon could still contend that "the moral is to the material as four is to one"; but now no technologically primitive nation, whatever its size, can hope to withstand an advanced nation unless it has comparably advanced allies or its superior adversary wills not to use its weaponry to the hilt. Ultimately, a nation that wishes to act independently, or even to be relatively secure, must undertake to develop weapons comparable in number and advancement to those of the strongest power on earth.

But the technology of weaponry is radically progressive; the weapons of ten years ago have been replaced by ones of greater power, accuracy, and specificity, and there is every reason to believe that this process will be repeated in coming decades. Moreover, it appears impossible to halt the process. No great power can cease to develop new weapons without risking subjuga-

tion or annihilation; in fact, no international agreement would be
viable in the long run if even one nation of adequate resources and
immoderate ambition refused to participate.

Nations do not necessarily like or choose military technology; it is
in a sense an alien force that imposes itself upon them.* It affects
every aspect of national life: the allocation of resources, the
structure of education, the organization of economic life, and the
practice of politics itself. It serves all modern regimes equally; it is
incompatible only with regimes that prize simplicity or the
ancestral.

Technology ultimately depends on science, "pure" research
that is not initially directed to a particular practical end; technology
is progressive because science is progressive. Its insights are cumulative because the first or most primary questions have been settled;
it is not necessary continually to return to the origins; a discovery
that is the outcome of decades of thought and research is fully
comprehensible even to the latecomer who does not concern
himself with its genesis. But science is dependent on nature; it
claims to discover a substratum that is preexisting, at least partially
independent of fantasy, projection, imagination, or "conceptual
frameworks." The precise direction or content of its forward movement cannot be fully known in advance. We may therefore
confidently expect the weapons of the future to be more powerful
than, even different in kind from, those of the present; but we
cannot know what they will be, what further perturbations or
revolutions they will produce in political life.

If the centrality of technology is an essential feature of
"modernity," and if the core of technology is science, then the
self-transformation of science is an important ground of the
changes that modernity has undergone and will undergo. It would
follow that changes cannot be understood as purely random or
particular but must to an extent be viewed as reflections of a
process that is ordered and rational. The problems of politics are
"historical" insofar as they are subject to this process. The
understanding of "whither we are tending" rests on the unity of
the apparently chaotic events befalling us—that is, on "history"

*For an exhaustive survey of the literature on this question see Winner, 1973.

viewed not as sequential randomness or accident but as a domain the partial intelligibility of which stems from a moving force that both recapitulates the rationality of the progressive comprehension of nature and mirrors the discontinuity between ignorance and knowledge.

In addition, modern politics is characterized by the progressive sway of the belief in freedom and equality. Monarchy and aristocracy have become completely illegitimate; the benevolent rule of a part for the sake of all is not permissible. Forms of government or authority vary, but all claim to be "democratic"; the few exceptions are visibly doomed. "Natural" inequality is dismissed as either nonnatural—a product of environment and conditioning—or politically and morally irrelevant. Freedom and equality expand extensively and intensively: no portion of the globe can long remain unaffected by them, and they continually deepen in meaning.* A government can exclude them only by ruthlessly isolating itself from the rest of the world; this increases their attractiveness and may no longer even be possible. In nations that already embody them in fundamental law, it becomes clear that they constitute a moving force that breaks the shackles of custom and expediency. The young, the poor, the "oppressed," the deviant and rebellious, all make claims on the basis of freedom and equality that can no longer be denied on the basis of any publicly defensible principle. Both the deepening and the actualization of the ideas of freedom and equality constitute a progressive and rational development of their original principles. To the extent that they constitute the horizon within which modern politics must operate and which it cannot challenge, politics is in the grip of the historical.

Finally, modern politics is increasingly dominated by the desire for material comfort and well being. This "revolution of rising expectations" is so obvious as to have become a commonplace. In part it reflects the belief in equality: extremes of wealth and poverty have become indefensible, for not even moral and intellectual distinctions among men are relevant to the distribution of

---

*This thesis is hardly novel, as every reader of Tocqueville will recognize. (See *Democracy in America,* "Introductory Chapter.") Philosophy of history may be viewed as the attempt to provide a secular-rational explanation for the great egalitarian movement that Tocqueville appears to ascribe to the "will of God."

property, to say nothng of the accidents and injustices that usually determine its distribution. But in former times equality of wealth might well have meant universal poverty. The modern desire reflects the belief that the universal abolition of extreme poverty is a genuine possibility because the total of available wealth can be multiplied almost limitlessly. Whatever qualms "advanced" nations may be developing about the unintended natural and social by-products of increasing wealth, the populations of "underdeveloped" nations long irresistibly to escape from poverty and will not indefinitely tolerate governments that do not visibly advance this desire. Rigorous and self-denying modes of communal organization are accepted only as means to this ultimate end. Arguments favoring poor or tribal existence are not so much rebutted as swept aside in a massive onrush of peoples. Only those few small societies that have been accidentally insulated from all knowledge of the wealth promised by modernity have failed to desire it, and the first contacts with modern civilization invariably occasion an irretrievable loss of innocence. Modern politics is circumscribed by the desire for wealth in that the idea spreads irresistibly and makes impossible any simple defense of the customary or ancestral. In this sense also, politics is historical.

Pondering these diverse historical phenomena of modernity, we come to realize that their underlying ground of unity is science. It is obvious that science provides the basis for military technology and for civil technology that makes possible the overcoming of poverty. The relation between science and the belief in freedom and equality is less clear. We may provisionally make the following observations.

1. The modern idea of equality first emerges in Hobbes as a consequence of his effort to study men "scientifically," as matter in motion. Men are physically equal because "the weakest has strength enough to kill the strongest, either by secret machination or by confederacy with others. . . ." Men are mentally equal because "prudence is but experience, which equal time equally bestows on all men. . . ." (Hobbes, 1957, p. 80). Experience is "much memory, or memory of many things" (p. 10), memory is "decaying sense" (ibid.), and sense is simply the effect of "external body or object which presseth the organ proper to each sense. . . ." (p. 7). The qualities of objects that we discern are "in the object

that causeth them but so many several motions of the matter by which it presseth our organs diversely. Neither in us that are pressed, are they anything else, but divers motions; for motion produceth nothing but motion" (pp. 7-8).

Hobbes demonstrates the mental equality of all men by reducing mind to prudence and prudence to material motion, i.e., by explicitly "setting aside the arts grounded upon words, and especially that skill of proceeding upon general, and infallible rules called science; which very few have, and but in few things..." (p. 80). Men are then unequal in regard to science, but according to Hobbes this is politically irrelevant. He does not explicitly justify this "setting aside"; for the present, we need only note that it implicitly restricts politics to the sphere of the bodily or material. Equality as the principle of political justice is established by a specific abstraction from the only activity or faculty that, on the basis of Hobbes's premises, might even be claimed to be peculiarly human.*

2. The philosophical justification of aristocracy, the doctrine of natural inequality among men, rests on the assertion of qualitative differences among men, and among the "parts of the soul" within each man. This is undermined by the reductionist tendency of modern science—the reinterpretation of observed "surface" differences as more or less complicated permutations of a few underlying causes or variables whose status is equal. This is expressed formally in the attempt to take geometry, or an axiomatized system, as the model for natural science.

3. If men are equal in the most important respects, then no man is set above another "by nature"; there is no genuine title to rule. But being ruled is the fundamental restriction of political freedom. Equality implies that politics begins from the freedom of every man; it may be tempered by conventional agreements but always constitutes a legitimate basis for resistance against oppressive authority.

4. The inherent materialism of science claims to be competent to study man in the same fashion as animals and inert matter; it tends to obliterate the distinction between the human and the

*For the difficulties inherent in Hobbes's account of speech or science see Strauss, 1965a, pp. 171-77, esp. 173-74 n., and 1959, pp. 174-82.

nonhuman. But any political practice that takes controversial moral-political questions seriously ultimately rests on the assertion that there exists a distinctively human sphere. Since the claim of science to complete jurisdiction over the material sphere seemed undeniable, it became necessary to define the human sphere negatively, as the nonmaterial or nondetermined—that is, as freedom. The assertion that the essence of humanity is (and can only be) freedom underlies the social and political doctrines of our time, even though its transposition from the metaphysical to the political realm is profoundly ambiguous.

Not only does science underlie these distinctive features of modern politics; it creates the conditions of their emergence. Technology provides the material basis of ideology—the means of rapidly promulgating ideas to distant, unseen millions. In similar fashion it creates the very possibility of an enduring, large nation-state that is well governed, civilized, and free.

To comprehend the truly revolutionary nature of such a nation-state, we need only recall Aristotle's reasoning concerning the best size for a political community.

Cities, like all other things . . . have a definite measure of size. Any object will lose its power of performing its function if it is either excessively small or of an excessive size. Sometimes it will wholly forfeit its nature; sometimes, short of that, it will merely be defective. We may take the example of a ship. A ship which is only 6 inches in length, or is as much as 1,200 feet long, will not be a ship at all; and even a ship of more moderate size may still cause difficulties for navigation, either because it is not large enough or because it is unwieldily large. The same is true of cities. A city composed of too few members is a city without self-sufficiency (and the city, by its definition, is self-sufficient). A city composed of too many will indeed be self-sufficient in the matter of material necessities (as an uncivilized people may equally be); but it will not be a true city, for the simple reason that it can hardly have a true regime. Who can be the general of a mass so excessively large? And who can give it orders, unless he has Stentor's voice? [*Politics* vii. 4. 1326a 35–b 7].

In the same way that scientific technology has made a 1,200-foot ship possible, thus revealing as merely contingent or historical a limitation that Aristotle viewed as natural and necessary, it seems to have made "true regimes" possible for political communities ten thousand times as large as the city of one hundred thousand that he declared to be "no longer a city" (*Ethics* ix. 10. 1170b 33). "Stentor's voice" has been transformed from myth or Aristotelian *reductio ad absurdum* to an unremarkable commonplace of everyday life, and the scope of vigorous political and military leadership correspondingly expanded.

But Aristotle adduces two other arguments against the nation-state. First, "experience shows that it is difficult, if not indeed impossible, for a very populous state to secure a general habit of obedience to law (*Politics* vii. 4. 1326a 25-27). Second,

both in order to give decisions in matters of disputed rights, and to distribute the offices of government according to the merit of candidates, the citizens of a city must know one another's characters. When this is not the case, the distribution of offices and the giving of decisions will suffer. Both are matters in which it is wrong to act on the spur of the moment; but that is obviously what happens when the population is overlarge [vii. 4. 1326b 14-20].

The widespread concern in our times over the increase of lawlessness, and the distortion or "image-making" that occurs through the organs of mass communication that attempt to convey the characters of political candidates to citizens who will never know or even meet them, suggests the possibility of transhistorical problems inherent in nation-states and not fully soluble by technological advances.

If it is true that the two great forces of modern life are science and the idea of progress or history, it is also true that science is the more fundamental. Science is the seemingly unshakable foundation on which the various practices and beliefs of modernity are erected. It is science that underlies the ideology and "expertise"— or, more generally, the interpenetration of theory and practice—so characteristic of our times. It is science, and science alone, that makes it nearly impossible for us to conceive of a return to the beliefs and conditions of former times. The idea of progress emerges from science: for modern politics is determined by science, and science is progressive. Only the relentless movement of science can make it plausible to characterize modernity as "historical," as the progress of an idea.

It follows from this analysis that adequate knowledge of "where we are" presupposes coherent reflection on the adequacy of science and of the grounds of its union with politics. In recent years there has been a tendency for uncritical acceptance of science to be replaced by an equally uncritical rejection. This tendency has in part been produced by disenchantment with technology. But it ought to be clear that the truth of a proposition does not depend on its salutary character. The revulsion against technology has been reinforced by a form of epistemological relativism that considers all intellectual activity as self-reinforcing group behavior and all reality as "socially constructed." In addition to being patently self-refuting, the relativistic attempt to explain away science as mass delusion ignores the distinction between desire and capability. Men of all ages have desired to fly to the moon, but only in our time has this been achieved. That this movement from desire to action is mediated by a *kind* of knowledge will be admitted by all those whose common sense has not been obliterated by antiscientific animus. That science has produced difficulties on both the practical and theoretical levels cannot be denied; if there is a "crisis of modernity," it consists in the growing conviction of the insufficiency of science coupled with the frustrating inability to elaborate coherent alternatives to it. The present task of serious thought is, not to attack and annihilate science, but rather to create a systematic structure within which the strengths of science can be acknowledged and its inadequacies explained and resolved by legitimating other modes of inquiry in those areas with which science is clearly incompetent to deal.

Kant and the Idea
of Rational History

We must now distinguish more fully between progress and "history" in the modern sense. Progress is that political movement from worse to better that is directly engendered by the movement of science. Its explicit premises are that the increase, wider promulgation, and more skillful application of scientific discoveries necessarily results in the improvement of political life, and that this improvement is inevitable because science is inherently progressive. Science, it is argued, is progressive because it has solved the most fundamental questions of orientation and "methodology"; it has defined the range of "meaningful" questions and knows in principle how to arrive at answers to them. It is not compelled to return again and again to the first questions; it resembles the construction of a building from agreed-on architectural plans. Science improves politics not only because technology provides power and wealth, but because science provides the model for a successful political founding that eliminates civil strife by securing universal agreement on fundamental principles. To the extent that political life becomes "scientific," it loses its essentially controversial character and becomes peaceful.

If we may say that the idea of progress characterizes what we call the Enlightenment, then the modern idea of history must be traced to the revolt against the Enlightenment initiated by Rousseau and, as it were, codified by Kant. It began with the observation that the political application of scientific discoveries seemed to lead, not to peace and contentment, but to massive disruptions of customary political life and to increasingly terrible wars; political progress appeared to be essentially discontinuous with scientific progress. Further, it was asserted that the attempt to interpret the entire visible world scientifically had led both to a skepticism or reductionism willfully blind to moral phenomena and, in principle, to the obliteration of the distinction between the human and the nonhuman on which politics as well as morality ultimately depends. However, this revolt preserved the primary elements of the idea of progress: the conviction that peace was the highest goal of political life and the certainty that science provided the only valid knowledge of the material world. The essential step, which first emerges clearly in the thought of Kant, is the assertion that the human—the moral and, to a certain extent, the political—sphere, stands outside the sphere within which science is competent. Science deals with the natural world, each of the parts of which has an external source of motion; the human is the self-moved, the spontaneous, autonomous, or free.

As first manifested in Kant, therefore, the idea or philosophy of history has the following aspects. (1) While fully recognizing the divergence between political and scientific progress, it seeks to show that the catastrophes unleashed by science ultimately contribute to,

and are in fact required for, the realization of that "perpetual
peace" that is mankind's highest goal. (2) While rejecting the
Hobbesian or "bourgeois" reduction of morality to "the sum of
rules which have to be obeyed if there is to be peace" (Strauss,
1965a, p. 187), it tries to show that restored, nondebased morality is
compatible with or converges toward peace, that the world is so
ordered that morality and peace are mutually reinforcing.* (3)
History is human history; it therefore tends to become identified
with the human sphere, freedom. The dualism of nature and history
reflects the fundamental distinction between nature and freedom.
Yet history is a force, cause, or purpose that stands above individual
human intention. Moreover, it is a domain with internal laws or
regularities; it is analogous to the natural sphere and distinct from,
though not wholly independent of, the moral sphere. History
appears to circumscribe human freedom, and therefore to challenge
man's very humanity by threatening to subject him once again to
the external or "heteronomous" causes against which the idea of
freedom was to defend.† And if history is neither purely natural nor
purely human, it is difficult to see the source of its asserted
regularities, or even the sense in which it can stand as a demarcated
and self-subsisting "object" of investigation. The philosophy of
history must therefore begin by demonstrating the noncontradictory character of the relation between history and freedom; it
must prove that history can and ought to be viewed as the "first
development of freedom" and the "progression of freedom"
("Conjectural Beginning," p. 53 [VIII:109]). And it must establish that history is in fact an independent realm that can be studied
philosophically, i.e., that history is not merely the sum of human
actions, but in some sense stands apart from and unifies them into a
meaningful whole.

To grasp the full scope and complexity of this task, let us briefly
glance at the position of the most fully developed nonhistorical
philosophy. For classical Greek philosophy, history is an intrinsically
nonphilosophic discipline. Philosophy consists in the movement

*The question of whether Kant believed them to be capable of actualization will
be considered in chaps. 4 and 5.

†For an elegant statement of this problem and description of Kant's attempt to
deal with it see Fackenheim, 1957, pp. 381-98.

from the particular to the universal; but history, the record of past human deeds, consists entirely in particular instances (Aristotle *Poetics* 8. 1451b 5). It is not that human deeds as such are so chaotic or radically individuated as not to be subject to philosophy in any way; classical philosophy emphatically claims that the particular human deeds that constitute everyday experience are meaningfully differentiated, ordered, and related to universals that can be treated philosophically—for instance, in ethics.

History is akin to epic or tragic poetry; both are speeches about sequences of actions. Poetry necessarily begins and ends, and reaches its height when every incident, every word, is perfectly correlated to and necessary for the realization of its intention. As a whole, human deeds have neither a beginning nor an ending; and it cannot be said that each deed is necessary, for the whole lacks that purpose or direction in light of which the "necessary" emerges. Poetry achieves its perfection through excluding and abolishing the accidental or random; but human deeds are inescapably subject to chance. Poetry is pure making that can select and organize freely; history is limited to actual occurrences in the order of their occurrence.

Ethics may use history as a source of examples; but the fact that a brave or just act occurred in the distant past, as opposed to the present, is ultimately irrelevant. Moreover, the standard by which the past is judged cannot be discovered through any chronicle; the fact that a man is condemned, a regime overthrown, proves nothing about the justice or necessity of these catastrophes.

This view of history rests on three related premises. (1) History can be "universal" only if each event has a permanent and worldwide significance. But events are local and temporary; even the most significant advances have a restricted impact. Everything human is subject to an endless cycle of disappearance and rediscovery, in part because of the intrinsic difficulty of transmitting ideas and practices from generation to generation, and especially from political community to political community. In the words of Aristotle, all institutions "have been invented in the course of the years on a number of different occasions—indeed on an indefinite number" (*Politics* vii. 10. 1329b 25). It follows that "almost everything has been discovered already" (ii. 5. 1264a 3). This applies equally to

political institutions and to philosophy and the arts (*Metaphysics*
xii. 8. 1074b 10).

(2) Human affairs are punctuated by repeated cataclysms. "The
world of men has often been destroyed by floods, plague, and many
other things, in such a way that only a small portion of the human
race has survived." The survivors "must necessarily have been
unskilled in the arts generally...," for "all implements were lost,
and ...everything in the way of important arts or inventions that
they may have had—whether concerned with politics or any other
wisdom—perished at that time..." (Plato *Laws* 677a). On this
basis, it is impossible to speak of a progress in the succession of
events taken as a whole; there may be a sort of upward movement
within each cycle, but the peaks of the cycles are fundamentally
equal. At the very least, since nearly all traces of each cycle are
destroyed, it is virtually impossible for the next to determine what
heights of political organization and learning it had reached.
Moreover, the number of these cycles is "indefinite"; there is no
first cycle, no beginning. The implied eternity—backward, if not
necessarily forward—of the world and the human species makes it
impossible to view history "as a whole," and therewith impossible
to characterize it as progressive.

(3) Within each cycle, there is a disjunction between intellectual
and political progress. All arts are susceptible of beneficial change,
or progress; and since politics is in part an art, it would seem also to
be progressive. But political change is mediated through law,
whether slowly or through revolutions that establish wholly new
legislation.

To change the practice of an art is not the same as to change the operation
of a law. It is from habit, and only from habit, that law derives the
validity which secures obedience. But habit can be created only by the
passage of time; and a readiness to change from existing to new and
different laws will accordingly tend to weaken the general power of law
[*Politics* ii. 8. 1269a 19-24].

With the greatest possible effort, it is impossible to put into practice
all, or indeed very many, novelties of thought, even political
thought. At any rate, such novelties do not automatically or
inevitably transform themselves into the desired practice. Moreover,
political communities must work unceasingly to habituate each new

generation to their laws and principles; unlike the arts, politics is almost wholly unprogressive because it is forever condemned to repeat, from the beginning, its most essential task.

Kant is the founder of the philosophy of history because he is the first to deal in a comprehensive manner with both the classical and modern objections to it. He accepts the classical distinction, restored by Rousseau, between intellectual and political progress, but argues that this need not lead to a denial of the possibility of political progress. He blurs the classical distinction between art and law by severing the connection, and in fact establishing an antithesis, between law and habituation. He argues that the classical assertion of the essential limitation or particularity of human affairs has been refuted: important events will become known to, and influence, all nations and all future generations. He can therefore speak of "universal history" and confidently address its lesson to posterity. He attempts to delineate the bounds of the domain of history and to provide an intelligible account of its relation to human freedom. He gives reasons for believing that cataclysms in the classical sense are unlikely, and challenges the validity (or rather undermines the meaning) of the doctrine of the eternity of the world.

For this and related reasons, Kant effects a limited rapprochement with biblical religion and contributes to the tendency to make philosophic use of Christian categories that becomes so pronounced in Hegel and Heidegger. It has in fact become a commonplace to argue that the philosophy of history is nothing but a secularized messianic vision and has therefore been refuted because Christianity has been refuted, or at least extruded from genuine philosophy. The implicit premises of this argument are that the idea of history is indistinguishable from that of divine Providence, and that Providence, understood as God's will working inexorably toward a secular millenium, is a truly Christian conception. We cannot here enter into a detailed discussion, and note only the considerable evidence that the idea of history arose on the basis of purely secular problems and premises, and that the traditional notion of Providence was reinterpreted in light of the philosophy of history, rather than the reverse—that in its truly Christian form, Providence was incompatible with the idea of secular history (see Löwith, 1962, esp. pp. 182-207). Finally, in affirming the evident refutation of

Christianity, critics of the philosophy of history are casually dismissing Kant's effort to demonstrate that the human intellect is incapable of so doing, and returning to the Enlightenment critique of religion as though nothing has happened since.

But to distinguish more concretely between biblical religion and the philosophy of history and, therefore, to establish history as a concept that can be elucidated within philosophy and whose political consequences can be understood on the purely secular plane, let us begin by examining Kant's "Conjectural Beginning of Human History," which boldly stakes out history's claims in the guise of a commentary on the Book of Genesis.

2

Sacred and Secular:
*The Conjectural
Beginning of
Human History*

Analysis of the Essay*

The "Conjectural Beginning of Human History" may be divided
into five sections. The introduction seeks to distinguish conjectures
about the beginnings of human history from pure fiction, to
indicate the rational component of such conjectures, and to justify
the use of the Book of Genesis as a guide to them. The next section
describes the beginnings of human history—the transition from an
"uncultured, merely animal condition to the state of humanity..." ("Conjectural Beginning," p. 60 [VIII: 115]). The third
section evaluates and justifies this transition from the standpoint of
the betterment of the human species. The fourth describes the
transition from the first stage of human history, "labor and strife,"
to that of "unification through society" (p. 63 [VIII: 118]). The
final section describes the distress that afflicts the thoughtful observer of human affairs and the part that the proper understanding of
human history can play in alleviating it. Since this section contains
the clearest indication of the concerns that led Kant to ascribe
importance to the beginnings of human history, it is proper to
examine it before proceeding to the systematic development of the
essay.

Kant begins as follows:

A thoughtful person is acquainted with a kind of distress which threatens
his moral fibre, a kind of distress of which the thoughtless know nothing:
discontent with Providence which governs the course of this world. This

*For an excellent analysis see Fackenheim, 1957, pp. 384-89.

distress he is apt to feel when he considers the evils which oppress the human species so heavily and, apparently, so hoplelessly [p. 66 (VIII: 120-21)].

It is not necessary to be thoughtful to perceive the evils of the human condition; as Kant will indicate, even those of "childish judgment" can observe them. Thoughtfulness rather consists in a particular response to these evils.

The view of the thoughtless man will perhaps be restricted to those evils that afflict him alone, or his family and friends; he may not rise to a general view of the afflictions of the human species. He may have achieved such a view but, judging from a purely secular standpoint, have accepted this as mankind's eternal lot. Finally, if he is able to view human affairs in the light of Providence, he sees no contradiction between Providence and the existence of evil on earth. God is unfathomable; His Will is accomplished on earth as it is in heaven; the apparent evils of this life lose their force and meaning in light of the promise of the afterlife.

Kant's argument implies that the thoughtful man must contemplate the situation of the human species from the standpoint that evil in this world is incompatible with the very nature of a ruling Providence. He implicitly rejects the views that human knowledge of good and evil is insufficient to judge the workings of Providence and that justice in the afterlife fully redeems or nullifies the evils of this world. The thoughtful are thus driven to deny the efficacy of Providence. But belief in Providence is an underpinning of morality; disbelief "threatens" the "moral fibre."*

The discontent of the thoughtful leads to the wish that human affairs be ordered differently. There are three major objects of dissatisfaction: war, the shortness of human life, and civilization itself. Kant acknowledges that war and the incessant preparation for war are "the greatest source of the evils which oppress civilized nations" (p. 66 [VIII: 121]). Natural resources and culture itself are directed toward warfare; freedom is restricted and harsh demands imposed by the state on its citizens. Yet, Kant argues, fear of war is the source of much existing culture, of social unity, of large populations, and of freedom itself. "In the present state of human culture,

---

*Whether this threat necessarily issues in the destruction of morality, whether morality requires as well as draws strength from the idea of Providence, is one of the most difficult questions of Kantian thought. For a discussion see below, pp. 249-56.

then, war is an indispensable means to the still further development
of human culture. Only in a state of perfect culture would perpetual
peace be of benefit to us, and only then would it be possible" (p. 67
[VIII: 121]). Not God, but the human race, by virtue of its imperfect culture, is the source of the evils of war. But if, as Kant points
out, "God alone knows" when perfect culture will be achieved, the
question necessarily arises why the human race was not created with
this perfection rather than being condemned to struggle for it.

Dissatisfaction with the shortness of human life, the wish to
prolong it, has a more ambiguous status. In the first place, unlike
war, there is no explicit indication that the shortness of life will be
eradicated by any foreseeable progress of culture (although Kant
implies that the indefinite prolongation of human life cannot be
known to be impossible, and may not in fact be impossible).
Second, shortness of life is not an unmixed evil. Since life is merely a
"game of unceasing war with troubles," he who wishes to prolong it
must be a poor judge of its value. And, since even the short span for
which means and future enjoyments must be sought leads to a mass
of cares and injustices, the attempt to provide for a longer period
would merely increase woe and vice. Yet Kant notes that he "cannot
find fault with those of childish judgment who have no love of life
and yet fear death" (p. 67 [VIII: 122]). Further, he elsewhere
objects to the attempt to value human life according to pleasure and
pain. We shall return to this problem in examining his discussion of
the decisive case, that of the thinker who is prevented from making
"the greatest discoveries" by old age and death (see below, pp.
85-86).

Kant distinguishes the dissatisfaction with civilization as a whole,
the wish for a precivilized Golden Age, from those previously
discussed: it is "an empty yearning rather than a genuine wish, for
those who have it know that its object is forever beyond human
reach" (p. 67 [VIII: 121]). According to these critics, civilization is
characterized by "imagined needs" produced by an unbridled
sensuality, while precivilized life consists in the satisfaction of
"natural needs," enjoyment of a carefree existence of dreams and
play, and is characterized by "universal human equality and
perpetual peace" (ibid.). In a sense, dissatisfaction with civilization

is the most comprehensive discontent, for civilization appears to be the origin of war and, if not of death, at least of the fear of death.

Kant's critique is very simple: even if a genuine choice between civilization and the Golden Age were possible, the preference for the age of simplicity and innocence reflects a purely hedonistic standard. "The existence of such yearnings proves that thoughtful persons weary of civilized life, if they seek its value in pleasure alone, and if, reminded by reason that they might give value to life by actions, fall back on laziness, to counteract this reminder" (p. 68 [VIII: 122]). Whatever value may consist in, it is distinct from simple pleasure. Moreover, there is no real choice between innocence and civilization. Because man as man necessarily perceives or divines the distinction between pleasure and value, he cannot rest content with innocent natural needs or simple pleasure: "The... presentation of man's original state teaches us that, because he could not be satisfied with it, man could not remain in this state, much less be inclined ever to return to it..." (p. 68 [VIII: 123]). Yet men are inclined to return to it, at least in their imagination; the distinction between pleasure and value necessarily raises the question why the world is not so constructed that men invariably obtain pleasure from worthy actions. More generally, both innocent pleasure and civilized (rational) action appear not to afford that comprehensive satisfaction that is man's deepest yearning.

Let us summarize. The discussion of war leads to the question of why Providence condemns men to struggle for perfect culture rather than endowing them with it. The discussion of death raises the question why Providence creates obstacles to man's achievement of culture. The discussion of innocence raises the question why Providence erects a disjunction between pleasure and culture.

According to Kant, there are two aspects of discontent. The first is the sense of impotence in the face of evils that appear to be imposed by fate. If they are thought to be imposed by fate, the natural inference is that they can be removed only by fate. It is unnecessary (and perhaps even impious) to seek to alleviate them through individual or collective human effort. But morality and culture rest on precisely such efforts. Kant therefore attempts to restore human responsibility for the human condition: "Our own failings...are perhaps the sole cause of all the evils which befall us, and we might seek help against them by improving ourselves" (p. 66 [VIII: 121]). Man is responsible for his own failings since they resulted from dissatisfaction with his origins: "He must, after all, ascribe his present troublesome condition to himself and his own choice" (p. 68 [VIII: 123]). But might it not be argued that man has been condemned to woe by an unwise choice of his first ancestors, not by his own choice, and thus is not fully responsible? The history of the beginnings, Kant replies, teaches man that "under like circumstances, he would act exactly like his first parents, that is, abuse reason in the very first use of reason, the advice of nature to the contrary notwithstanding. Hence he must recognize what they have done as his own act, and thus blame only himself for the evils which spring from the abuse of reason" (ibid.).

But if man is so constituted as necessarily to abuse reason, can we say that the abuse is a free act, a choice, an imputable deed? Must we not say that the abuse of reason is an outcome of Providence? And even if man is only condemned to be free, what is the point of freedom that leads to apparently hopeless, perpetual evil and misery? The second and deeper root of thoughtful discontent is despair over the outcome of reason or freedom. Kant's apparent response is hope: the philosophic reconstruction of human history teaches us that "the course of human affairs, considered as a whole...is not a decline from good to evil, but rather a gradual development from the worse to the better; and nature itself has given the vocation to everyone to contribute as much to this progress as may be within his power" (ibid.). But this response is manifestly inadequate. Why should man be condemned to progress painfully from the worse to the better? Is the existence even of remediable or transitory evil compatible with the idea of Providence? The deepest task of a philosophic history is somehow to demonstrate the superiority, the higher goodness, of human satisfaction achieved through the painful struggle of generations as compared to the satisfaction of immediate and spontaneous Grace.

The longing for an innocent and simple Golden Age reflects the dissatisfaction with the entire venture of civilization and with humanity itself. Civil society no longer appears preferable to anarchy or solitude, or humanity to animality. The justification of man's fate must include the justification of humanity and civil society. This is the most obvious reason why Kant feels impelled to write a conjectural beginning of human history—to trace the coming-into-being of humanity and society and to discover in the reasons for their emergence the proof of their necessity and worth. There is an obvious difficulty with this procedure: other similar accounts of the origin have failed to support the conclusions Kant wishes to establish. The two most influential opponents are Rousseau and the Bible. Rousseau's *Discourse on the Origin and Foundations of Inequality* appears to constitute a theoretical basis for dissatisfaction with civilization. The Bible appears to trace the origin and misery of humanity and society to original sin and to deny any solution of the human problem in this world. Kant will argue that Rousseau's work, properly interpreted, constitutes a vindication of history. And he boldly bases his own history on the Book of Genesis, implicitly advancing a most heterodox interpretation.

Kant begins by attempting to establish the cognitive status of his conjectural history. He distinguishes between conjectural history, which joins two known facts by means of intermediate facts or causes, and fiction, in which a conjecture forms the basis of one or both of the allegedly "known" facts. But if the first facts or beginnings of human history are not known, then any account linking them with later facts would appear to have the status of fiction. Kant is thus compelled to distinguish between two types of facts and between two correlative modes of knowing. Facts of the "progression of the history of human actions" or the "progression of freedom" can be based on records alone. But facts of the first beginning of human action, "the first development of freedom from its original predisposition in human nature," can be established on the basis of pure conjecture insofar as this beginning is made "by nature." Nature is known through experience, which presupposes the persistence of uniform law through time. Just as the attempt to specify the past configuration of planets (or matter in general) requires the assumption that laws currently held to be valid were operative in the past, the attempt to derive past history from experience "presupposes that human actions were in the first beginning no better and no worse than we find them now—a presupposition which is according to the analogy of nature...."*

Whatever the validity of this presupposition, Kant's distinction between history based on records and the beginnings based on inference is at least consistent with his later assertion that culture, hence records, originate with civil society, which also constitutes the *terminus ad quem* of the "beginnings." But, it must be noted, this distinction is valid only for purely secular records. The Bible does not permit us to distinguish between conjecture and history: the account of the Creation makes the same claim on our belief as the books of Chronicles. The problem of conjecture arises only if the beginnings are unknown; but the Bible asserts that they are known. The principle underlying Kant's procedure contains an implicit reservation against the biblical account.

For Kant, the core of the phenomenon of history is freedom: history is the progression of freedom, and the beginning of human history coincides with the "first development of freedom from its original predisposition in human nature" (p. 53 [VIII: 109]). The problem is to elucidate the sense in which freedom can develop from nature (can appear or come into being), and the motive or force impelling its development. It would seem that the development of freedom cannot be an act or consequence of freedom; freedom must somehow flow from unfreedom. Yet the original human "predisposition" to freedom stands somewhere between freedom and unfreedom. Is there any such middle ground? We must attempt to discover why these difficulties did not induce Kant to make the apparently simpler assertion that "man was born free."

---

*P. 53 (VIII: 109). By this Kant does not mean to suggest that human actions have not changed, but rather that the change has the property of continuity or linear transformation of the origins (on the model of the formation of planetary systems from gaseous nebulae). In particular, he is delicately rejecting the possibility of a *moral* discontinuity—i.e., of a supernaturally occasioned Fall.

An obvious answer would be that the ascription of original freedom to man merely removes the problem from the plane of nature to that of cosmology or theology. Yet, as the very beginning of the actual account demonstrates, Kant is not unwilling to move beyond nature. He explicitly states that human reason cannot derive the existence of man from "prior natural causes" and rejects "irresponsible" attempts to do so. Human existence thus appears to require a special creation; this suggests an immediate and profound justification for Kant's selection of Genesis as a map or model. Yet, strikingly, he refuses to make direct use of the biblical account of the creation either of the world or of man; we begin with human beings whose existence is radically mysterious and whose relation to or rank within the whole is not established. But common to the biblical and Kantian accounts is the assertion that there was a "first man"; Kant silently rejects the possibility of the eternity of the human race.

Following a portion of the biblical account, Kant begins with a single adult pair; among other reasons, he asserts that a greater number would have led to an immediate state of war. There is harmony and peace between the original man and woman, who are made to live together: humans are at least partly sociable by nature. Further, a single pair implies the descent of all men from the same ancestors, which is the "most suitable means to bring about the highest end intended for man, namely, sociability"; it appears that man is intrinsically directed to some form of group life that transcends the family (p. 54 [VIII:110]). Deviating from the Bible, Kant argues that speech and thought are skills that man had to acquire for himself, though they are present as "powers" from the beginning: the original "natural state" is one of "crudeness." He refuses to trace the development of speech and reason from the origin both because of the highly speculative nature of such a reconstruction and because his purpose is to consider the development of manners and morals, which presuppose these skills. Thus, although man does not begin with developed speech and reason, they are potentials toward the development of which he is intrinsically directed. The Bible refuses to posit a state of nature even in Kant's restricted sense; speech and reason are coeval with the human species. For both Kant and the Bible, man's first surroundings are bountiful and beneficent, and his first needs easy to satisfy. For Kant, the first garden is richly endowed "by nature," while the Bible asserts its specifically Divine creation.

Kant and the Bible agree that reason preceded knowledge of good and evil. What then guided man's actions? The biblical account asserts that Adam received a commandment from God forbidding him to eat the fruit of the tree of knowledge of good and evil and threatening him with death for disobedience. One would be tempted to say that Adam was at first guided by simple unmediated obedience, by the inability to imagine violating God's command; yet the presence of an explicit threat strongly suggests the possibility of disobedience. Further, the threat could not be meaningful if Adam lacked all knowledge of death; it could not be efficacious if Adam did not somehow fear death and prize life, if he did not implicitly deem death bad and life good. Adam might be said to agree with God about the goodness of life; he would therefore appear to begin by possessing some knowledge of good and evil.

Kant denies that man began with any such knowledge or that his original action was regulated by a commandment appealing to reason in any way. He argues that the first man must have been guided "by instinct alone, that voice of God which is obeyed by all animals" (p. 55 [VIII: 111]). The Bible appears to distinguish between the grounds of animal and human action; in the crucial case at least, man's action is regulated, not by instinct, but by a sort of rational commandment. The concept of "instinct" is of course foreign to the Bible; Kant's employment of it is strictly parallel to his notion of the original crude natural state, similarly excluded from the biblical account.

Whatever the nature of the prohibition, the crucial problem is to account for man's disobedience. Kant argues that reason and innocence are an inherently unstable combination; as soon as man is confronted with novel experiences, reason is compelled to seek to enlarge human knowledge by comparing the unfamiliar to the familiar. This comparison weakens the voice of God, for "reason has this peculiarity that, aided by the imagination, it can create

artificial desires which are not only unsupported by natural
instinct but actually contrary to it."*

The original stirring of reason was "man's first attempt to
become conscious of his reason as a power which can extend itself
beyond the limits to which all animals are confined" (p. 56 [VIII:
112]). Reason emerges as the source of the "artificial" or "unnatural," the active negation of the natural. The struggle for
self-consciousness was at the same time "the first attempt at a free
choice" (ibid.): the self-consciousness of reason becomes the
consciousness of freedom. The consequence of consciousness is
"anxiety": the negation of nature brings man to "the brink of an
abyss," for the overcoming of nature leaves man with as yet no
principle of choosing among the infinity of objects of desire. Nor is
it possible to return to the "state of servitude" from the "state of
freedom"; the first or primary effect of freedom, the negation of
natural or instinctive determination of choice, is irreversible.

But, Kant indicates, the liberation from instinct, the unrea-
soned affinity for certain objects as the satisfaction of desires, is not
a liberation from desire itself as the determining ground of choice.
Reason remains the servant of the desires. As long as desire remains
on the purely animal plane, it is "transient" and "periodic"—the
alternation of short periods of want and satisfaction with longer
periods of dormancy. If satisfaction is correlative to want, it can be
increased only by increasing want. Desire wishes, not to annihilate
itself, but to extend itself indefinitely. Imagination, by removing
the object of desire from the senses, by affording a mode of
possessing and yet not possessing the object, is the means for this
extension. The infinite extension of desire is however an idea of
reason: the very act of "rendering an inclination more inward and
constant by removing its object from the senses...already reflects
consciousness of a certain degree of mastery of reason over
impulse" (p. 57 [VIII:113]). This "refusal" is the origin of love,
the idea of beauty, and morality.

*Pp. 55–56 (VIII:111). Kant does not explain the origin of imagination,
which was not among the skills or powers initially presupposed. Nor is the
relation between the unfamiliar and the imagination clarified. This difficulty is
parallel to a crucial problem in Rousseau's *Second Discourse:* the absence of an
adequate genetic account of *amour-propre.*

Morality stems from the "sense of decency" that resembles love and beauty in that its characteristic mode is concealment. But while love appears to conceal or sublimate its object in order to heighten and prolong its consciousness of that object, decency seeks to bring its object—the respect of others—into existence by concealing "all that which might arouse low esteem" (ibid.). The desire for respect is purely spiritual or human because respect cannot be a mode of purely animal gratification but can only be apprehended through reason; it is not and can never become an "object." It is, moreover, "the real basis of all true sociability" (ibid.). Kant suggests that society cannot be understood simply as the consequence of the desire for self-preservation; society is the indispensable arena for the achievement of esteem. Morality is presented as a certain relation to other men. It presupposes their presence; it is intrinsically social.

It has now become clear that the beginning of human history consists in the progressive self-development of reason. In Kant's presentation, reason is apparently "stirred" or "aroused" spontaneously; it contains its own principle of motion that is not, strictly speaking, brought into being or even affected by external influences. The first two "steps" of reason involve its transformation of the two fundamental needs or instincts. The next steps are wholly independent of animal beginnings.

The first of these is the "conscious *expectation of the future*," which Kant emphatically states is the "most decisive mark of the human's advantage" (pp. 57-58 [VIII: 113]). Being human requires the ability to work toward "distant aims," which can only serve as grounds of action if they are present in consciousness. Kant links enjoyment with total absorption in the present: although foresight has profound worth or value, it is the source of care and trouble—the fear of labor, subjection, and death. Unlike sexual sublimation, but like the original liberation of desire from instinct, it is perceived as burdensome; unlike original liberation, it is not accompanied by even a fleeting "moment of delight." The capacity that is most distinctively "historical" is the most burdensome or painful for man. It leads for the first time to explicit hatred of reason, the unrequitable yearning for the return to innocence.

The first three steps of reason might roughly be characterized as the development of powers or capacities. Only the fourth and final step is knowledge. Man comes to understand that he is "the true end of nature, and that nothing that lives on earth can compare with him in this regard" (p. 58 [VIII: 114]). All that is nonhuman serves only as means and tools for human ends. This implies that human beings cannot serve as mere means for the ends of other men; in the crucial respects, men are not ranked with respect to one another, but all are "equal participants." This fundamental equality serves as the basis for the rational establishment of civil society; distinctions among men are politically irrelevant and perhaps ultimately groundless.

But what is an "end," and what gives man this character? It is man's reason—"reason considered not insofar as it is a tool to the satisfaction of his inclinations, but insofar as it makes him an end in himself" (p. 59 [VIII: 114]). It must be noted that we have not yet been given a clear account of reason in the latter sense: freedom from instinct continues to "serve impulse"; morality, the culmination of refusal, is an "inclination"; and foresight is fully as operative in the realm of desires and aversions as in the preparation for "distant aims." It appears, in addition, that Kant's foundation of human equality might serve as the basis for distinctions among men, if the reason of some men is more in the service of desire than that of others.

However this may be, reason, which opens up a gulf between men and animals, abolishes in a sense the distinction between man and God: "man had entered into a relation of equality with all rational beings, whatever their rank...man is without qualification equal even to higher beings in that none has the right to use him according to pleasure" (ibid.). Man cannot be God's plaything; the interpretation of human history must show that man at every stage is treated as an end. History is irreversible and progressive; its principle of motion is "restless reason ... irresistibly impelling [man] to develop the faculties implanted within him" (p. 59 [VIII: 115]). This, not external conditions, renders impossible the return to innocence. The justification of history must then take the form of the proof that the progressive self-development of man is compatible with (indeed, required by) man's character as an end.

Kant begins this justification by characterizing the beginnings of human history as the transition from animality to humanity, from instinct to reason, from "the tutelage of nature to the state of freedom." This alteration is "honorable," from "worse to better," because it is a movement from the lower to the higher (p. 60 [VIII: 115]). The first difficulty is that the initial use of freedom is (and must be) an abuse that necessarily results in "vice," which is in a sense a "fall." Kant is thus compelled to introduce a distinction between the individual and the species: while for the species history is a movement from worse to better, the same is not true for the individual. But if the fall of the first man is somehow necessary for the good of the species, the first man (and indeed, men at every stage who are afflicted with vices and ills) would appear to be related to the species as means to ends.

A second and related difficulty may be formulated as follows. Kant teaches that vice is the abuse of reason and that the evils of the human condition are a (just) punishment for vice. As we have seen, he further asserts that all men would abuse reason if placed in the circumstances of the first man. "Hence the individual must consider as his own fault, not only every act of wickedness which he commits, but also all the evils which he suffers" (p. 60 [VIII: 116]). But on this basis not only are all men punished for vices that they were not truly free to avoid, but also it appears arbitrary and unjust that the members of any future generation could actually achieve liberation from vice and punishment. Their blessings would seem to flow from their position in a purely temporal sequence rather than from inner worth.

The third difficulty is that Kant explicitly presupposes that the human species is a "whole." The fate of the individual is intelligible only with reference to the fate of the species, which is more than the sum of individuals; it is itself a being with an internal structure and a unified destiny. But this concept of species remains without an adequate foundation.

Kant offers a second interpretation of evil that downgrades both the notion of punishment and the distinction between the individual and the species. Man, he argues, may be considered as both a "natural" and a "moral" species. Qua natural, he is directed toward the fulfillment of desire; qua moral, the vehicle of his development is "culture." Vice and evil are the outcome of the conflict between nature and morality, which is unresolved because "culture, considered as the genuine education of man as man and citizen, has perhaps not even begun properly, much less been completed" (p. 62 [VIII: 116]). Since nature serves man well in his original condition, it is a mistake to view natural impulse as the source of vice, which is rather the outcome of the simultaneous presence and mutual interference of nature and culture. The abolition of evil, the "ultimate moral end of the human species," lies in the final victory of culture over nature, when "finally art will be strong and perfect enough to become a second nature" (pp. 62–63 [VIII: 117–18]). Moral education requires the complete denaturization of man. Moreover, this education is in an important sense political and although according to Kant there is a distinction between man as man and as citizen, there is no essential conflict or tension.

The question necessarily arises whether culture or education can possibly accomplish this end. Kant considers at length three of the major obstacles to morality or culture: sexuality, death, and inequality. We note that in introducing these examples he refers to the conflict between man's moral destiny and the *"unalterable* subjection to laws fit for the uncivilized and animal state" (p. 61 n. [VIII: 116 n.]). There is a tension between the unalterable character of such laws and the moral requirement that culture become a second nature.

Natural sexuality is the desire and power to reproduce; it implies the family. In the "state of nature," the onset of this desire poses no problem because needs are simple; a man can provide for a family from a very early age. The complexity and needs and responsibilities of civil society require the delay of reproduction; for manhood, the ability to provide for oneself and one's family, requires extended preparation. Since the desire to reproduce perseveres unaltered and comes to precede the onset of family life, a tension arises that results in vice.

Remarkably, Kant does not argue that the answer lies in culturally imposed self-restraint, even if it were possible: "Surely nature has not endowed living beings with instincts and capacities in order that they should fight and suppress them" (p. 61 n. [VIII: 117 n.]). Rather, civil society must be reshaped to conform to the demands of natural sexuality. Thus, the solution is political, a "perfect civil constitution," which is the "ultimate end at which all culture aims" (ibid.). Kant does not elaborate, but we may well suppose that since the delay of the family in civil society is linked to needs that require both the ability to acquire property and property itself, the solution must entail a distribution of wealth guided by the political order.

It would appear that the conflict between nature and culture must be interpreted in light of Kant's distinction between natural and "artificial" desires. Culture cannot hope to alter the original natural desires; at best it will govern or perhaps eradicate the artificial desires that are the product of the transformation of the natural effected by reason and imagination. And, to the extent that the final solution constitutes a return to nature on the level of civil society, nature functions as a sort of standard: the yearning for the natural sexuality of the Golden Age is in accord with morality. Finally, natural sexuality does not point beyond itself to civil society; since sexuality is adequate for "the preservation of man as an animal species," civil society is not necessary for preservation. Its genesis and function must be understood in other terms.

The phenomenon of political inequality, inequality with regard to "civil right" or "universal human right," is more complex. Kant appears to argue as follows. Natural inequality (inequality of talent) exists among precivil men but cannot be translated into domination and subordination. Civil society provides an arena for domination, and reason justifies it by linking it to the natural inequality that has manifested itself through the differentiated development of talents into "human skills." Civil inequality is "inseparable from culture, so long as the latter progresses without plan, as it were; and this is for a long time inevitable." Civil inequality is unjust because inequality of talent or skill is irrelevant to the question of civil rights, which are based on "freedom" that all men possess equally by "nature." Freedom becomes "right" through limitation by reason; but the limitation is derived from the essence of freedom, and all men are limited equally. The knowledge of the nature of civil right is a discovery or "skill" that can be acquired "only at a late date," i.e., only by means of a long period of civil society that is ignorant of true right. Thus, inequality is the "source of. . . many evils but also of everything good" (p. 62 n. [VIII:117–18 n.]).

The attempt to fit this account into Kant's distinction between morality and unalterable laws of animality is exposed to the difficulty that there is neither servitude nor dominion in the precivil state and thus that inequality is a purely civil phenomenon. It is already the result of the transformation of nature by reason and thus corresponds far more closely to concupiscence or the unnatural desires of the imagination than to natural sexuality. Because civil inequality is not a fact of nature but rather is produced by changeable human will, the civil order can ultimately induce men to "rise above" civil inequality, whereas it can only reach a successful accommodation with sexuality.

In the crucial example, the problem of death, Kant's original distinction appears to have been decisively transformed. He focuses on the great innovative thinker, the "single man of talent" who could further the arts and sciences more than many whole generations of scholars if he were permitted to live for several lifetimes. In fact, the natural life span is long enough to permit only preparation for the "greatest discoveries," but not the discoveries themselves; the following generations must recapitulate his efforts and face the same difficulty. Thus, "nature has apparently disposed concerning the length of human life with ends other than the furtherance of the sciences in view" (p. 62 n. [VIII: 117n.]). The shortness of human life is a major obstacle to progress, which is subject to "ceaseless interruptions"; mankind appears to be perpetually in danger of reverting to "ancient savagery."

Kant's argument appears to presuppose the following premises. (1) The arts and sciences are essentially progressive in the sense that it is not of the essence of knowledge perpetually to recur to the first questions; "discoveries," the culmination of extended intellectual labor, can be comprehended without the necessity of recapitulating that labor and hence can serve as the foundation for future efforts. (2) There is in this regard a distinction between discovery and "preparation." (3) It is of the essence of reason to issue in discoveries that are essentially public, i.e., expoundable in the form of propositions. (4) Once made, discoveries are not forgotten

but remain the permanent property of, and properly comprehended by, future generations. (5) Accordingly, the progress of
the thought of the great man is necessarily the progress of the
generations and even of the species. (6) The progress of the arts
and sciences is ultimately compatible with, indeed essential to,
that progress of "culture" that promotes the ultimate moral end
of the human species.

There appear to be two main conclusions to be drawn from the
shortness of human life. First, as we saw earlier, Kant argues that a
longer life span for nearly all men would increase beyond all
bounds the force of self-interest and calculation at the expense of
morality. There is therefore a tension between the precondition of
the moral life and the requirements of the arts, and between the
immediate good of the many and that of the talented few. Second,
if the present evils of the human condition are intelligible only in
light of the ultimate victory of morality and science, and if death
prevents any one man from achieving this victory for himself, then
the explanation of history and of man himself is radically dependent on man's character as a "species being" who somehow
benefits from the accomplishments of the past and, adding
through his own efforts, transmits them to the future.

The remainder of the "Conjectural Beginning" is devoted to the
origin of civil society. The transition from animality to humanity
produces a period of "labor and strife." The fundamental conflict
is between those whose way of life requires stability and property
(e.g., farmers) and those whose interests are opposed to any fixed
property, such as herdsmen. Civil society comes into being as
mutual defense of property owners against the attacks of the
propertyless. It soon gives rise to trade, culture, art, entertainment,
and public justice. Justice requires government, which possesses an
authority unknown to wanderers who, lacking masters in the strict
sense, recognize only God as their lord. Warfare breaks out
between nomads and city dwellers that, through creating a condition of continual danger, guarantees the liberty of the contending
parties. However, the nomads, at length irresistibly attracted by
the charming luxury of the cities, come to join civil society. The
result is peace coupled with despotism, slavery, and unmitigated
sensual indulgence. The human race, abandoning its task of

progressive self-development, becomes unworthy of continued existence (pp. 63–65 [VIII: 118–20]).

War, therefore, is justified because civil society cannot be understood simply as serving the end of security, preservation, or peace; rather, it is the vehicle for the development of culture and freedom. Peace may ultimately be the crown or culmination of this development; but it both presupposes cultured freedom and gains its value from it alone. Moreover, freedom is opposed to sensuality and self-indulgence; but war demands self-sacrifice and issues in pain. Thus, even though in a sense it results in the curtailment of freedom, it has a fundamental kinship with free or moral action.

Finally, the general justification of war must be distinguished from the reasons given by civil societies for particular wars. Men may believe that they are fighting for self-preservation, for property, for empire, for a way of life; but ultimately any particular war must be seen as serving a distant end of which the participants are not aware. The reasons for a particular war (and hence its justice or injustice) are ultimately irrelevant; the perspective of the citizen or statesman is fundamentally flawed because it regards as serious, even crucial, ends that are transitory and epiphenomenal. Yet if war is necessary, individual wars must be taken seriously, for they are in fact serious business. The knowledge of the end of history, the true nature of war, the "historical sense," would seem to militate against taking the particularity of human history seriously and lead to cynicism and quietism. It might well appear that the movement of history depends on the ignorance of historical actors concerning the meaning and end of history.

The division of the earth into a multiplicity of closed civil societies is strictly correlated to the need for war. The premature unification of the human species would make real progress impossible and corruption inevitable. The need for closed societies disappears only when the need for war disappears. Conversely, freedom and culture are compatible with the existence of a universal society at the end of history; freedom is linked to the existence of small, war-making societies, not intrinsically, but merely historically. In making the most crucial decisions, therefore, true statesmanship requires more than a knowledge of the end and judgment (the skilled subsumption of the particular under the general); it depends as well on the evaluation of one's position within the "historical process"—that is, on a new kind of theoretical knowledge coupled with a new kind of judgment.

Critique

Let us now examine the extent to which the "Conjectural Beginning" serves as the explanation and justification of history that Kant explicitly wishes to provide. We may approach this problem by completing our comparison of the Kantian and biblical accounts.

In the first place, it is instructive to note the temporal limits of Kant's narrative. He begins with man in existence and placed in Eden; he concludes with man mired in vice, deserving to be "wiped from the face of the earth." The beginning and ending of Kant's narrative exclude, on the one hand, original Creation and, on the other, God's intervention through the Flood and covenant with Noah.* He attempts to give a purely human, immanent, non-miraculous account of history. Kant, like the biblical account, tells the story of antedeluvian man's decline into vice. But while the Bible suggests that man required Divine intervention, a miracle amounting almost to a second Creation, to turn back toward virtue and become worthy of law, Kant does not admit this intervention. He interprets man's moral improvement as secular and self-wrought.

In addition, the biblical account is much more ambivalent than Kant in its judgment of the departure from Eden. While for Kant the Fall is the transition from animality to humanity, in the Bible man is fully human from the moment of his creation. (This implies in particular that man cannot ascribe his humanity to his own efforts.) Kant's heterodox intention is especially manifest in his treatment of the founding of civil society. Like the Bible, he attributes the first city to the farmer; but he represents the strife between Cain and Abel as resulting from a conflict over property in which Cain's claims are at least as justified as Abel's. Kant ignores God's preference for Abel and hence is able to deny that

*For the relation of this procedure to Kant's theoretical position see Kelly, 1969, pp. 114–15.

Cain was moved by envy (while asserting that Abel was moved by hatred!). While conceding that Cain was the first to resort to force, he argues that it was "to end the nuisance which the other had created" ("Conjectural Beginning," p. 63 [VIII:119]). Kant does not suggest that Cain was guilty of any wrongdoing; force or violence, even fratricide, is not, ipso facto, a crime. Kant's Cain is not marked (even by remorse) and neither is the city he founds. For the Bible, the first city is possible only because God spares Cain in spite of his evident guilt; one can at least say that the city participates in the ambiguity of Cain's lenient punishment.

Moreover, the Bible gives to the origin of human evil (the Fall) an ambiguity that, at least on the surface, the Kantian account lacks. Man's disobedience of God begins with, and presupposes, the evil of the serpent. But the serpent in his subtlety is an integral part of the Creation. The unanswerable question necessarily arises whether some evil is not intrinsic to the notion of the Creation, or at least to the notion of good. In addition, in arguing with Eve, the serpent can do no more than assert (correctly) that eating the forbidden fruit will produce knowledge of good and evil, making man "as God." Eve must supply the crucial premise that wisdom, or the imitation of God, is good because God is good; but this premise was the tacit basis of God's original command and man's initial obedience. Why was man given "eyes" if they were not to be opened?

These indications might make it appear that original sin, the origin of human evil, was inherent in the Creation, hence inevitable. The massive objection is that man's disobedience evokes a dire punishment, which implies that evil was somehow avoidable; this objection is weakened but not overcome by the suggestion that linking punishment to the existence of true choice might implicitly presuppose certain nonbiblical premises or doctrines.

At any rate, Kant appears to resolve this ambiguity: "The history of nature... begins with good, for it is the work of God, while the history of freedom begins with wickedness, for it is the work of man" (p. 60 [VIII:115]). The distinction between nature and freedom is of course wholly nonbiblical; there is not even a biblical word for "nature" (see Strauss, 1967, p. 6). Further, the

maintenance of this distinction requires the unspoken premise that
man and man's deeds are in a crucial respect not God's handiwork.
But, as we have seen, freedom both presupposes reason and is its
inevitable consequence. Man chooses neither the potential for
reason nor the mode and fact of its actualization. It is a spontaneous and irresistible welling up from within. But if it is not man's
deed, it is God's work, and therefore good. The problem of evil
(and therewith the problem of history) is on the basis of Kant's
premises necessarily transformed into the question of why man as a
rational being condemned to painful self-actualization should
exist at all.

If Kant's procedure and intention are to be understood, the
significance of this question must be grasped, at least provisionally. Kant begins with the phenomenon of distress engendered
by the existence of evil, a distress that threatens the possibility of
morality. We must ask why this distress should threaten morality.
For what reason is morality, the clear perception of the ought or
the good, incompatible with the discontent engendered by the
failure of the actual world to conform to it? Kant may be said to
provide four different indications.

First, the moral man is not simply concerned with self-perfection, or even the status of his own civil community; he is compelled
to concern himself with "the evils which oppress the human
species" ("Conjectural Beginning," p. 66 [VIII: 121]). Second,
discontent produces fear of the outside world, a sense of hopeless-
ness or despair when confronted with it; but morality requires
"courage." Third, discontent leads to the sense that evils are
radically other, are imposed by "fate"; but morality requires the
conviction of responsibility and of the possibility of efficacious
action. Finally, the moral man begins with the premise that
"Providence... governs the course of this world" (ibid.). Distress
over evil becomes discontent with Providence; the premise is not
questioned but rather becomes the basis for the questioning of
God's goodness. But God's goodness is inseparable from His being:
the presence of unexplained evil leads to the sense that He is radically mysterious, that He has "hidden his face." If good and evil can
ultimately be comprehended only in light of God's mystery, then
all purely human morality that seeks to understand good and evil

in rational terms is radically defective, even vain and foolish. Rational morality must be abandoned, and man must trust in and subordinate himself without question to God's will, to Providence.

Kant must reject this conclusion because of his fundamental premise that man can know good and evil, that insofar as he becomes conscious of being an end in himself he enters into a "relation of equality with all rational beings, whatever their rank...." Morality itself seems to require that Providence be intelligible to men, that God's will be infallibly guided by those determinations that become manifest to fallible man as the constraints of moral law. Kant may be said to be guided by Abraham's questioning of God concerning the destruction of Sodom rather than by his unquestioning obedience to God concerning the sacrifice of Isaac.

Given the tension between distress and morality, how can the philosopher seek to alleviate it? There are, it would appear, two main alternatives: the first, the demonstration that good and evil will be eternally copresent, locked in earthly combat, and that distress over evil reflects an "empty yearning"—i.e., the dashing of an expectation to whose impossibility both hope and despair are blind; the second, the suggestion that current evils must be interpreted as a necessary prelude to the victory of the good. Kant clearly chooses the latter course; he rejects the assertion that the eternal presence of evil is compatible with the idea of Providence or of morality.

We must say, then, that Kant's project in the "Conjectural Beginning" ultimately rests on premises the truth or necessity of which is by no means self-evident: the governance of the world by Providence; the moral requirement that Providence must be intelligible; and the assertion that perpetual evil is incompatible with the idea of Providence. The idea of history comes into being through these premises; its two constituting elements are Providence and rational morality. Providence without morality leads to faith; morality without Providence leads to stoicism. To put it another way: history in Kant's sense accepts as legitimate the questions posed by the biblical account but rejects as unsatisfactory the answers it provides. It is legitimate to ask what is the purpose of man's presence on earth, but it cannot suffice to answer that man is made in the likeness of God; for why should God require or make a likeness, particularly such an imperfect one?

If it is true that the Bible ultimately teaches that the perplexity of human existence must be traced back to the mystery of Creation and hence of God, then Kant radicalizes the question by accepting, and putting himself into the service of, the demand that the inexplicable be rendered evident to human reason. This demand appears to have its source in Kant's view of morality that, in the "Conjectural Beginning," reveals the following aspects: (1) the distinction between means and ends, with only man and the other "rational beings" designated as ends; (2) the distinction between pleasure and worth; (3) the distinctions between nature and culture, and nature and freedom, culture and freedom somehow serving as constituting elements of morality; (4) the distinction between nature and reason, reason being understood as the prerequisite for, and the servant of, freedom; (5) the assertion that morality is intrinsically social or, more broadly, that it leads to concern for the entire human species. The problem is twofold: first, to establish the ground or justification for this characterization of morality; second, to show how morality so defined necessarily leads to or requires the existence of an intelligible Providence.

There is the further difficulty of the ambiguous relation between Providence and nature, which stems from the apparently ambiguous view of nature employed in the "Conjectural Beginning." On the one hand, as we have seen, Kant distinguishes sharply between nature and freedom, equating nature with the subhuman or prehuman and excluding it from the realm of morality altogether. On the other, Kant states that "nature has given us two different dispositions for two different purposes, the one for man as an animal, the other for him as a moral species" pp. 61-62 n. [VIII: 117 n.]). He can thus argue that "the progressive cultivation of [the] disposition to goodness" is the task "assigned" to the human species "by nature" (p. 65 [VIII: 120]). But almost immediately afterward he speaks of this progressive cultivation as a toilsome road that "Providence has assigned to us" (p. 66 [VIII: 121]). Again, in the concluding sentence of this work, it is asserted

that "nature itself has given the vocation to everyone to contribute . . . to this progress" (p. 68 [VIII: 123]). It might be argued
that nature is a sort of independent cause that merely establishes a
potentiality the actualization of which is guided by Providence. In
fact such a distinction is untenable, as is shown by Kant's crucial
assertion that "the history of nature. . . begins with good, for it is
the work of God..."; for whatever Providence is, it is surely the
work of God (indeed, God in the act of providing). Yet nature and
Providence cannot be equated, for while the core of being human
consists in the escape from "the tutelage of nature," it also
requires contentment with the Providence "which governs the
course of this world."*

Kant and Rousseau

Kant variously describes history as the progressive realization of
reason, of freedom, of morality, and of culture. The relation
among these constituting elements of history must for now remain

---

*See Kelly, 1969, pp. 139-41. Kelly's animadversions against ascribing an
"animistic" view of nature to Kant are well taken. But his assertion that nature
for Kant is both mechanistic (Newtonian) and teleological (Aristotelian) obscures
Kant's distinction between "regulative" and "constitutive" principles and blurs
the real rigor of Kant's thought.

We shall return to this issue in chap. 5. At the present juncture it suffices to
emphasize that Kant is not piously employing a traditional notion of Providence
derived from Christian faith or theology. The following expresses most clearly the
movement of his thought: "The guarantee of perpetual peace is nothing less
than that great artist, nature (*natura daedala rerum*). In her mechanical course we
see that her aim is to produce a harmony among men, against their will and
indeed through their discord. As a necessity working according to laws we do not
know, we call it destiny. But, considering its design in world history, we call it
"providence," inasmuch as we discern in it the profound wisdom of a higher
cause which predetermines the course of nature and directs it to the objective final
end of the human race. We do not observe or infer this providence in the cunning
contrivances of nature, but, as in questions of the relation of the form of things to
ends in general, we can and must supply it from our own minds in order
to conceive of its possibility by analogy to actions of human art. The Idea of the
relationship and harmony between these actions and the end which reason
directly assigns to us is transcendent from a theoretical point of view; from a
practical standpoint, with respect, for example, to the ideal of perpetual peace,
the concept is dogmatic and its reality is well established, and thus the
mechanisms of nature may be employed to that end. The use of the word 'nature'
is more fitting to the limits of human reason and more modest than an expression
indicating a providence unknown to us" (*Perpetual Peace*, pp. 106-8 [VIII:
361-62]).

unclarified; following Kant's apparent procedure, let us use "culture" as a general term encompassing them. Culture is opposed to nature; discontent with history is essentially discontent with culture and takes the form of a desire to return to nature. Kant traces the doctrine of the opposition between nature and culture to Rousseau and ascribes the preference or yearning for nature to a popular misinterpretation of Rousseau. Kant advances the following interpretation: whereas the *Discourse on the Sciences and Arts* (*First Discourse*) and *Discourse on the Origin and Foundations of Inequality* (*Second Discourse*) demonstrate the opposition between culture and man's "natural end" (happiness or contentment), *Emile* and the *Social Contract* show how culture is to progress in order to achieve man's moral end and to eliminate the opposition between nature and morality. He ascribes to Rousseau the view that morality is without qualification superior to happiness and that culture is capable of changing men so completely as to eliminate the yearning for premoral happiness ("Conjectural Beginning," pp. 60–61 [VIII:116]; see Kelly, 1969, p. 100).

The "Conjectural Beginning" points back to a study of Rousseau for several reasons. First, Kant appears to accept the premise underlying the *Second Discourse,* that the history of man's movement from animality to humanity is essential to the understanding of mankind's present dissatisfaction. But whereas the "Conjectural Beginning" provides only a moral or practical justification, the *Second Discourse* furnishes this premise its scientific or philosophical underpinnings. Second, Kant accepts the discontent of the thoughtful as the proper beginning-point for the study of human history: the problem of evil or of culture is the correct question. But, as Kant indicates, it is Rousseau who supplies the premises on the basis of which evil comes to be unbearable and culture to be seen as its cause. Third, as we have seen, Kant resolves the problem of evil on the basis of the distinction between the good of the individual and of the species. The premises that underlie this distinction are articulated by Rousseau, but he understands it in an altogether different manner. Kant's intention and characteristic assumptions cannot be understood without clarifying the status of the individual. Finally, although Kant refrains from making the connection explicit, it is

Rousseau, and not merely the "poets," who stimulates yearning for the Golden Age. The question is whether this widespread effect results merely from a "misinterpretation" or rather reflects a genuine ambiguity in Rousseau concerning not only the efficacy of culture in overcoming nature but also the relative worth of these two great forces. A comparison of Rousseau and Kant will therefore clarify the basis on which Kant is able to decide unequivocally in favor of the power and worth of culture.

The "Conjectural Beginning" is thematically parallel, and partially a response, to the *Second Discourse,* to which we must direct our attention to grasp fully the consequences of Kant's procedure. We begin with a series of surface comparisons that lead to the central issue.

Whereas Kant intends to produce contentment with history, Rousseau explicitly states that his analysis will produce discontent and the wish "to be able to go backward in time" (*Inequality*, p. 104 [III: 133]). Kant begins with the biblical account, while Rousseau repeatedly and emphatically rejects all reliance on "supernatural knowledge" and explicitly proceeds in a pre- or nonbiblical manner; he imagines himself in the "Lyceum of Athens" (p. 103 [III: 133]). Insofar as Rousseau relies on any source, it is Book V of Lucretius' *De rerum natura*. We may say that Kant, basing his account on Genesis, attempts a correction of Rousseau in the same manner that Rousseau, basing his account on Lucretius, attempts a correction of Hobbes. Rousseau's history emerges through a meditation on "natural law" or "right"; for Kant, natural law seems to have disappeared as an explicit issue.

Kant and Rousseau agree that it is somehow necessary to recur to the origins of the human species (and its history) in order to understand the present and future status of man; following Hobbes, both identify the origins with "nature" or the "state of nature." Further, they agree that there was an origin of human history, or first man; that is, they implicitly reject the classical hypothesis of the eternity of the human species. Finally, whereas both the Bible and Lucretius provide accounts of the origins of the universe that describe the creation or emergence of man and his place within the whole, Kant and Rousseau begin with the universe and man already in existence; they implicitly suggest that humanity can (and perhaps must) be understood without reference to specific cosmological principles.

Beyond this fundamental agreement, the accounts of the purely human origins diverge. Kant's first men begin with speech, reason, the family, and a natural tendency toward sociability (membership in civil society). To be sure, speech and reason are "acquired skills," but only in the sense of developing from preexisting powers; their acquisition does not, in Kant's opinion, pose any insoluble theoretical problems. Rousseau's natural man lacks speech, reason, and any tendency toward society or even the family. He is intended to form the basis for an explanation of all the characteristics of civil man "without the necessity of introducing [the principle] of sociability..." (p. 95 [III:126]). For Kant, the emergence and progress of reason is an immanent or self-moved development that is intrinsically necessary: reason is "restless" and "could not be satisfied" with simplicity or primitivity. Rousseau argues that natural man had no internal principle that directed him away from animality; reason emerged in response to external mechanical causes that might never have impacted on him and without which he would forever have remained in the state of nature. Finally, Rousseau's natural man begins with a rudimentary sort of compassion or pity; although the discussion is extraordinarily complex and ambiguous, one can say that pity plays an important role in both the natural and civil states. Kant omits pity altogether from his account of the origins and indicates his general view in the statement that the "restraints [of reason]...are far more essential for the establishment of a civil society than inclination and love" ("Conjectural Beginning," p. 59 [VIII:114]).

In analyzing the movement from the first beginnings to civil society, similar differences emerge. For Rousseau, the central phenomenon is pride, the desire for reputation or the esteem of others, which is the prime motive for the development of both the social virtues and of the natural faculties (the arts and sciences). In his account, pride is responsible for the greater part of human misery, of unnecessary endeavor, and of unnatural needs; it operates, moreover, largely in opposition to genuine social morality. Kant deemphasizes the role of pride. He stresses, as we have seen, the self-actualizing character of the natural faculties. And in his discussion of sociability, the place of pride is taken by the related sense of shame or decency. For Kant, the desire to be respected or esteemed is ultimately admirable because it is linked to a divination of morality.

In the case of property, Rousseau argues that the origin of civil society lies in a plot by the rich to defend and legitimate their usurpations. Civil society is characterized by an inevitable self-contradiction because its subsequent efforts to establish justice fail to eradicate the effects of the original injustice. Kant agrees that civil society originated as a defense of property, but claims that men of roughly equal wealth banded together to defend their holdings against nomads whose way of life was altogether opposed to private property. The primary distinction is not between the rich and the poor but rather between the city and the tribe.

This is but one indication of the fact that civil society is not as radically problematic for Kant as it is for Rousseau. Another is the general question of inequality. Rousseau and Kant agree that there exists a natural inequality of talent and that, as Rousseau puts it, civil society, "instead of destroying natural inequality...substitutes a moral and legitimate equality for such physical inequality as nature has been able to produce among men...while possibly unequal in strength or character, they all become equal as a matter of...right" (*C.S.*, I, 9 [III: 367]). Kant goes to the end of this road by asserting that natural inequality is politically irrelevant and cannot serve as the basis for the distribution of honor or power; under the perfect civil constitution, natural inequality is completely disregarded and the equality of "civil right" prevails. However, Rousseau is unwilling to sever completely the link between nature and civil right. He argues that political inequality is "contrary to natural right whenever it is not combined in the same proportion with physical inequality" (*Inequality*, p. 180 [III: 193]). This suggests that the justice of the equality established in the *Social Contract* is in direct proportion to the physical or natural equality that exists among the citizens. But, as Rousseau also argues, it is civil society itself that is primarily responsible for the development of natural inequality, which is "barely perceptible in the state of nature, and...its influence there...almost null..."

(p. 140 [III:162]). Civil society is responsible for the problematic status of civil right.

Rousseau and Kant agree that morality is fully possible only within civil society and that morality is the standard by which civil society ought to be judged. But Rousseau argues that morality conflicts with the other major consequence of civil society—the development of the arts and sciences. Without now attempting to elucidate the ambiguous concept of virtue or morality that he defends, we may say that his morality is akin to liberty, to "strength and vigor of the soul," to the honest expression of one's feelings, to simplicity, to innocence, to duty and labor, to courage and endurance, and to "conscience," all of which are endangered by the leisure, luxury, and sophistication engendered by the arts. Kant is perfectly aware of this problem but radically deemphasizes it. The man of talent who furthers the arts and sciences is at the same time furthering the "progress of culture" that is the vehicle of man's moral development. In fact, Kant's concept of "culture" appears intended to blur the distinction between science and morals. This perhaps occurs because Kant conceives of the application of morality to civil society as an "art" or "skill" and thus can view morality much less ambiguously than does Rousseau as a mode of knowing (see Delbos, 1926, p. 284).

In addition, it is apparent even from the "Conjectural Beginning" that Kant holds out the possibility that history culminates in the universal victory of the perfect civil constitution, which will abolish war and at least make possible the triumph of morality. Rousseau's good or legitimate constitution is much more ambiguously situated in history; Rousseau speaks of the "inevitable abuses of such a constitution," for "the vices that make social institutions necessary are the same ones that make their abuse inevitable" (*Inequality*, pp. 169, 172-73 [III:185, 187]). And in the *Social Contract*, where the principles of legitimacy are worked out much less provisionally, he argues that a given civil society can receive a free or good regime only once in its history, at its "maturity"; the history of civil society is not a continual progress but rather resembles the life of the individual—an ascent from birth to maturity, followed by decline and dissolution. The peak of history is not necessarily the end of history (*C.S.*, II, 8 [III:

385–86]). Besides, Rousseau does not foresee an end to war; at best, the perfect civil constitution comes into existence in one country or scattered countries. The solution to the political problem is not world-historical. In addition, while Kant praises war as an instrument of morality at a given stage of history, Rousseau appears to view the "warlike qualities" as constituents of morality itself (at least one side of morality). He therefore distinguishes between offensive and defensive war and views the best possible case as one in which not even defense is really necessary. If the citizens of the good regime are trained in warfare, it is "to maintain in them that warlike ardor and that spirited courage which suit freedom so well and whet the appetite for it, rather than from the necessity to provide for their own defense" (*Inequality*, p. 81 [III:113]). But warlike aggression is superior to peaceful luxury and decadence; Rousseau is compelled to approve of the imperial republicanism of Rome. Kant links the abolition of war to the political unification of mankind, although he argues that political divisions play a positive role for a time; Rousseau assumes that the human species will be perpetually divided into small, closed, and mutually hostile political communities. He can approve of this division to the extent that small communities are the necessary condition for the practice of civic morality.

Finally, Rousseau and Kant agree that historical progress or civilization produces a tension between the good of the individual and the species, but they construe this conflict in opposite senses.* Rousseau argues that "the development of enlightenment and of vices occurs always in the same proportion, not in individuals, but in peoples" ("Beaumont," p. 471). He explicitly argues that the few great men, of the caliber of Bacon, Descartes, and Newton, have through their study of the sciences and arts both fulfilled their "vast genius" that irresistibly impelled them to intellectual exertion and raised "monuments to the glory of the human intellect" (*Sciences and Arts*, p. 63 [III:29]). Enlightenment is good for such men (and perhaps for other types as well), but bad for peoples, considered politically, as citizens. On this basis, the political problem of the arts consists in determining whether, or to

---

*Delbos, 1926, p. 297, observes the similarity on this point between Kant and Rousseau but fails to emphasize the differences.

what extent, the misery and vice of the many can be justified as means to the development of the few superior men. For Rousseau the rigor of this antinomy is mitigated solely by the faint possibility that kings will be receptive to the advice of philosophers. Kant argues, in the first place, that "while for the species the direction of [culture] may be from worse to better, this is not true for the individual"—i.e., the reverse of Rousseau's contention ("Conjectural Beginning," p. 60 [VIII:115]). He does not distinguish in this regard between the few and the many; insofar as every individual is concerned with his own self-interest or satisfaction, the transition from animality to humanity or civil society will be perceived as a decline. And he argues that, at the end of history, the tension between the individual and the species will disappear: the perfect civil constitution solves the political problem and the problem of the individual simultaneously. They are in fact the same problem.

These are the most important practical disagreements between Kant and Rousseau. The real difficulty is not to list them but to discover the fundamental considerations that give rise to them. I would suggest the following points. Kant has no doubt that the transition from nature to society is good for man, contributes to his "perfection"; "whether man has won or lost in this change is no longer an open question" (ibid.). For Rousseau it is indeed an open question. In a crucial passage in the *Social Contract*, he states: "If the abuses of this new condition [humanity and civil society] had not often degraded him below that which he left, he ought to bless unceasingly the happy moment which tore him away from [the state of nature] forever and which, from a stupid and limited animal, made an intelligent being and a man" (*C.S.*, I, 8 [III: 364]). Rousseau assumes without hesitation that, in and of themselves, reason and humanity are preferable to, higher than, stupidity and animality. The difficulty is to balance the "abuses" of these faculties against their proper employment. In this respect the difference between Kant and Rousseau may be expressed as follows: Kant implicitly argues that all human action, even morally evil actions, are, ipso facto, superior to merely animal innocence; Rousseau argues that while morally good actions do indeed stand high above animality, evil or degraded acts of humanity are in a crucial sense lower than animality (see Kelly, 1969, p. 120). In addition, in the *Second Discourse* Rousseau appears to argue that the abuse of humanity is virtually inevitable, at least for most men in civil society: "The savage lives within himself; the sociable man, always outside of himself, knows how to live only in the opinion of others; and it is, so to speak, from their judgment alone that he draws the sentiment of his own existence" (*Inequality*, p. 179 [III:193]). To this fundamental difference he traces deception, dishonor, shallowness, cowardice, sensuality, and "indifference" to the distinction between good and evil; and he describes these as "the spirit of society" (p. 180 [III:193]).

Rousseau's refusal simply to affirm the superiority of civil society or of humanity, and therewith his disagreement with Kant, may be traced to two related problems. First, Kant and Rousseau agree in making a distinction between natural and unnatural desires and in tracing the unnatural to the liberation of reason and the imagination. For Rousseau, this distinction is the basis for the distinction between the "low" and "high" pleasures or, more simply, between pleasure and true happiness. In the "Conjectural Beginning," the distinction between pleasure and happiness is inconsequential, perhaps even nonexistent; at any rate, it has no immediate moral relevance. Rousseau in a way accepts the distinction between morality and happiness; but he cannot totally disregard the claim of happiness to share in the determination of human choice. One may say that for Rousseau morality and happiness are the fundamental aspects of the good, that they stand in considerable tension with each other, and that their relative rank is ambiguous. This is linked to the fact that while for Rousseau and Kant pleasure is infinite and simply relative to human particularity, Rousseau refuses to relativize happiness. For Rousseau there may be more than one way of human life that can lead to happiness, but there is not an infinite number of such ways. The fact (if it is a fact) that men in the state of nature were happy while men in civil society are miserable must give Rousseau pause. Kant is not blind to the problem of human wretchedness; as we have seen, it constitutes the starting point of his analysis. But because he views happiness as completely relative to the individual and thoroughly subordinate to morality, he can face with equanimity the unhappiness of large numbers of individuals, of entire generations, as long as morality is served.

Second, Kant and Rousseau agree that the criterion for judgment of civil society is to a large extent a measure of the extent to which it promotes or makes possible morality. Further, they agree that morality ultimately derives its character and worth from the fundamental freedom of individuals. Thus, the problem of history or of progress is the problem of the actualization of freedom in civil society and in each individual. In the "Conjectural Beginning," Kant sees no ultimate contradiction between individual and civic freedom; this may be traced to his view that the original animality, subjection to instinct and nature, was totally devoid of freedom. Kant argues, in short, that all freedom is civil or moral freedom. Rousseau's view of the relation of freedom to civil society is much more ambiguous. This ambiguity can be traced back to the ambiguity of the notion of freedom in Rousseau's thought, and the problematic relation of freedom and nature. And, insofar as Kant's strict distinction between morality and happiness is parallel, and correlated, to the distinction between freedom and nature, it may be asserted that the status of happiness is grounded in and clarified by the analysis of the status of nature.

We recall that Kant explained the existence of morality or freedom in civil man through its development from an "original disposition in human nature" and that this explanation apparently had the effect of rendering "nature" equivocal or of calling into question the distinction between nature and freedom. Further, we recall that Rousseau attempts to avoid positing any immanent impulse of natural man toward humanity or toward freedom in the moral sense. The examination of Rousseau's effort to explain on this basis the coming-into-being of freedom will clarify the genesis of the idea of freedom in Rousseau's thought, its ambiguities, and its contribution to the peculiarly Kantian view of freedom.

3

Morality and Happiness: *The Dualism of Freedom and Nature in the Thought of Rousseau*

The Problem

In the *Social Contract*, Rousseau distinguishes three types of freedom: natural, civil, and moral (*C.S.*, I, 8 [III: 365]). Civil and moral freedom presuppose civil society; natural freedom is pre-political, characteristic of man in the state of nature. In the state of nature, man's actions lack all "morality"; they are motivated by "instinct," "physical impulsion," "appetite," and "inclination." And, according to Rousseau, "the impulsion of mere appetite is slavery" (ibid.). The state of nature is moral slavery. Rousseau nevertheless describes a "natural freedom" that "has for limits only the powers of the individual." This suggests a distinction between freedom externally and internally considered; the naturally free man is not constrained in his actions by any other man. More precisely, it suggests a distinction between subjection to human will and subjection to nature. The problem is to establish a ground for this distinction.

In the civil state, man's actions are influenced by "justice," "morality," "duty," "right," and "reason." Civil freedom "is limited by the general will," the needs or desires of all members of the community, expressed in law. Moral freedom is "obedience to the law which one prescribes for oneself" (ibid.). Rousseau does not give any indication of the content of the moral law. Moral freedom appears to be the ground for civil freedom, since civil freedom consists in obedience to a particular sort of self-prescribed law. Conversely, civil freedom in a way is the model for moral freedom; civil freedom clearly requires some sort of participation in the making of law, while it is less evident that moral freedom stands in a necessary relation to self-legislation. Rousseau appears to view law as necessarily proceeding from, as well as concerning, the entire people: "that which a man, whoever he may be, prescribes on his own authority is in no way a law" (II, 6 [III: 379]). Yet the argument that moral law is simply the product of the general will does not provide a ground for the distinction between moral and civil law, since Rousseau does not specify any limitation on the scope of the civil law emanating from the general will or any distinction between public and private. Life itself, to say nothing of property or action, is at the disposition of the sovereign.

Rousseau does distinguish between morals and "right" (*Inequality*, pp. 227-28 [III:222-23]). Right consists in the conformity of "actions" to law; the proper sphere of law is the ordering or ranking of actions. Morals are bound up with character or intention. Law does not require (in fact is not competent to make) inferences from action to intention. This inference requires an "exact measure," judgment or finesse, which the generality of the law cannot supply. The distinction between morals and right implies a disjunction between morality and law taken as a standard of public judgment. However, adequate public judgment of morals is always possible. "It is up to public esteem to establish the difference between evil and good men...the people are the true judges of morals: an upright and even enlightened judge on this point, sometimes deceived but never corrupted." Standards of morals and of public right have the same source but a different mode of expression. Just as Rousseau is driven to discuss the question whether the general will can err, he must consider whether public opinion can err. He suggests that the people always know the true standard of morality but in particular instances fail to apply it rightly out of ignorance. Yet every society is divided into "evil and good men," and it is difficult to imagine that the evil will always agree with the good concerning the standards by which they are to be condemned. If the true standard of morality does not consist in universal agreement (or even the opinion of the majority in times of corruption), by what means is it established? Must it be willed before it is apprehended, as the general will might appear to be? At this point, abstracting from the problem of the content or standard, we can only observe that there is a tension between the concept of morality as originating from the individual through self-prescription and the concept of morality as law, if, as Rousseau asserts, law cannot be viewed as originating from any individual. This tension might be said to point forward to the view that morality necessarily consists in the capacity of the individual for generalization, for recapitulating in the movement of his own will the willing of the community.*

It is clear that civil and moral freedom are akin in a crucial respect: both are grounded in the notion of a specifically human freedom that enables man to oppose the impulsion of the instinct, appetite, or inclination within him. This freedom is not coeval with man; man in the state of nature, possessing natural freedom, is simply ruled by instinct or appetite. It thus becomes necessary to furnish an account of the state of nature and the transition to civil society that can render intelligible the coming-into-being of civil or moral freedom. In the *Social Contract*, Rousseau merely assumes this transition; in particular, his account of the motive or efficient cause of man's departure from the state of nature is explicitly a supposition (*C.S.,* I, 6 [III:360]). Further, the description of the transition rests on the premise that the state of nature actually existed in the past and that man was then characterized by natural freedom. Rousseau does not attempt in the *Social Contract* to establish the actuality of the state of nature. But natural freedom is not only an affair of the past; it is the standard for civil freedom. The *Social Contract* is said to provide the means whereby men coming together to form civil associations remain "as free as before" (ibid.). Finally, there appears to be a complete disjunction between natural freedom (subjection to appetite) and civil or moral freedom (the capacity to oppose

---

*See the discussion in Kelly, 1969, pp. 52-55. I do not think his conclusion that in the *C.S.* morality is "dispersed" between nature and civil law or "subsumed, collectivized and turned into a 'general will' " can be sustained. Within the legal or juridical perspective of the *C.S.*, Rousseau explicitly perceives the philosophical existence (and to a certain extent the political relevance) of "personal morality," which is not simply the product of the general will. See *C.S.*, I, 8 (III:365), and II, 12 (III:394).

appetite). Rousseau must provide an account of the common quality by virtue of which they are all "freedom" and which alone could allow natural freedom to serve as the standard for civil freedom. In these respects, the *Social Contract* rests on a demonstration of the existence and character of the state of nature, that is, on the fundamental investigations of the *Second Discourse*.* A crucial difficulty has already emerged: the coming-into-being of moral freedom cannot be understood as an effect of moral freedom. It must somehow be the consequence of premoral or nonmoral causation.

Nature and Freedom in
the Second Discourse

Introduction

Rousseau begins the *Second Discourse* with an epigraph, a quotation from Aristotle's *Politics* that occurs in the course of a thematic discussion of slavery: "Not in corrupt things, but in those which are well ordered in accordance with nature, should one consider that which is natural" (*Politics* i. 4. 1254a 36-37). Nature is the standard of judgment; but it is not evident, particularly in the case of animate beings, in what nature consists. Aristotle suggests that the natural may be discerned in those things that are well ordered. The natural ordering emerges when each element or part is fully developed. To be incompletely or imperfectly developed is unnatural. Aristotle concludes that it is natural for the soul to rule the body and for mind or reason to rule the appetites. All men whose lack of mental capacity places them in the same relation to other men as that of body to soul are naturally slaves and benefit from being enslaved. The crucial assertion is that reason should rule the appetites. As is well known, Rousseau questions this assertion and the conclusion that follows from it. He is then compelled to question the conception of nature and the natural that underlies them. The crucial premise of Rousseau's correction

*For a thoughtful discussion of these themes see Fetscher, 1962, pp. 29-56.

of Aristotle is in a sense supplied by Aristotle himself. In Book 7, Aristotle appears to redefine natural slavery as the lack of desire to preserve one's independence (vii. 7. 1327b 25-31, 1328a 6-7). Rousseau will argue that this lack of desire is itself unnatural. The epigraph draws our attention to the problem of what is natural by alluding to a practical disagreement between Rousseau and Aristotle that points back to the conflicting characterizations of the natural. Further, the disagreement concerning freedom and servitude is of crucial practical and theoretical importance for Rousseau. At the same time, the epigraph points to a crucial area of agreement; there is a distinction between the well ordered and the depraved without which a natural standard of worth cannot be seen. In proposing a new content for this standard, Rousseau radically alters the content and status of freedom.*

Freedom must be considered in relation or contradistinction to nature. But for Rousseau, nature appears to bifurcate into the human and the nonhuman. The study of nonhuman nature (natural science), Rousseau believes, has achieved striking successes based on a particular hypothesis concerning nature in general and a novel procedure or method that reflects that hypothesis. The question inevitably arises whether the study of human nature cannot in turn be advanced through this method or hypothesis. The preface to the *Second Discourse* outlines the structure of the knowledge of man viewed from this novel perspective and suggests the implications of and difficulties inherent in such a transformation of the traditional understanding.

Natural Science and the Science of Man

Rousseau's argument suggests the dependence of political science on natural science. Both an account of the origin or "real foundations of human society" and the standard of judgment, "the true definition of natural right," rest on a knowledge of natural man. This knowledge requires "experiments," which are in fact "the only means we have left" to achieve it. Simple

---

*For further discussion of the epigraph see Starobinski's note in *O.c.*, III: 1255.

observation will no longer suffice, since natural man has been obscured: "He who would try to determine exactly which precautions to take in order to make solid observations on this subject would need even more philosophy than is generally thought" (*Inequality*, p. 93 [III:123]).

According to Rousseau, the knowledge of man is the "most useful" and "least advanced" of all human knowledge. This assertion is surely not self-evident or even clear. For what is this knowledge useful? Why is it more useful than knowledge of nonhuman things? Moreover, an object generally held to be useful is generally sought after; is there something that obscures the importance of this knowledge or, that lacking, creates barriers to its achievement? A quotation from Buffon, which Rousseau emphatically endorses as "solid and sublime reason" (pp. 182–83 [III:195]), provides an indication. Men are provided by nature with external senses and internal sense. The external senses are directed toward the world, receiving "foreign impressions," for the purpose of self-preservation and the gratification of the passions. These powerful motives lead to an incessant increase in man's receptivity to and control over the external world. Yet in mastering the world, man gives himself over to the world: "We seek only to extend beyond ourselves, and exist outside ourselves" (ibid.). The distinction between man and the world, or the separation of the truly human from the foreign, can only be achieved through inner sense; this sense reduces us to our true dimensions and provides the only basis for self-knowledge and self-judgment. The exercise of inner sense is opposed by the preoccupation with the outer world—not only by the passions, but by the knowledge of the external world that stems from passion, "the illusions of our mind" (ibid.). It would seem to follow that knowledge of man rests on an effort that would make possible a return to introspection. Rousseau appears to endorse this conclusion by referring to the Delphic inscription "Know thyself." However, this transforms the question of knowledge of man in general into that of individual self-knowledge. Individual knowledge can serve as the basis for general knowledge only if the particular individual can be taken as a model; but this procedure appears to presuppose a fundamental equality or similarity

among members of the human species in crucial respects. There is,
then, a connection between the moral or political problem of
inequality and the method of inquiry.*

The path to knowledge of man is further complicated by an
apparent peculiarity of man. The "physical scientist" finds his
objects of investigation—minerals, plants, animals—ready to
hand; they are, as they appear to the investigator, an adequate
starting point for the accurate and impartial observations or
"experiments" that will lead the investigator to knowledge of
them. This procedure cannot be applied to man. The most careful
examination of modern man as he appears to us will never suffice,
since modern man is not "man" simply. The essential task is to separate man's "own stock," man "as nature formed him," from the
impact or products of "circumstances and progress" (p. 91 [III:
122]). There is a point in time that can be identified as the
"natural" for man and from the standpoint of which knowledge
of man must be acquired. The impact of the sequence of time and
things obscures this point; the events of this sequence do not
contribute to knowing man. Whatever the mode of investigation
one adopts, then, it will not suffice to observe or even to question
the men around us to discover the truly natural, since modern man
is at best a compound of the natural and something else.

Yet it is difficult to see how the very distinction between the
natural and the non-natural could result from simple observation
of modern man. In a sense, this distinction must be the starting
point (hypothesis) of Rousseau's analysis. Nature is a sort of cause;
it "formed" man. Original man is natural because he is the effect
of a single cause, nature. The movement away from the original
condition is brought about by "a thousand continually renewed
causes" whose common element appears to be "society" (ibid.).
But if the "sequence of time and things" or "circumstances
and...progress" are not natural or a product of the natural, what
are they, and what is their origin? If they are present from the
beginning, is the reduction of primitive man to the natural
tenable? If they are natural, what additional principle enables
Rousseau to identify any point in time as distinctively natural? All

*For precisely the same problem see Hobbes, 1957, p. 6.

that one can say with certainty is that Rousseau equates the natural with the original or primitive, and hence that progress, or the effects produced by society, is not natural; nature does not have the character of an unfolding or progressive realization. The changes that befall man are the "impact" of external causes and have no internal or immanent cause. They are, moreover, a down-going or decline from "fixed and invariable principles" or "heavenly and majestic simplicity" to the "ugly contrast of passion which presumes to reason and understanding in delirium" (p. 92 [III:122]). The human soul has not merely changed its appearance in civil society; its very nature and principles have been altered, and for the worse.

The distinction between the natural and the non-natural is of particular importance for the study of man because man appears to be more fundamentally mutable than the other beings. It is not the case that other beings are unchanging. The animals of each species were originally very similar to each other until "various physical causes...introduced into certain species the varieties we notice" (p. 92 [III:123]). There is no suggestion, however, that the varieties produced by physical causation constitute an inevitable deformation of nature. To be sure, the diverse qualities they acquired were "not inherent in their nature"; the physical causes transformed the original animals in accidental or unpredictable ways. But these qualities may be "good or bad," and the transformation either a perfection or deterioration. Hence the standard of judgment cannot simply be whether a quality is original or present from the beginning. This is perhaps related to the fact that changes among animals were brought about only by "physical causes," whereas changes in man stemmed from causes not all of which were self-evidently physical. Rousseau uses the analogy between men and animals to explain "in general" the origin of diversity or inequality, but while the cause of diversity among animals is fairly clear, it is more difficult to discover the "true causes" of human diversity "with precision." The analogy is explicitly based on the "common avowal" that men were originally equal; this appears to presuppose the results of the inquiry. There are, then, two closely related problems: the nature of the origin, and the causes of the departure from it. The distinction between these problems depends crucially on the general understanding of nature as external rather than immanent causation (ibid.).

Rousseau reformulates the first problem as follows: "to separate what is original from what is artificial, in the present nature of man..."(ibid.). The original is that which is formed "by nature." To maintain the distinction between the original and the artificial, the artificial must be that which is not formed by nature. The distinction is not merely between the original and subsequent products of physical causation, since animals are altered by physical causes without being rendered artificial. What then is the cause of the artificial? Suppose man himself has the power or capacity to form the artificial within himself. This capacity, being part of his nature, is itself either original or artificial. But it cannot be artificial; this would imply a capacity to form a capacity to form the artificial, merely pushing the question back one step and producing an infinite regress. It follows that man's capacity to form himself is original, i.e., formed by nature. The artificial is produced by a power formed by nature. The sole remaining ground of distinction would then be that the power is produced by nature but that its operation is not caused by nature. The apparent outcome of the distinction between the original and the artificial is the conclusion that nature itself can and does produce an active agency that supplements or even *opposes* its own causation.

If the nature of man is natural man (man in the state of nature), and if the state of nature is both the standard of natural right and an actuality at some point in the past, and if nature is viewed as necessity or physical causation, then man's behavior in the state of nature was characterized by complete conformity to natural right. Rousseau is compelled to discover a sanction for, or ground of obedience to, natural right that guaranteed its actualization. He clarifies his views through a critique of previous efforts to use nature as a standard. The outcome of these efforts was natural law rather than natural right. The question of the nature of law thus becomes crucial. In addition, these efforts resulted in disagreement concerning the most important premise of Rousseau's argument, the derivation of the natural standard from the particular nature of man.

Rousseau divides his predecessors into three main groups.* The "ancient philosophers" are dismissed without analysis because of the contradictory character of their principles. The "Roman jurists" subject both men and animals to the same law because they take law as "the expression of the general relations established by nature among all animate beings for their common preservation" (*Inequality*, p. 94 [III: 124]). This view implies that natural law is not deduced from the particular nature of man, but rather from what man has in common with the animals. The Roman view of law as that which nature imposes on itself is distinguished from law considered as "prescribed"; prescription, though here undefined, apparently implies a principle requiring rational apprehension for obedience. The "moderns" define law as prescription, and directed to a moral being "intelligent, free, and considered in his relations with other beings" (ibid.). These criteria imply the limitation of natural law to man.

Rousseau's criticism of the "modern" view may be formulated as follows. Prescription implies that understanding of the natural is a necessary ground of obedience to it. But natural law based upon reason is so difficult to comprehend that unenlightened men could never have understood it, hence could never have obeyed it. But enlightenment presupposes society. There is therefore no presocial knowledge of natural law. The establishment of society could not have rested on an understanding of natural law, hence could not have been undertaken in conformity with it. This critique, then, indicates a tension between the proposition that obedience to natural law implies rational knowledge and the assertion that civil society is founded through knowledge of natural law. This in itself is not a refutation of the first proposition, for the latter assertion may be abandoned. This would lead to the conclusion that society was founded on injustice or passion or ignorance and that natural law could form the basis for a critique of society. In the *Social Contract*, Rousseau traces the unwillingness of the "moderns" to

---

*For discussion and specific citations see Starobinski's note in *O.c.*, III: 1296-97.

accept this conclusion to their desire to justify the existing order of
society as natural—in particular, the institution of monarchy.
Natural law must buttress the duty of the people to obey. Grotius,
for example, "stopped at nothing in order to despoil peoples of all
their rights and vest them, with all possible artistry, in kings"
(*C.S.*, II, 2 [III:370]).

Rousseau moves from this implicit political critique to a more
general explicit criticism: all existing definitions of natural law
presuppose knowledge that man does not naturally have and
advantages that can be comprehended only after man has left the
state of nature. Natural law must be based on what man knows or
what suits him in the state of nature. Existing definitions also have
the fault of presupposing the notions of "common utility" and
social agreement in an uncritical manner. The proof that a law thus
grounded is natural rests on the mere assertion of its socially
salutary effects rather than on the demonstration that men by
nature do stand in such a relation to one another.

Rousseau then offers his own formal description of natural law:
"For it to be law, not only must the will of him who is bound
by it be able to submit to it with knowledge; but also, for it to be
natural, it must speak directly by nature's voice" (*Inequality*, p.
95 [III:125]). This appears at first to be a combination of the
Roman and modern theses. Rousseau in a way accepts the modern
view of law as prescription, although he shifts the emphasis from
reason simply to will informed by knowledge as the ground of
obedience. But his view of nature as prompting actions directed to
reasonable ends, in particular, self-preservation, through non-
rational means common to animals and men, seems much closer
to the Roman view.

This definition provides an indication of why Rousseau immediately replaces the question of natural law with that of natural
right. His reasoning may be summarized as follows. In the state of
nature, nature's voice speaks clearly, but reason, hence law, is
completely absent. In civil society, reason is present; but reason
itself has "by its successive developments...succeeded in stifling"
nature's voice (p. 96 [III:126]). The very notion of natural law
contains two divergent or contradictory elements; more precisely,
there is no point in time in which rational apprehension of law and

the natural sanction of law are copresent. This dilemma points in two directions: to the notion of presocial behavior that follows nature's voice and lacks "law"; and to the notion of civil law as a law of reason the ground of obedience to which cannot be sought in nature. The former is what Rousseau calls natural right. There is no distinction between the content of natural right and its sanction: nature's voice, the passions or sensations "anterior to reason," is an inner impulse that issues in "rules." Natural right is in one sense the standard for civil rights; the rules of natural right can later be reasonably obeyed. In fact, it is possible to submit rationally to all rules engendered by nature's voice; reason reestablishes them on "other foundations" but does not alter their content. The natural, or once actual, coincides with the rational; but the nature and binding power of the new "foundations" are not clear. Natural right is correlated to the nature of primitive man but not that of modern man; the actualization of right was guaranteed in the state of nature but is no longer (pp. 95–96 [III: 125–26; see also 1299]).

The suggestion that natural right must be derived from the nature of natural man is somewhat complicated by the account of that nature that Rousseau provides. The principles "anterior to reason" appear to be those traits that man has in common with the animals. Self-preservation is not a specifically human drive or desire; and Rousseau will later contend that the limited pity that natural man experiences can be observed in animals. But these, with their associated pleasures and pains, constitute the content of "sensitivity," which is a "quality . . . common to beast and man" (p. 96 [III: 126]). This quality, in the absence of wisdom, is the foundation of "duties" as well as rights. It would seem to follow that natural right is common or reciprocal, i.e., that animals have duties as well as rights. According to Rousseau, it was asserted by previous thinkers that being human implied developed reason or philosophy, since humanity implied the capacity for duty that rests on reason. Rousseau argues that duty does not rest on reason, or the "belated lessons of wisdom"; duty can in fact be grounded on "impulse" (ibid.). But he appears to accept the proposition that humanity implies the capacity for duty. This proposition stands in tension with the reduction of duty to that which is shared by animals and men and points toward the conclusion that natural man is virtually indistinguishable from the animals.

There is, however, an ambiguity concerning the relation between natural right or duty and reason. The rules of natural right are said to flow from "the conjunction and combination that our mind is able to make" of the original principles. The question arises whether this operation of the mind was characteristic of natural man, and whether it requires reason, or at least some specifically human quality, or rather is purely mechanical and animal. In addition, the original principles are explicitly intended to eliminate the necessity for the hypothesis of sociability; yet pity appears to require the ability to distinguish sensitive from insensitive beings and men from other animals, and a natural inclination not to see other men suffer that is not based on sexuality or any other physical need.

Finally, Rousseau had previously asserted that only a "specifically 'scientific' procedure" (see Strauss, 1965a, p. 268) could lead to knowledge of natural man. In agreement with this assertion, he here rejects that science that is based on the uncritical or naïve observation of modern men or "men as they have made themselves." However, he claims to discover the first principles of the human soul, not through the experiments that he previously declared to be the only means, but through a sort of "meditation." Rousseau does not elaborate on this method; but since he is later to describe himself as a modern man who cannot return to the state of nature, it can scarcely be a simple introspection. Nor, by hypothesis, can it be a simple observation of the men around him. At one point, Rousseau asserts that his researches are "hypothetical and conditional reasonings...like those our physicists make every day concerning the formation of the world" (*Inequality*, p. 103 [III: 133]).

I would make the following suggestion. The origin of humanity, like the origin of the world itself, cannot be an object of direct investigation. At best, one can begin with a hypothesis concerning the origin and attempt to demonstrate that it is, without the employment of implausible or ad hoc premises, capable of being transformed into the effects that one can observe directly. In the case of the Newtonian physicist, this procedure requires the view that there is only one type of causation, whose character is that of strict necessity, such that from one configuration of matter at a given point in time, one and only one configuration is possible (and necessary) at any given future time. Rousseau's procedure is Newtonian to the extent that his attempt to explain the present with reference to a hypothesis concerning the origin involves the notion of a single type of causation with a mechanical or necessitarian character. His hypothesis is composed of two related elements: the hypothesis concerning the character of original man, and the hypothesis that the transition from original to modern man can be explained on the basis of mechanical causation.* As shown by contrast of natural and civil right, Rousseau must distinguish human action viewed externally from the "impulse" or "motive" of soul that underlies it. His hypothesis must then provide a satisfactory explanation of both human action and the "successive developments" of the dimension of human inwardness, which issues ultimately in reason and freedom. And it must either provide a foundation for the distinction between men and animals or demonstrate the nonessential character of the apparent differences between them.

Natural Mechanism and the Perfectibility of Man

Rousseau divides the description of natural man into two parts: the "physical" and the "metaphysical and moral." The physical description consists in a comparison of natural man with the animals and with civil man, without any coherent attempt to specify what distinguishes man as man from the animals, i.e., to specify what civil and natural man have in common. The metaphysical description begins with this attempt; it therefore begins by dropping the distinction between natural and civil man and speaking simply of "man" (p. 113 [III:141]). An animal is an

---

*Kelly, 1969, p. 38, distinguishes between a "subjectivist foundation" and "scientific experimentalism," arguing that it would be a mistake to attribute the latter to Rousseau. The argument sketched above suggests that in Rousseau's view subjectivism and experimentalism were not necessarily opposed. For evidence of Rousseau's experimental orientation see *Inequality*, pp. 93, 208-9 (III:123-24, 211).

"ingenious machine" directed toward self-preservation "by instinct" and provided with senses in support of instinct. Man is also
a machine directed toward self-preservation; he even feels the
command or impetus of nature, but he is at the same time a "free
agent." Freedom is the ability to resist or negate instinct. Both
instinct and freedom are imperfectly related to self-preservation.
Animals bound by instinct are restrained from acts that would
conduce to their preservation, while freedom enables man to
destroy himself. For instance, Rousseau argues that dissoluteness or
sensual excesses occur when the mind and will overpower the
senses and nature in general. Nature provides a limitation on
desire that only man's free will can override. Limitation of desire,
then, arises from what man has in common with the animals.
Freedom is the necessary and perhaps sufficient condition for the
emancipation of desire. Yet nature is somewhat imperfect; nature's means, instinct, inadequately serves her end, self-preservation. The most natural end requires at least a partial emancipation
from nature. The concept of freedom as the unlimited or undetermined lacks positive content; it is here viewed as the negation of
nature, nature being the source of limit or determination (necessity). The view of nature as mechanism requires the rejection of the
traditional definition of man as the "rational" animal. Ideas are
merely sense perceptions, and "physics" or "the laws of mechanics" "explain in some way the mechanism of the senses and the
formation of ideas." The specific difference of man consists in
freedom and the consciousness of freedom.*

Rousseau's reasoning may be summarized as follows. The whole
of nature is characterized by a fundamental homogeneity that can
be explained by physics, that is, by laws of mechanical necessity. If
man is distinguished from nature or the natural beings, it must be
by virtue of some quality that radically transcends the domain of
mechanical necessity. All human senses or powers that receive
impressions from nature must be explained through their interaction with nature, i.e., mechanically. The distinctively human
power must be purely nonreceptive or inward or spontaneous. Only
the power of choosing can be conceived of as free or spontaneous.

---

*For additional discussion see Starobinski's note in *O.c.*, III: 1316–17.

But, to repeat, Rousseau's concept of freedom arises through a negation of nature viewed as necessity (*Inequality*, pp. 113-14 [III:141-42]).

Rousseau refuses to rely on this redefinition of man, on the grounds that his reasoning fails to eradicate the "difficulties" or "dispute" surrounding "these questions" (p. 114 [III:142]). He specifies neither the character of the dispute nor its scope. He was not unaware of the relation between freedom of the will and certain established theological doctrines or of the problematic status of an argument that assumes a disjunction between consciousness and sensation. There is, however, a more central difficulty. In seeking a definition of man, Rousseau is compelled to abstract from the differences between natural and civil man. Yet his definition must be compatible with his account of these differences and of the transition from the natural to the civil. Rousseau cannot assert that natural man is characterized by freedom without calling into question the identification of natural man with the animals, whose cares and desires are limited by nature, and raising the question whether the transition from the natural to the civil ought not to be explained with reference to an immanent predisposition or impulse rather than external causation. But if natural man is not free, then *ex hypothesi* he is not really man at all. Further, it then becomes necessary to explain the generation of the freedom of civil man through mechanical causation, which surely calls into question the assertion that "the laws of mechanics explain nothing" about freedom. The positing of "potential freedom" would not obviate this difficulty.

Rousseau is therefore compelled to replace freedom with "perfectibility." Perfectibility, or self-perfection, on the surface would appear to imply development in a desirable direction: yet Rousseau immediately suggests that it is "the source of all man's misfortunes" (p. 115 [III:142]). The other possibility is that perfection means completion. Perfectibility is said to be a "faculty" that develops all the other faculties (p. 114 [III:142]). Rousseau speaks repeatedly of "potential faculties" (pp. 97, 127, 140, 204 [III: 127, 152, 162, 208]), the extent of whose possible development is determined by preexisting limitations. He distinguishes these faculties, which are said to be "natural," from their successive

developments, which are not natural (pp. 97, 140 [III:127, 162]).
The final form that civil man assumes, with all his faculties
developed, is not random or accidental but rather inherent in his
beginning. But the impulse for their development was not
immanent but external: "time," "circumstances," or "accidents." Perfectibility is not simply equivalent to malleability,
lack of limitation, or openness to change: it is the capacity for
change in a particular direction.

Yet, in the first place, perfectibility is only one among several
faculties (e.g., foresight, imagination, mind, the "social virtues")
that are presented as distinctively human (p. 140 [III:162]). What
then is the ground for selecting it as the specific difference of man?
In fact, can perfectibility be anything more than a general
characterization of the openness (receptivity) of the other human
faculties? Further, perfectibility is said to be the ground or cause of
the development of all the other faculties. Yet perfectibility is said
to "depend on" general ideas, which presuppose speech (p. 124
[III:149]). But "although the organ of speech is natural to man,
speech itself is nevertheless not natural to him ..." (p. 207 [III:
210]). It is therefore a faculty that rests on perfectibility. Moreover,
perfectibility is not fully present in the beginning; it is "received
in potentiality" like the other faculties (p. 140 [III:162]). Man
"in his primitive condition" is not characterized by perfectibility
any more than by the other potential faculties. Finally, perfectibility is "almost unlimited" (p. 115 [III:142]); it is not therefore
unlimited. The potential faculties have inherent configurations or
bounds; for instance, "mind" is described as having a "limit of
the perfection of which it is susceptible" (p. 155 [III:174]). At
some point, man will be characterized, not by perfectibility, but
by perfection or completion. There is thus a tension between the
notion of perfectibility as openness and the concept of natural or
potential faculties. Perfectibility appears to characterize neither
man's beginning nor his end, but only, so to speak, his coming-
into-being. It is therefore difficult to see how perfectibility can be
the specific difference of man as man.

That this is not an accidental error on Rousseau's part but rather
a consequence of his most fundamental concerns may be shown as
follows. According to Rousseau's own assertion, the argument that

man's development, and in particular the development of his reason, is the product of accident or externality, "the chance combination of several foreign causes which might never have arisen,"* rests on the demonstration that perfectibility is not natural but only potential. If perfectibility is actual from the beginning, man's development is produced, not by external causation, but rather by an immanent impulse. The doctrine of the nonnatural development of the potential faculties would collapse. This would necessitate the view that the traditional definition of man was essentially correct; in particular, that reason and sociability were fully natural rather than accidental. Yet Rousseau is unwilling to argue that the form as well as the existence of the perfected faculties of civil man is entirely accidental; the notion of potential faculty mediates between simple animality and the developed faculties of civil man. More precisely, Rousseau cannot present a view of the origin that leads to the conclusion that the faculties of civil man could never have developed, for these very faculties constitute the beginning point of all inquiry; they may be explained or reinterpreted but never denied. He implicitly argues that openness to external causation does not fully explain the existence and character of human faculties; he must therefore posit a specifically human predisposition or pre-formed receptivity. The tension or ambiguity of perfectibility points to a difficulty in the attempt to use nature viewed as the primitive or original, or as mechanical causation, as the ground of explanation for the characteristics of civil man.

Let us reconsider perfectibility from a slightly different standpoint. Animals are characterized by blind obedience to natural impulsion or instinct (p. 113 [III:141]). Instinct is invariant and prevents the animals from acquiring anything in addition to their original constitutions (p. 115 [III:142]). Perfectibility is the negation of the sway of instinct. But perfectibility is not original, but rather an acquired product. The question therefore arises

---

*P. 140 (III:162). When Rousseau speaks of "chance" or "accident," he is not, as Kelly suggests, invoking a *tertium quid* standing between human will and mechanical necessity (Kelly, 1969, pp. 42–43), but rather is underscoring the lack of intrinsic relation between human inwardness and mechanical externality. Natural necessity impinges on man and thereby initiates his development, but nature is not teleologically ordered toward that development.

whether primitive man prior to the acquisition of perfectibility is
an animal in the sense that he is ruled by instinct. On this point
Roussseau provides us with a bewildering variety of suggestions.
He begins by arguing that each species of animal "has only its own
proper instinct" while man, "*perhaps* having none that belongs to
him," appropriates the various instincts of the animals (p. 106
[III: 135]; my emphasis). This appropriation rests on the abilities
to "observe" and "imitate" the animals, abilities that are
apparently present from the beginning (p. 105 [III: 135]). Original
man is then characterized by openness—absence of instinct—and
faculties that can substitute for or rather "develop ... the instinct
of the beasts." Yet the "perhaps" indicates a certain hesitation to
affirm simple openness. Rousseau later gives an example of an
animal that has a capacity for imitation and declares that this
capacity can exist in the absence of perfectibility (p. 208 [III: 211]).
Imitation cannot then be specifically human and must be expli-
cable as a purely animal—that is, instinctive or at least mechanical—function. Conversely, perfectibility cannot be viewed as
simple absence of instinct, that is, as purely passive or animal
receptivity to mechanical causation in the determination of action.
Rousseau's next attempt to characterize the relation of instinct and
perfectibility reinforces this ambiguity. "Savage man, by nature
committed to instinct alone, or rather compensated for the instinct
he *perhaps* lacks by faculties capable of substituting for it at first,
and then of raising him far above nature, will therefore begin with
purely animal functions" (p. 115 [III: 143]; my emphasis). Rousseau wishes to characterize man's beginnings as purely animal,
or natural, but at the same time he views the outcome of man's
perfectibility as "above" nature (ibid.). If man begins with instinct, perfectibility must be viewed as a faculty capable of opposing
or overriding instinct. But Rousseau has previously argued that such
a faculty is or must be derived from freedom of the will, and
perfectibility is intended not to depend on this disputed or
questionable freedom. Perfectibility so conceived is only compatible with the assumption that man begins without instinct. Yet
Rousseau again emphasizes his doubt; man "perhaps" lacks
instinct. To add to the perplexity, he later repeatedly argues that
natural man was in fact ruled by instinct. He states that natural man

"had, in instinct alone, everything necessary for him to live in the state of nature" (p. 127 [III: 152]). And, further on, it is said of natural man that "the products of the earth furnished him with all the necessary help; instinct led him to make use of them" (p. 142 [III: 164]).

What is the origin of this apparent vacillation? Instinct is presented as a natural limitation of desire or action. Animality is characterized by instinct and sensation; instinct determines the reaction to sensation but is not fundamentally altered by sensation. But sensation (more generally, mechanical causation) is the only force or cause that impinges on animals. Instinct is therefore invariant. Man's origins are unlike his completion; in particular, a fundamental change has occurred with respect to the character and objects of his desire. Man is the changeable animal. If man was originally ruled by instinct, some force other than mechanical causation was required to change or counteract his instinct. But mechanical causation is the only force in the external world. The force that counteracts instinct must then be found within man. However, the sole ground of internal opposition to instinct is metaphysical freedom (freedom of the will). If, on the other hand, man was originally devoid of instinct, then, first, there is from the beginning a fundamental discontinuity between the animals and man, for animals are uniformly the possessors of instinct. Second, instinct in animals performs the functions of deliberation and choice in civil or rational man—the determination of the response to external causation. If original man is devoid of instinct, he is also, according to Rousseau, quite without deliberation. What then is original man's ground of action? As we have seen, Rousseau is compelled to propose a capacity for observation and imitation through which man develops instincts; but either imitation is itself an animal instinct, as Rousseau himself once appears to suggest, or there is a specifically human imitation, distinguished from animal imitation. If the latter, what gives it its specific humanity? At best, the human capacity for imitation would be an indication of the difference between men and animals rather than the true ground of the distinction. Further, human imitation is an activity. But, *ex hypothesi,* it can arise neither from instinct nor as an unmediated response to pure sensation. In this crucial respect, it has a formal, in fact more than formal, similarity to the concept of metaphysical freedom.

Though logically persuasive, there is insufficient textual support for the conclusion that Rousseau believed freedom to be the necessary ground of distinctively human imitation. I would venture, however, the following conclusion. Rousseau's apparent vacillation concerning human instinct stems from the fact that both the explicit affirmation and explicit denial of instinct in original man appear to issue in the necessity to posit something like the concept of metaphysical freedom. But the problem of instinct is made central by the positing of perfectibility as man's specific difference. The concept of perfectibility, which came into being as a replacement for freedom, appears to imply or require once again the positing of freedom as a human faculty.

The Ambiguity of "Freedom"

It is, therefore, not surprising that Rousseau returns to the question of freedom. Savage man is said to be a "free being" who exists "in freedom" (p. 127 [III: 152]). Savage man "breathes only repose and freedom" (p. 179 [III: 192]). Rousseau calls the freedom of the savage "natural freedom" (p. 170 [III: 185]). The problem is to elucidate the content of natural freedom. Rousseau begins with the assertion that sociality is not natural to man; original man is solitary. No man in the state of nature does or can significantly limit the physical movements of any other; original man wanders without constraint. Further, original man is "self-sufficient"; he has "no need of his fellow-men" (p. 137 [III: 160]). But "the bonds of servitude are formed only from the mutual dependence of men and the reciprocal needs that unite them"; original man is therefore "free of the yoke..." (p. 140 [III: 162]). Natural freedom is the absence of "reciprocal needs." Original man has few needs, and they are all (or almost all) purely solitary; these are his "true needs" (p. 137 [III: 160]). Natural freedom is obedience to the impulsion of true needs, which are given by nature (are necessary) and are in no way the outcome of will or choice. Since true needs are few, their satisfaction requires a very small proportion of the myriad of objects that nature presents.

Original man is therefore characterized by "his profound indifference for all other objects" (p. 179 [III: 192]). He is unaffected by
or independent of nature except to the limited extent that natural
objects are required for, or hinder, the fulfillment of his needs.
Accordingly, Rousseau describes man at the end of the state of
nature in the following manner: "Having formerly been free
and independent, behold man, due to a multitude of new needs,
subjected so to speak to all of nature and especially to his
fellow-men...." (p. 156 [III: 175]). Natural freedom is contentment with a severely limited range of pleasures; original man
enjoys "repose." Natural freedom may then be said to be
somewhat austere; in this regard, Rousseau compares original
man to the Stoic (p. 179 [III: 192]). But whereas the austerity of
the Stoic is achieved by an effort of will, by a ruthless repression of
desire, the austerity of original man stems from the natural
operation of the unfettered original desires, from "the simple
impulsion of nature."

This account would suggest that the eventual emancipation of
the desires that issue in civil society would obliterate natural
freedom. But Rousseau later broadens his analysis. Man has a
"natural disposition" for freedom or against servitude and oppression. This may be seen from the examples of the behavior in
captivity of animals that were born free; of barbarous man; and of
"all free peoples." Servitude is here viewed as physical constraint;
more precisely, the cage of the wild animal is the analogy through
which civil oppression is understood. The desire for freedom is as
fundamental, natural, or original as any of savage man's true
needs. In fact, the desire for freedom appears to take precedence
over the other needs; "savages scorn European voluptuousness
and endure hunger, fire, the sword, and death to preserve only
their independence...." Free men sacrifice "pleasures, repose,
wealth, power and life itself" for the preservation of freedom. If savage man "breathes only *repose* and freedom," it is also the case that
he "prefers the most *turbulent* freedom to tranquil subjection"
(pp. 163-65 [III: 180-82]; my emphasis). Freedom, Rousseau
clearly argues, is (and is naturally perceived to be) a higher good
than life itself. It follows, first, that even if civil society is viewed as
subordinate to or the product of individual human desire, its

genesis and nature cannot be explained simply as a deduction from the desire for self-preservation. Second, the core of the freedom so ardently desired is the absence of subjection to another human being. Moreover, since freedom so defined is natural, natural freedom constitutes the standard for the judgment of civil society and of civilized man in general. Finally, freedom in this sense is in an important respect akin to natural freedom viewed as limited need or desire; freedom is the basis of austerity, or actions not directed to "voluptuousness" and endless pleasure. Freedom may ultimately be bound up with a pleasure; but it is not sought for that pleasure, and it is preserved or regained through pain. The desire for freedom is the ground of the distinction between high and low pleasures.

If freedom is the highest desire, and if human nature is to be understood with reference to "the first and simplest operations of the human soul," which are "anterior to reason," it would follow that man's essence or humanity ought to be understood in large measure as freedom. Rousseau does not hesitate to follow this course. Freedom is one of the "essential gifts of nature"; by giving it up, "one degrades his being" (p. 168 [III:184]). "No temporal goods" can compensate for the loss of freedom; it is beyond price; it has absolute worth or what comes to be called "dignity" (*Foundations*, p. 53 [IV:435]). Again, "freedom is a gift they [i.e., all children] receive from nature by being men ... the jurists, who have gravely pronounced that the child of a slave would be born a slave, have decided in other terms that a man would not be born a man" (*Inequality*, p. 168 [III:184]). It is by virtue of freedom that man is man; freedom is not an accidental or conventional quality, but rather "essential."

It thus appears that Rousseau, having at the outset rejected freedom as man's specific difference, returns as it were dialectically through the notion of perfectibility to the view that freedom is indeed man's distinguishing quality. This view is exposed, however, to a fundamental objection. The desire for freedom, and freedom itself, are said to be natural to animals as well as to men. If freedom is the essence of man, it cannot be freedom viewed either as absence of constraint or as the natural limitation of desire, for animals participate in freedom in both these senses. There is,

moreover, a tension between these two senses of freedom. Freedom viewed as the limitation of desire vanishes at or prior to the
inception of civil society. All men come to share a fundamental
dependence or servitude; man becomes a "slave" to his fellow
men "even in becoming their master" (p. 156 [III: 175]). Freedom
viewed as absence of constraint persists, at least as an ardent desire,
in civil society. In relation to this kind of freedom, the distinction
between master and slave, or between free man and slave, far from
being a matter of mere opinion or appearance, is fundamental. It
would seem that freedom in this sense, which preserves an
unbroken continuity of existence between the state of nature and
civil society, must be the natural freedom that provides the ground
for civil freedom. Yet Rousseau explicitly argues that "the origin of
society . . . destroyed natural freedom for all time. . . ." (p. 160
[III: 178]). It follows that if civil freedom exists, even as a coherent
idea, it must be understood as discontinuous with, or fundamentally different from, natural freedom. Yet there is almost nothing
in the *Second Discourse* that would enable us to provide this
merely negative concept with any concrete content or character.

Rousseau's dilemma stems from his faithfulness to his original
"scientific" program. His return to the notion of freedom takes
place on the level of nature; freedom comes to consist in a
particular sort of desire, or absence of desire, which can be
understood as a natural or even animal phenomenon. His final
characterization of freedom reflects his unwillingness to rest the
analysis of human or political affairs on the disputed concept of
metaphysical freedom. In the course of that characterization, he
states that he "will not stop to inquire" into the notion of
freedom as opposition to instinct or simple animality. And he
suggests that freedom so conceived must be viewed as the gift or
product of a "sublime workman," "the author of one's being,"
and not merely as an "essential gift of nature." The problem of
metaphysical freedom is evidently linked to broader cosmological
or theological considerations (p. 167 [III: 183]). As in the first
discussion, Rousseau does not suggest that metaphysical freedom is
absurd or self-contradictory; he appears to incline to the view that
it is both "noble" and compatible with the human phenomena as
they emerge within the perspective of the citizen and even within

political inquiry. However, the proof or demonstration of this freedom is outside the scope of his inquiry, and perhaps altogether impossible; human science constructed in the image of natural science is incompetent to judge of metaphysical questions. To repeat, metaphysical freedom is at best a permissible but non-demonstrable hypothesis.

Nature, Freedom, and the Problem of History

Let us return to the beginning of our inquiry. The *Social Contract* embodies a qualified praise of civil society as against the state of nature; in civil society, man's condition can be better as well as worse than in the state of nature. Not only are natural man's ideas limited, his sentiments and soul undeveloped; but, also, his actions are entirely premoral. He is moved only by instinct, physical impulsion, appetite, self-interest, and inclination. The passage from the state of nature to the civil state produces in man "a very remarkable change"; his actions come to be characterized by "justice," "morality," and "other principles" that can successfully oppose the instinctual or merely animal within him (*C.S.*, I, 8 [III: 364]). This praise of civil society rests then on the contention that nature is low and that civil man is elevated above nature by a specific sort of freedom that can oppose nature. Rousseau does not say that civil man is happier than natural man; the possibility of morality or justice, and not happiness, is the ground of distinction between the high and the low.

It is for this reason that there is a tension between the *Second Discourse* and the *Social Contract* concerning the status of civil society. Since Rousseau refuses to rely on metaphysical freedom in the *Second Discourse,* he is compelled to give a purely "natural" account of freedom and thus to cast grave doubt on the possibility of morality and justice in the strict sense. Thus whereas in the *Social Contract* he argues that "to relinquish one's freedom is to relinquish ... one's duties" and that "to strip all liberty from one's will is to strip all morality from one's actions" (I, 4 [III: 356]), he speaks in the *Second Discourse* of the "duties" of natural man and alludes to a premoral conception of virtue as those qualities that conduce to preservation, "in which case, it would be necessary to call the most virtuous the one who least resists the simple impulses of nature" (*Inequality*, pp. 96, 128 [III: 126, 152]). He goes so far as to suggest the possibility of "natural virtue" (p. 130 [III: 154]). The blurring of the distinction between virtue and "natural goodness" is the necessary consequence of the lowering or redefinition of freedom in the *Second Discourse*. This ambiguity allows (or perhaps compels) Rousseau to recur to happiness as a standard of judgment. Civil society is inferior to the state of nature because civil man is discontented or miserable while natural man is content or happy (pp. 178-80 [III: 191-93]).

   Ultimately, then, the political science based on natural science is not fully compatible with the political science incorporating metaphysical freedom as a standard. This tension, however, does not lead Rousseau to discard the permissible hypothesis of freedom in favor of the apparently more solid or demonstrable conclusions of natural science. Rousseau begins from the phenomenon of morality as self-denial, austerity, or opposition to instinct, that is, from the perspective of the good citizen or the moral man. Citizen virtue, the "sublime science of simple souls" (*Sciences and Arts*, p. 64 [III: 30]), has for him a sort of self-evidence; the question is not to demonstrate the existence of morality but rather to describe the structure of the world in such a manner that the possibility and dignity of morality are preserved. Rigorous natural or scientific explanation reduces morality to desire. Theological or metaphysical explanation preserves the dignity of morality but lacks rigor or certainty; it may weaken moral conviction by grounding morality on abstract premises that will always be in dispute. The dignity and self-evident certainty of morality cannot together be defended either from "below" or from "above." Morality must somehow serve as its own ground or justification or source. Yet it is surely vulnerable to attack from both below and above. Rousseau's analysis establishes the need for, and points forward to, a negative defense that will silence "all objections to morality ... in Socratic fashion, namely, by the clearest proof of the ignorance of the objectors" (*Pure Reason,* p. 30 [B xxxi]). Nonetheless, he is unwilling to sever completely the link between nature and morality, or between natural science and political science. The ambiguity of "natural freedom," which cannot ultimately be distinguished from moral slavery, is but one indication of Rousseau's inability either to surrender to nature completely or to abandon the attempt to find in nature as known through natural science the ground and content of specifically human virtues or qualities.

This problem is by no means peculiar to Rousseau. The central theoretical difficulties of Hobbes's political thought stem from a never-resolved tension between political science as "phenomenology" and as deduced from natural science; the latter procedure, while apparently more rigorous, cannot help but abolish all politically relevent distinctions between man and the rest of nature, rendering political science as an independent sphere of inquiry impossible and leading irresistibly to the Spinozistic conclusion that might (viewed as power common to all beings) makes right.*

That the *Second Discourse* takes the form of a history follows from the fact that Rousseau ultimately preserves the distinction between the natural and the human that is the ground for the difference between original and civil man. History is necessary and important only if the passage of time changes mankind in the most fundamental respects; as Rousseau emphatically states, "the human race of one age [is] not ... the human race of another ... the soul and human passions, altering imperceptibly, change their nature so to speak ... our needs and our pleasures change their objects in the long run..." (*Inequality*, p. 178 [III: 192]). Therefore, as Collingwood emphasizes, the existence of history in the modern sense is absolutely incompatible with the doctrine that the essential boundaries of human nature are fixed and that the changes that occur are (in both the common and the philosophical sense) merely "accidents" (Collingwood, 1967, pp. 20-25, 42-45, 71-76, 81-85, 223-31, 315-20). Modern science contributes negatively to the establishment of history by making plausible the contention that the apparently eternal heterogeneity of things, each with its own nature, must by viewed as transitory modifications of one primordial substance. However, as the case of Spinoza showed most clearly, the complete immersion of humanity in the determined

---

*For the classic exposition of this dilemma see Strauss, 1965b, pp. 15-21, 229-41; 1963, pp. 1-29, 129-70; 1959, pp. 174-82; 1965a, pp. 165-77 (esp. 173 n.), 201.

natural order made history impossible. History is grounded on the apparently contradictory requirements that a distinctively human sphere exist over against "mere" nature and that humanity have no fixed or specifiable essence. This demand could be satisfied only by the concept of a human substance whose essence was to have no essence and could therefore provide the ground for indefinite modification of humanity without ceasing to be itself. (As can be seen even from this formulation, any attempt to describe this substance further necessarily "hypostasizes" it and therefore contradicts itself.) It is in the thought of Rousseau that this conception of humanity first emerges. Whatever the contradictions within and among the notions of natural freedom, perfectibility, and moral freedom, their common substratum is absence of structure or determination. History becomes central for Rousseau's analysis of humanity precisely because he is compelled to view the essence of man as negative: freedom or absence of determination.

There are two related difficulties. Rousseau sees that human freedom requires an attack on the doctrine of human teleology (in fact, what nature and freedom have in common is lack of purpose). Accordingly, he argues that the present characteristics of man have only accidental existence: they "could never develop by themselves ... in order to develop they needed the chance combination of several foreign causes which might never have arisen..." (*Inequality*, p. 140 [III: 162]). In Aristotelian terms, the various features of civil man are present in natural man as formal causes, but the efficient causes of their development are found only in material motion, i.e., nature. In a sense, history is determined by nature, for man's alteration in time does not occur solely as a consequence of what he is.* Thus, as we have seen, although Rousseau insists that freedom manifests itself in "purely spiritual acts about which the laws of mechanics explain nothing," his attack on teleology seems to lead to the consequence that material causation is the only source of human motion (i.e., action). The independence of man and history is jeopardized by the apparent dominance of nature.

Moreover, although Rousseau calls his account of history a "system" or "philosophy," in fact the very existence of history (to

*For a fuller exposition of the position see "Philopolis," III: 230–32. For the argument to which Rousseau was responding see *O.c.*, III: 1383–84.

say nothing of the particular course it has taken) is contingent or accidental. In speaking of the "chance" combination of natural causes he does not mean that a portion of nature is mechanically undetermined but rather that nothing in the ceaseless flux of matter is directed toward the emergence of historical motion. History fills no void in the cosmos; it is a sequence of accidents; it is meaningless or absurd. But if history is to be a "realm" or "field" separate from nature and subject to philosophical investigation, while it need not consist of essences or objects, it must have some sort of structure, and its parts, some relation to a whole or organizing principle.

Generally, we may say that human freedom is the ground of "historicity" but not of history; more precisely, it is the necessary but not sufficient condition of history. History requires in addition both that freedom be purely self-subsisting, i.e., contain an immanent source of change or motion, and that this motion constitute a structure that is ordered or significant and whose form emerges purely out of itself.

4

Kant's Philosophy of History: *The Convergence of Morality and Natural Science*

Introduction

For Kant, philosophy of history emerges as the necessary completion of politics, the only possible (or permissible) means for the actualization of the just political order. The direction of the movement of history (hence its very nature) can only be understood with reference to the just order. This order purports to be deduced from the character of morality. The core of Kantian morality consists in the radical rejection of any natural guidance and of the orientation toward happiness and in the assertion that morality or the good can only be understood as internal freedom. We may say that Kant begins from Rousseau's antithesis between happiness and the moral life and from Rousseau's characterization of the moral as the free; but he resolutely rejects Rousseau's inability to choose unambiguously between morality and happiness. We are necessarily and irretrievably human, as Rousseau virtually admits; but according to his own premise, the core of humanity or human dignity is freedom. Insofar as happiness is irrelevant to freedom we must ignore it; insofar as it endangers freedom we must resist it. It may be tolerated as a thoroughly subordinated wish but cannot be the guiding object of moral desire. In fact, morality must be understood as altogether unrelated to desire.*

---

*The foregoing, of course, rests on an *interpretation* of the essential tendency of Kantian moral thought. For a more extended discussion of the problem of happiness see below, pp. 180–83, 252–55.

Kant's depreciation of happiness in large measure must be seen as the outcome of his analysis of natural science, an analysis far deeper and more complex than that of Rousseau, though thoroughly in accord with his fundamental tendency. Yet even a cursory reading of the crucial moral works reveals that Kant also felt compelled to attack the status of happiness on its own level without overtly recurring to scientific principles. Kant's radicalization of Rousseau required an attack on the entire "eudaimonistic" tradition, of which Rousseau was only the very ambivalent heir. The classic and most comprehensive attempt to present morality within the horizon of human striving for happiness is to be found in Aristotle's *Ethics*.

At first glance, the *Ethics* appears to move within the sphere of the ordinary moral consciousness; one may quarrel with the account given of particular virtues, but by and large the description possesses a remarkable force and evidence. It is, as it were, a gallery in which the statues of the virtues are displayed. By contrast, Kantian morality may appear arbitrary, forced, and nearly unrecognizable in spite of its explicit claims to be nothing more than a clarification of the ordinary moral experience. But these first impressions cannot be maintained. In crucial respects Aristotelian morality stands in tension both with itself and with our most fundamental notions of the basis on which praise and blame ought to be assigned. There is a direct dialectical path from these difficulties to the most characteristic tenets of Kantian morality, which may be viewed as an attempt to provide an account both less paradoxical and more faithful to our (largely unexamined) experiences. We begin, therefore, with a critique of the *Ethics,* implicitly guided by what will emerge as the major premises of Kantian morality.

The Problem of Morality

Internal Tensions in
Aristotle's Ethics

The central argument of Book 1, which sets forth the outline and scope of the inquiry, may be roughly summarized as follows. All human activities are directed toward an end. Different activities are directed toward different ends, but there is an order or hierarchy among ends. There is a highest end, which is the end of politics. The highest end is happiness, which consists in virtuous activity coupled with good fortune (bodily and external goods). As this argument is propounded in Book 1, many serious difficulties emerge, of which for present purposes we need note only five.

1. The argument for a determinate highest good appears to rest on the assertion that there exists a more or less invariant and easily specifiable hierarchy among the various human activities, but in practice it seems peculiarly difficult to ascertain dominance and subordination except in very particular situations. (a) Aristotle's subordination of horseback riding to strategy is based on the assertion that riding is a "military action." But riding has now ceased to be of military relevance; rather, it is a leisured activity pursued for its innate pleasure, hence akin to those activities to which Aristotle himself subordinates the "unleisurely"arts of war (*Ethics* x. 7. 1177b 8-10). The hierarchy of the arts seems not to be natural or fixed but rather to depend on particular circumstances or on "history." (b) To pose the problem more sharply, let us consider the relation of courage and strategy. This procedure is legitimated by Aristotle himself who, having given examples of hierarchical ordering of activities and ends, remarks that "it makes no difference whether the activities themselves are the ends of the actions, or something else apart from the activities . . ." (i. 1. 1094a 16-18). Strategy must make use of courage; every general must know which are his best troops and which tasks ought to be assigned to them. Yet strategy is subordinate to the overall political order and, as Aristotle emphasizes, that order is directed toward the nurture of moral virtue, of which courage is a conspicuous part. That courage is used by strategy does not mean that the end of strategy is to be preferred to the end (i.e., activity) of courage. Moreover, it is questionable whether the strategist who makes use of the courage of his troops is necessarily courageous or virtuous in any sense. He may merely be clever, i.e., able to do the things that "conduce to the proposed aim," whatever it may be (vi. 12. 1144a 25). The order of rank of art, even architectonic art, and virtue is far from evident; the courageous enlisted man may

well be the equal or superior of the noncourageous but strategically
excellent general.

2. The proposition that there is a highest end is fundamentally
hypothetical. Aristotle states: "*If* our actions have an end that we
wish for itself and *if* we wish other things for that end, and not
each thing on account of another (for this would involve us in an
infinite process, making our desire useless and in vain), then
obviously that will be not only a good end but a supreme end" (i. 2.
1094a 19-23). Aquinas elucidates the implied premises as follows:

> If we should proceed to infinity in our desire for ends so that one end
> should always be desired on account of another to infinity, we will never
> arrive at the point where a man may attain the ends desired. But a man
> desires fruitlessly what he cannot get; consequently, the end he desires
> would be useless and vain. But this desire is natural, for it was said that
> the good is what all beings naturally desire. Hence it follows that a
> natural desire would be useless and vain. But this is impossible. The
> reason is that a natural desire is nothing but an inclination belonging to
> things by the disposition of the First Mover, and this cannot be frustrated
> [Aquinas, 1964, p. 13, ¶ 21].

(Among other things, this argument would appear to imply that
since the desire for wisdom is natural, wisdom in principle must be
available to men.)

In addition, the argument depends on an essential unity of
human nature, which is assumed rather than proved. Aquinas
brings out Aristotle's premise as follows:

> If . . . there should be some end immediately apparent to which all the
> products of all arts and human activities are directed, such an end will be
> the good unqualifiedly sought, that is, the end intended in all human
> operations. But if at this point many goods arise to which the different
> ends of different arts are ordered, our reason will have to inquire beyond
> this number until it arrives at this one thing, that is, some obvious good.
> There must be, indeed, one ultimate end for man precisely as man
> because of the unity of human nature, just as there is one end for a
> physician as physician because of the unity of the art of medicine. The
> ultimate end of man is called the human good which is happiness [pp.
> 47-48, ¶ 106].

3. The proposition that the highest end is the end of politics is
established through the premise that politics governs all other
studies and pursuits. But there is a distinction between the
practical and the theoretical. Architectonic knowledge dictates

what is to be done by subordinate arts and sciences and uses them for its own ends. As to the first, political science governs both the existence and specific operation of the practical, but only the existence of the theoretical, not its operation or subject matter. As to the second, political science governs the use of the practical things only. Politics can attempt to govern the theoretical fully (e.g., Lysenkoism), but perverts it thereby for, as Aquinas says, the theoretical is "not subject to the human will nor . . . ordered to human living but . . . depends on the very nature of things" (p. 14, ¶ 27).

4. The claim that politics is harmonious or coextensive with ethics rests on the assertion that the ends of the individual and of the city are the same; yet, as Aristotle explicitly indicates, this assertion is at best hypothetical, an object of investigation rather than a proposition secure enough to serve as its foundation. It is not evident that a city can be "happy" in the way that individuals are. The statement that a city is "just" has a possible meaning that does not necessarily reduce to the assertion that all of its citizens are just, but the same does not seem to be true of happiness. Yet political science deals with men in the city rather than in the family or as individuals.

5. Aristotle establishes that the good for man is the activity of the soul in accordance with virtue (excellence) through a theoretical or scientific deduction from the distinctively human functions or faculties. But the content of this excellence is not so deduced; the equation of excellence with moral virtue as commonly understood is merely asserted on the basis of respectable opinions. Moreover, the specific content of moral virtue is not deduced, but only described and clarified; this phenomenology, it seems, can command assent only through self-evidence. But one need not be immoral or contentious to doubt that Aristotle's descriptions of particular virtues are incontrovertible; it suffices to refer to the dispute between classical and Christian ethics over the status of magnanimity and continence. The appeal to common sense does not seem capable of coping with the most profound moral questions.

These, though serious difficulties, in a sense remain on the surface. To understand both the connection and the tension

between the alleged self-evidence of Aristotelian ethics and its
extraordinarily equivocal status, we shall have to proceed somewhat more systematically. The following inquiry deals with three
major themes in the *Ethics:* the relation of moral virtue to
theoretical philosophy or science; the relation of moral virtue to
politics and law; and the relation between moral virtue and
happiness.

Moral Virtue and Theory

For Aristotle, the nature of moral virtue cannot be understood
without reference to its rank. He defines wisdom as "knowledge of
the highest objects"; consequently, "it is strange to think that
politics or prudence is the most worthy, if man is not the best thing
in the cosmos." But "there are other things much more divine in
their nature even than man, the most visible being the things of
which the heavens are composed" (*Ethics* vi. 7. 1141a 20-b 2).
Accordingly, the *Ethics* culminates in the praise of the contemplative life, since "not only is *nous* the highest thing in us, but these
things with which it deals are the highest of knowable things" (x.
6. 1177a 21-22). But man can contemplate truth, not by virtue of
the specifically human, but insofar as something divine is present
in him; and "by so much as this is superior to our composite
nature is its activity superior to that which is the exercise of the
other kind of virtue" (x. 7. 1177b 29-30). Moral virtue, on the
other hand, is specifically human; it seems "even to arise from the
body, and virtue of character to be in many ways bound up with
the passsions." Moral virtue and prudence, indissolubly linked to
each other, both connected to the passions, must belong to our
"composite nature" and are (merely) human (x. 7. 1178a 14-22).
   There are some difficulties, however. We may set aside the
question of whether the celestial bodies are truly divine in any
sense (and whether Aristotle fundamentally believed them to be)
since they were offered only as the most visible and concrete
example, and one fully in accord with conventional piety. The
most manifest difficulty is that Aristotle explicitly distinguishes
"contemplation" from "philosophy"; contemplation is not the
yearning or quest for wisdom but activity in accordance with

wisdom; it presupposes that the quest can come to an end, that the highest things are ultimately knowable. But this is an unfounded assumption in the absence of a completed inquiry into the whole. The contemplative life comes to light as the culmination of the quest for happiness, as the answer to the question "What is happiness?"; but if the quest for knowledge in principle cannot be requited, does the situation of the inquirer (philosopher) not resemble that of men (discussed by Aristotle at the very beginning of the *Ethics*) whose desire is infinite, hence "empty and vain"? Clearly it cannot be known prior to inquiry whether inquiry is vain; and it may be that precisely the essential limitations of reason cannot become evident to reason. The inquirer is, it seems, like a prospector who sets out not knowing in which direction his treasure might lie, whether he can reach it if the direction is determined, or whether he can unearth it if it is reached—with the added difficulty that whereas every real prospector knows the appearance of the valuable object sought, the determination of what is to be found is precisely the problem for the inquirer. (It cannot be argued that inquiry is the outcome of the necessity for every natural faculty to be fully developed, for this alleged "necessity" is the outcome or conclusion of a prior inquiry into nature.) It might then appear that inquiry is the outcome of a groundless act of pure faith, a choice. The knower stands higher than the inquirer; but what is the relative rank of the inquirer and the virtuous man if the possibility of successful inquiry is in question?

One might argue that man as man cannot help what he should do in particular situations and that the mere description of diverse virtues cannot satisfy him; he must ultimately ask what makes the virtues good, binding, appropriate guides for action. The subordination of moral virtue to inquiry is implicit in the very notion of human action. The most striking feature of the *Ethics* is Aristotle's refusal to permit this subordination. As presented in Book 10, moral virtue is lower than contemplation because the aim they share, happiness, is more perfectly achieved through contemplation and because the human is lower than the divine. But there is no indication that moral action rests on contemplation, that there is a necessary dialectical path leading from the humblest questions of practice to the most exalted objects of theory. The

cognitive independence of moral virtue preserves the possibility
and dignity of moral action; given the infrequent occurrence of
men capable of inquiry or contemplation, the dependence of
moral action on theory would make it impossible for nearly all men
to share in the distinctively human happiness. Nature (and, indeed, the divine things) would have to be considered in light of
this near-universal frustration of human desire. But Aristotle
asserts that happiness will be "very generally shared ... since
everything depends on the action of nature is by nature as good as
it can be, and similarly everything that depends on art or any
rational causes, and especially if it depends on the best of all
causes" (i. 8. 1099b 18-20).

Setting aside the question of natural and divine beneficence, the
central difficulty may be formulated as follows. Aristotle seeks to
give a nonmercenary or nonutilitarian account of moral virtue as
choiceworthy for its own sake; yet the question of virtue emerges
from the desire for happiness, and the analysis of the common
unexamined notion of happiness shows that moral virtue cannot
achieve happiness in the full or highest sense. Further, he insists
that the highest happiness is accessible, at least in some cases,
because completed wisdom is available. There is then a tension
between the notion of the moral as action for its own sake and
happiness as the full satisfaction of human desire. To preserve the
moral phenomena as they appear, on their own level, two steps
seem to be required. First, if it is controversial whether knowledge
of the highest things is available, it may be that man is the highest
being who can in any meaningful way be known. One can then
wonder whether the rational or theoretical knowledge of man is
higher in rank or dignity than the insight into the human good
that accompanies moral action. Second, if one ceases to view
morality within the horizon of happiness, i.e., refuses to take
human desire as the starting point for inquiry into the human
good, then the moral can preserve its status, whatever the
consequences of other modes of human activity. We will see later
how the phenomenon of courage or, more generally, the heterogeneity of the noble and the pleasant, forces Aristotle to move
along the second path. As for the first, the following brief remarks
must now suffice.

Aristotle begins the discussion of contemplation with the

observation that it is the activity of the highest within us, "whether it be *nous* or something else that is this which is thought to be our natural ruler and guide, whether it be itself also divine or only the most divine thing in us ..." (x. 6. 1177a 14-17). He appears to waver between characterizing the human intellect as divine simply, or divine only in comparison to the body (x. 7. 1177b 27-1178a 2). In distinguishing between theoretical and practical wisdom, it was argued that the "good" is relative to the different species and even to the individuals within each species, while theoretical knowledge is absolute: "What is healthy or good is different for men and for fishes, but what is white or straight is always the same" (vi. 7. 1141a 22-24). But one might argue that it is hardly self-evident that white and straight are perceived similarly by men and other animals, that Aristotle's willingness to accept the human intellect as competent to render absolute judgments in the theoretical sphere while denying it that power in the moral sphere is not adequately grounded. More precisely, if the human good is not an object of theoretical knowledge because "there are other things much more divine in their nature even than man," then the human intellect might well be different from, and lower than, the divine. We have no right to assume that contemplation is of the same character for gods and men, that the human intellect is capable of coming to knowledge of the highest things or that it is not deceived when it believes itself to have done so.

The same issue emerges in the *Metaphysics*. Having described the mode of existence of the First Mover, Aristotle at first suggests that human contemplation differs from the divine only in that it is linked to a body: the divine is an activity "such as the best which we can enjoy, and enjoy but for a short time (for it is ever in this state, which we cannot be) ..." (*Metaphysics* xii. 7. 1072b 15-16). Yet shortly afterward he observes that "if God is always in that good state in which we sometimes are, this compels our wonder; and if in a better, this compels it yet more. And God is in a better state" (xii. 7. 1072b 24-26). God's contemplation must be of the highest thing, which moreover is not external or other; "it must be of itself that the divine thought thinks ... and its thinking is a thinking on thinking" (xii. 9. 1074b 33-35). There are therefore two possibilities. If human intellect is strictly speaking divine, then it is its own highest object; human self-contemplation would be knowledge of God as God knows himself, and God ceases to be higher, or indeed other, than the highest potentiality of man. Aristotle's remark in *De Anima* that "the soul is in a way all things" (*De Anima* iii. 8. 431b 21) would be vindicated in the profoundest possible way. But this is absurd. God or the First Mover comes into view as an attempt to explain all motion, and the human intellect cannot easily be viewed as the source of motion of, e.g., the heavenly bodies. We must then say that the human intellect is divine only by relation or analogy. But, if so, it cannot know the highest things; it will at best know *that* they are but not *what* they are. In principle, the human intellect becomes the highest thing of which full or contemplative knowledge is even possible. But, if so, as we have seen, the object of practical wisdom is identical to that of theoretical wisdom. On this level, like the inaccessible highest, "the primary objects of desire and thought are the same" (*Metaphysics* xii. 7. 1072a 27).

According to Aristotle, the proper study of ethics rests on proper expectations; the inquiry is guided by a prior understanding of the general character of ethics. Ethics is threatened by the demand that it take as its model the precision and certainty attained by mathematics, for this results in two related extremes: the quest for fixed and invariable principles; and the conclusion that the noble and just things "exist only by convention and not by nature" (*Ethics* i. 2. 1094b 16). Ethics is not merely arbitrary or conventional, but neither does it have the character of law. Yet if, as Aristotle appears to suggest, ethical principles are true only "generally" or "for the most part," then either the exceptional cases (the deviations from the rules) are legitimated by reference to some higher principle that is not variable, or the exceptional is merely arbitrary and relative to the individual actor. Again, if the antithesis of conventional ethics is natural ethics, nature as understood by Aristotle provides a standard in light of which deviations are viewed as incomplete or defective. Why then could he not speak with the same confidence of natural ethics as of the nature of man, in light of which, e.g., a mentally retarded person is seen as not fully human in each particular case? In a sense, both natural science and ethics are concerned with particular instances; the ambiguous position of ethics cannot arise simply from the need in every case to subsume the particular under the appropriate universal (i.e., the necessity of good judgment).

Aristotle begins the discussion (i. 2. 1094b 13) by considering the noble and just things, the diversity of opinion concerning which leads to moral skepticism. He moves to the "good" things, giving the examples of wealth and courage. Here the problem is not a diversity of opinions—everyone, it seems, begins by assuming that they are preferable to poverty and cowardice—but rather an ambiguity in the ordinary notion of the good. It is generally assumed that good things have good consequences, but wealth and courage can lead to disaster. The case of wealth is not particularly serious, since Aristotle argues that its goodness is merely its utility, that the extent of its acquisition is regulated by higher ends, and that viewing it as a good in itself is simply erroneous. Courage, on the other hand, is unquestionably noble. It seems that the difficulty can be overcome only by severing the connection between courage and its "end." A courageous death is to be preferred to a cowardly life; courage may preserve life in certain circumstances but cannot be reduced to the requirements of self-preservation; it can only be its own end. This conclusion merely increases our perplexity: if the clarity of courage (or, more generally, virtue) is not obscured by the ambiguous relation to an ambiguous end but rather shines forth as the self-subsisting end of action, then whence the imprecision of morality?

Ethical inquiry is almost purely practical; "the end aimed at is not knowledge but action" (i. 3. 1095a 6). Yet the same might be said of the arts, many of which admit of a very high degree of precision. The distinction is that while the actions of the artisan rest on nothing except the knowledge of his art, virtuous action depends on a particular quality of choice and state of character; "as a condition of the possession of the virtues knowledge has little or no weight, while the other conditions count not for a little but for everything ..." (ii. 4. 1105b 2-4). An artisan may choose not to exercise his art and yet remain an artisan in the strict and full sense; the virtuous man cannot choose not to act virtuously without ceasing to be virtuous. Morality tends to collapse the disjunction between knowing and acting. This is supported by the consideration that a nonartisan may be perfectly qualified to judge the artisan's action; a man buying shoes can judge their utility and beauty without knowing anything about their production. Knowledge of the products of the arts is distinct from knowledge of the arts themselves. In contrast, virtuous actions can be properly judged only by men who are themselves virtuous. It is as though the virtuous man creates a product that is only visible to others of his kind. Since the virtuous man is produced by habituation, the "doing" precedes the "seeing"; fully developed, they are inseparable, since every seeing and judging is itself a moral act. Theoretical wisdom and the arts are akin in that each has a sphere of knowing that is at least conceptually distinct from any doing; it seems that the variability and imprecision of virtue must derive from the absence of any such sphere, from the peculiar centrality of action as such. But this account closes off morality too completely; could not moral habituation so presented be compared to putting on sunglasses and "discovering" that the world is green, a judgment shared only with fellow sunglass-wearers? Aristotle suggests that virtue and theoretical knowledge are not completely disjunct by referring emphatically to the virtuous man as acting "according to reason" (*kata logon*) (i. 3. 1095a 10).

This problem emerges more clearly through a comparison of the methodological discussions in Book 1. In the first, Aristotle remarks that it would be just as incorrect to demand demonstrative proofs from a rhetorician as to accept merely probable reasoning from a mathematician. Ethics is somewhere between rhetoric and mathematics; the acceptable degree of imprecision is directly related to the character of the subject matter. In the second, the imprecision is also correlated with the intention of the inquiry. The carpenter and the geometer investigate, e.g., the right angle in different ways: the carpenter, insofar as it is useful for his work; the geometer, to discover what it is, to lay bare all its attributes. Ethics is analogous to carpentry: it investigates and describes virtue only to the extent that it facilitates action. A "theoretical" ethics would ask "What is virtue?" and "Why is virtue good?"; it would seek to derive the virtues from higher principles. The precise description of the particular virtues would become theoretically uninteresting, subordinated to the problems of the status and class character of virtue. Moreover, the geometer is totally indifferent to what use the carpenter makes of the right angle. But we may compare the carpenter, not only to the practical inquiry into virtue, but to the virtuous man himself. A geometry of ethics would inevitably transcend the horizon of the virtuous man; in one sense it would be a completed knowledge of virtue, but it would lose touch with the specific level on which virtuous action occurs. The "carpentry" of ethics constructs the world view tacitly presupposed by the actions and opinions of the moral man; it looks around but not up. This analogy, however, is imperfect to the extent that the carpenter's interest in the right angle is subordinated to the overall end of his activity, while the virtuous man's interest in virtue is for the sake of virtue. Even if the virtuous man is not besieged by a wide variety of dangerous theories that lead him into perplexity and self-doubt, practical problems will inevitably engender difficulties that cannot be solved adequately on the level of the moral consciousness. The example of geometry appears to suggest that there are in fact axioms or fixed principles of ethics.

But the crucial point is that the carpenter does not require any *theoretical* training to know the existence and general character of the right angle; it is a direct perception, based on a kind of experience, of what Aristotle calls the "that" or fact. The moral virtues are of this character as well. Aristotle argues that we need not seek the "cause" in all matters; in some the establishment of the "that" will suffice. "Thus it is with the principles; and the that is a primary thing or first principle. Now of first principles we see some by induction, some by sense-perception [*aesthesis*], some by a certain habituation, and others too in other ways. But each kind of principle we must try to investigate in the natural way . . ." (i. 7. 1098b 1-5). Moral virtue is essentially connected with individual actions; all actions are "particulars or ultimates" that cannot be arrived at from higher principles. Aristotle goes so far as to say that the particular and variable facts (on which actions are directly based) are apprehended by the same faculty that grasps the nondemonstrable first principles of scientific knowledge: "This perception [*aesthesis*] is intuitive reason [*nous*]" (vi. 11. 1143b 6). Prudence, which is concerned with such facts because it mediates

between the state of character (habit) and the particular action to
be done, is the right reason (*orthos logos*) of virtue; virtue is
bound up with a sort of reason that consists only in a mode of
apprehending particular instances. But, as we shall see, virtue
supplies the end and prudence the right means; the rationality
seems to be confined to the means. Aristotle rejects the Socratic
view that the virtues are rational or forms of scientific knowledge;
the "reason" of prudence is not derived from, and does not imply,
a "rule" of virtue (vi. 13. 1144b 18-21). Individual actions are not
related to virtue as the particular to the general; it would be more
correct to say that virtue is the sum of particular actions but that it
is impossible to state in the form of a substantive rule or principle
what these actions have in common. This is not contradicted by the
extensive description of particular virtues, for Aristotle explicitly
characterizes this description as too general to guide actions: the
content of the "right reason" that must determine actions is not
revealed through a phenomenology of virtue.

It follows that Aristotelian moral virtue does not have the
character of commandment or universal law; it cannot be reduced
to a set of principles that can be taught and applied to all
instances. Virtuous men will tend to agree among themselves as to
the proper course of action, but there is no abstract code against
which a man's conduct can be measured to determine infallibly
whether or not he is virtuous. It is possible to specify actions that
always, or nearly always, aid or hinder the coming-into-being of
virtue. Thus law, which commands or proscribes classes of actions,
can be of some utility in developing virtuous habits. But law is
always subordinate to moral virtue, both because it is for the sake
of virtue and because virtue demands that full awareness of
constantly changing circumstances of which law by itself is incapable. Virtue is far more akin to the human qualities needed to
frame and alter laws than it is to knowledge of the laws.

Moral Virtue and Politics

For these and related reasons, there is a profound compatibility
between Aristotelian virtue and politics. Not only is virtue the end
of legislation, or politics in the highest sense; it is a practical end

that does not, in principle, undercut or transcend the specific level
on which politics moves and the necessities to which it always
responds. Without becoming either despairing or cynical, Aristotelian virtue is at the farthest possible remove from innocence. Yet
in a crucial respect the *Ethics* abstracts from political necessity. It
begins with the optimistic assumption that happiness, of which
the core is virtue, will be "very generally shared; for all those who
are not maimed as regards their potentiality for virtue may win it
by a certain kind of study and care," and the substantive
discussion proceeds on this basis (i. 8. 1099b 18-20). It ends with a
rather sharp distinction between the few who can be made virtuous
through speeches and the many who can be induced to act with
even minimal justice only through constant threat of punishment.
To the extent that the *Ethics* has a political teaching, it consists
primarily in the exploration of the tension between the demands
of virtue and its scarcity.

Aristotle begins the discussion that concludes the *Ethics* and
provides the transition to the *Politics* by remarking, as he has done
earlier, that ethics is inherently practical, but for the first time this
practicality is revealed as dual. We study ethics both to ensure and
deepen our own virtue and to be enabled to make others good.
The *Ethics* falls into the latter category; it therefore presumes that
its hearers can be improved through speeches. It is addressed only
to the few who are well brought up, lovers of the noble, "ready to
be possessed by virtue" (x. 8. 1179b 9-10). The many must be
forcibly restrained and punished through law. The distinction
between the few and the many is at least in part a question of
original natural endowment or predisposition. It appears that
teachers of ethics are uninterested in law, since it crucially affects
only those who cannot become virtuous. But this reasoning
presupposes well-raised young men as a condition; it forgets that
upbringing is greatly facilitated if not determined by proper laws.
This is not to deny that a good upbringing is possible in a regime
whose laws are indifferent or even hostile to the cultivation of
virtue. Parental education might even be thought superior, since it
can deal with particular individuals in a way that law cannot. But,
Aristotle argues, the proper handling of particular cases depends
on a sort of general knowledge of what is good for all men or for

people of a certain kind, i.e., an art or science; this is legislation, which must be mastered by anyone who "wants to make men, whether many or few, better by his care. . ." (x. 9. 1180b 23-24). The art or science of legislation combines the generality of law with the particularity of private education. But if the capability of legislation is knowledge of the human good, it is coextensive with ethics; if it is a science, then there is a science (theoretical apprehension) of the ends for which prudence supplies the means. This appears to call into question the assertion that it is moral virtue, in principle distinguished from any intellectual virtue, which provides the end of prudence. It might be argued that legislation is an art, since it necessarily is directed to a product. But Aristotle emphasizes that legislation in this sense does not necessarily issue in law as such, for one does not make laws for the guidance of one's friends, students, or children. In fact, this legislation appears to be general knowledge that the theoretical inquirer seeks for its own sake, even if he has no opportunity to use it; it transcends the implicit distinction between one's own good and the good of others with which the discussion began.

To return to the strictly political level, ethics must interest itself in legislation because bad laws can render men with good natures incapable of becoming good. But Aristotle seems to attach equal weight to the problem of those who cannot be made receptive to virtue through law—men whose passions or desires are so strong that habituation has little or no effect. Law is composed of two elements, force and reason. For educable men, compulsion is the ground of habituation that eventually becomes second nature, even pleasurable; the object of compulsion is the elimination of compulsion. For the incorrigible, however, compulsion is a life-long punishment that never has the slightest moral effect; the removal of painful constraint means an immediate resumption of forbidden acts. According to Aristotle, incorrigibility results either from natural disposition or defective habituation through law or family. Natural disposition "evidently does not depend on us, but as a result of some divine causes is present in those who are truly fortunate . . . ," while defective laws and family are hardly the fault of the child whose capacities they permanently stunt (x. 9. 1179b 22). Good laws inflict pain and punishment on men who do not seem to be responsible for their unfortunate condition and who cannot be significantly improved. This apparent (and not only apparent) injustice points back to the question of why ethics is compelled even to concern itself with the multitudes of incorrigible men.

Aristotle's first response (made explicit in the *Politics*) is that even forced obedience to law elevates men by linking their actions to an external rational principle in the same sense that "tame animals have a better nature than wild" (*Politics* i. 5. 1254b 11). The deeper response may be formulated as follows. Law is inherently political; it arises from and is addressed to the political community as a whole, which will always be divided into the few with the potential for nobility and the many who lack it. The legislator is inevitably faced with the choice between lax laws that do not punish the many but hinder the few in developing their potential and harsh laws that foster the growth of nobility but punish the many for inclinations and actions for which they are not responsible. The elimination of this dilemma would require not only the mass expulsion outlined in the *Republic* but also a continuing program of expulsion; and even this may be considered merely a radicalization of the problem insofar as expulsion from the political community is itself a dire punishment. For all practical purposes the coexistence of and tension between the few and the many is inescapable. If the legislator orients himself by the requirements of the few, he must argue that the possibility of nobility is incommensurable with the actuality of injustice; the relation of few to many is that of ends to means; by the very existence of the few, the many lose their claim to just treatment. But does this not mean that the many cease to be considered men in the full sense and are treated as slaves or animals? Does it not appear that the orientation of law toward the actualization of the virtues in principle requires a certain kind of injustice? This problem is particularly serious because, for Aristotle, virtue is at least as much concerned with the character of the means as with the content of the ends.

We can at least say that the wisdom of the law and its compulsory power form only a fragile unity that is disrupted by the disjunction of the few and the many; compulsion becomes

deracinated, separated from the end it ostensibly serves. The
distinction between the few and the many is by nature; but the
general human receptivity to virtue is also by nature (*Ethics* ii. 1.
1103a 24). If the incapacity of most men to be fully virtuous must
be ascribed to a defect of nature itself, an inability of natural end
or purpose to bring about a complete ordering of the human
things according to its full tendency, it is difficult to see how
human inequality can be the basis of reward and punishment, i.e.,
of praise and blame, in political life.*

The core of the problematic relation between Aristotelian moral
virtue and politics has been expounded in the following manner.
Political life seeks the common good, but this consists of two
heterogeneous elements—life according to virtue or justice and
the mere survival of the political community. In extreme situations, "in which the very existence or independence of a society is
at stake," there may be conflicts between "what the self-preservation of society requires and the requirements of . . . justice." In
such situations, self-preservation must take precedence over the
normal rules of justice. There is, in principle, no limit to the
actions that the requirement of self-preservation legitimates:
"Aristotle seems to suggest that there is not a single rule, however
basic, which is not subject to exception." Yet "the exceptions are
as just as rules." Moreover, "there is no principle which defines
clearly in what type of cases the public safety, and in what type of
cases the precise rules of justice, have priority. For it is not possible
to define precisely what constitutes an extreme situation in
contradistinction to a normal situation." In short, Aristotle holds
that "there is a universally valid hierarchy of ends, but there are no
universally valid rules of action," and that this discontinuity must
be traced to the frequent conflict between objectives that are
"higher in rank" and those that are "most urgent in the
circumstances" (Strauss, 1965a, pp. 160-62).

We can only sketch the difficulties to which this argument is
exposed. First, while it is clear that in practice every political
community will assign a very high priority to its preservation and
independence, it is far from clear that this priority is warranted in

*For a recent discussion of this question see Rawls, 1971, pp. 100-108.

all cases. Should a weak city or petty principality necessarily wage a ferocious struggle to avoid integration into a larger nation or federation, especially if this federation is likely to reduce the frequency of extreme situations? Second, the survival of the political community is nearly always a question of the survival of a particular form of government. (In World War II, for instance, the issue was not the physical survival of the German people but rather that of a regime that organized and mobilized them in a particular fashion.) Can we say that the "exceptions" an extremely repressive or unjust regime makes to preserve itself are as just as the normal rules of justice?

Further, moral virtue seems to transcend the distinction between "ends" and "actions"; it consists in actions that are chosen for their own sake, i.e., are ends. Moral virtue may be equally well characterized as the proper choice of means as of ends. In practice, the distinction between normal and extreme situations amounts to saying that unjust means are sometimes required. But means to what end? According to Aristotle himself, preservation is not coequal with but rather subordinated to living well. It follows that the movement of the political community toward justice inevitably requires the employment of injustice.

Finally, it appears that the city is permitted to consult its needs in a way that the individual is not. The individual may be faced with a choice between courageous action leading to almost certain death and cowardice that will preserve his life; *qua* moral man, he must subordinate even his most urgent and vital needs to the demands of virtue. However particular and delicate the problems of moral action may be, it is difficult to see in Aristotle's account any basis or higher principle on which moral situations for the individual can be divided into extreme and normal. This discontinuity between individual and political morality can be maintained or justified only if the preservation of the political community has a higher rank than the preservation of the individual; now, it is precisely this claim that every political community (even those explicitly founded to preserve the individual) must at some point make. But can this be generally maintained; what should we think about the good man who finds himself ordered to risk his life in an unjust war for the sake of a

corrupt regime? Even in a less extreme case, it appears that some
men die so that others may live, but it is difficult to see why the
life of one man should be subordinated to the lives of one or more
others.

These difficulties may be summed up in a single question:
What guides the decision whether "normal" justice is applicable
here and now? What do normal and extreme justice have in
common such that they may both be called just? One might be
tempted to answer—nothing; the nature of political life is such
that there is frequently an antinomy between the just and the
necessary. Not everything necessary is just. Without going to this
extreme, it can be said that if in "normal" situations the demands
of politics can be roughly coextensive with those of virtue, *the*
distinctively political phenomenon—that which necessitates the
distinction between the *Ethics* as "a kind of politics" and the
Politics as "political science"—is the "extreme" situation. Both
politics and morality are distinctively human—attributes, as
Aristotle says, of our composite nature—but while morality stands
or falls by the rigorous subordination of one element of this
nature, the bodily or animal, to higher principle, politics must
attend to the body as its first order of business and is able to strive
toward higher principle only in those respites of normality granted
by fortune.

Two conclusions appear to follow. First, from the standpoint of
morality the primary political concern must appear questionable;
the moral man wishes for long life and happiness but does not
pursue them when they involve forbidden means; morality is not
derived from or delimited by the requirements of mere existence.
Second, from the strictly political standpoint the greatest obstacles
to the emergence of justice are the extreme situations themselves—
that is, conditions of foreign war, scarcity, and internal conflict.
Peace, plenty, and harmony are the most urgent concerns of the
citizen or statesman who is a sincere partisan of justice. Peace
cannot be secured as long as the earth is divided into a multiplicity
of independent political communities, for even if each has enough
to satisfy its basic needs, not all wars are for the sake of necessities.
Plenty and harmony cannot be achieved within the framework of
laws that repress acquisition in the name of nature and moderation

or create divisions by cultivating and rewarding the abilities of the few while restraining and punishing the many. There seems to be a tension between the type of law that directly promotes morality and the type that serves morality by working toward the elimination of the extreme situation. This tension can be resolved either by abandoning the assumption that the law of the political community can or ought to be aimed directly at the development of moral virtue or by refraining from the hope that extreme situations with all their attendant horrors can ever be fully eradicated. The latter is Aristotle's conclusion. The former leads in turn to two problems. First, if the concern for morality is not simply to be abandoned, an account of morality must be given that demonstrates, in opposition to the claim of Aristotle, that it can develop fully in the absence of a favorable climate of public law. Second, it must be shown how morality so conceived can reasonably continue to serve as a standard or guide for public life.

Moral Virtue and Happiness

Aristotle divides the virtues into the moral and the intellectual. Of the intellectual, some deal with the invariable, some with the variable. In the sphere of the invariable, science (*episteme*) is the capacity to demonstrate, and intuitive reason (*nous*) grasps the first principles that form the basis of demonstration. Wisdom is knowledge of first principles coupled with knowledge of what follows demonstratively from them. The structure of the variable sphere is different. The variable is divided into making and doing, of which the virtues are art and prudence. Roughly speaking, prudence corresponds to science; it operates within a horizon provided by higher principles. In the same way that deduction from false premises is not science, practical consideration based on false principles of action is not prudence. Strictly speaking, the principles of action or ends of prudence are supplied by moral virtue, and "prudence makes us take the right means" (*Ethics* vi. 12. 1144a 8). Goodness, "in the strict sense," corresponds to wisdom: it is the combination or interpenetration of moral virtue (the right ends) and prudence (the right means).

The problem is that there appears to be no intellectual capacity that can apprehend moral virtue (i.e., that corresponds to *nous*). In Aristotle's division, moral virtue is definitely asserted to exist but there does not seem to be any way of knowing about it. This difficulty does not arise simply from the distinction between knowledge and opinion, for the entire sphere of the variable is the sphere of opinion. Prudence is a virtue of the part of the soul "which forms opinions," for "opinion is about the variable and so is practical wisdom" (vi. 5. 1140b 28). Is there no part of the intellect that can be said to be capable of right opinion about moral virtue? We must also ask whether moral virtue itself is in the sphere of the variable or invariable. In distinguishing between prudence and science, Aristotle argues that prudence cannot be science because "scientific knowledge involves demonstration, but there is no demonstration of things whose first principles are variable" (vi. 4. 1140a 33). But the first principles of prudence are, it seems, the moral virtues.*

Aristotle begins this entire discussion by referring to virtue as the habit of choosing rightly, choice being guided by right reason (*orthos logos*). He states that both the general discussion of virtue and the enumeration of particular virtues is insufficient so long as the content of this *orthos logos* is not determined. Thus, it looks as though choice is composed of a mixture of variable and invariable: it looks up to general rational determinations and down to particular situations. Right choice would be the correct sub-sumption of the particular to the general; the *orthos logos* is within the sphere of practical reason. Yet, as we have seen, the "rightness" of prudence is defined, not absolutely, but relative to preexisting right desire. The *orthos logos* is not, it seems, a determination of prudence. Aquinas comments as follows:

There seems to be some difficulty here. If the truth of the practical intellect is determined by comparison with a right appetitive faculty and the rectitude of the appetitive faculty is determined by the fact that it agrees with right reason, as was previously shown, an apparent vicious

---

*The problems stemming from these considerations have been extensively debated. The best recent discussion is provided by James J. Walsh, 1963, pp. 128-49. See also Milo, 1966, pp. 36-66; Ando, 1965, pp. 208-300; Ross, 1923, pp. 215-21; Michelakis, 1961, pp. 1-78; Oates, 1963, pp. 262-95; Aubenque, 1963, pp. 143-53.

circle results from these statements. Therefore, we must say that the end and means pertain to the appetitive faculty, but the end is determined for men by nature.... [Aquinas, 1964, pp. 546-47, ¶ 1130].

This solution will not suffice since Aristotle has explicitly denied that virtue comes to us or is developed by nature. We are naturally able to receive virtue but are not predetermined to comply with it; the moral habit is preceded and developed by repeated acts. But which acts ought to be repeated?

The following approach suggests itself. We can escape from the circle only if the content of virtue can be inferred from some being or quality that can be known, at least in outline, without reference to this precise content. The sphere or subject matter of moral virtue is human action, which characteristically aims beyond itself to some end. Perhaps then there is some end of action to which the moral virtues are related as means and in light of which their specific content emerges. This surmise seems fully supported by the most massive teaching of the *Ethics*: happiness is the aim of all action, can be grasped in general without prior discussion of the virtues, and requires them. Let us then investigate the hypothesis that virtue can be understood as the means to the attainment of happiness.

Aristotle states that "honor and pleasure and knowledge and every virtue we do indeed choose for themselves, for we would choose every one of them even if no advantage accrued to us. But we choose them also on account of happiness because we hope to become happy" (*Ethics* i. 7. 1097b 2-6). Virtue belongs to a class of ends intermediate between the instrument that is desired only for the sake of an end and happiness that is desired for no end, but only for itself. Aquinas explains this through an example—sweet-tasting medicine that is desired both for itself and for its contribution to health (Aquinas, 1964, p. 48, ¶ 109). It is desired for itself insofar as it is sweet-tasting. But it is questionable whether virtue is "sweet." This difficulty is indicated when Aristotle comes to discuss happiness: pleasure seems to be akin to happiness in that it is a "good not praised but is better than things praised, such as God and any good in itself," whereas virtue is simply praised (*Ethics* i. 12. 1101b 10-27). Later, Aristotle says that "even if,

among the activities of the moral virtues, political and military
actions stand out prominently both in nobility and in greatness,
they are without leisure, aim at some other end, and are not
desirable for their own sakes" (x. 7. 1177b 15-18).

The difficulty emerges most clearly in the following. Aristotle
distinguishes between the ends, for which we wish, and means,
about which we deliberate and choose. "The activity of the virtues
is concerned with means" (iii. 4. 1113b 5). The end is "assumed"
(iii. 3. 1112b 16). If virtue is an end, there must be a distinction
between the activity (*energeia*) of the virtues and virtue itself (the
habit or fixed disposition). But Aristotle insists that the end or
good is "the activity of the soul according to virtue": the habit
must be viewed in a way as the means to the activity (i. 13. 1102a
5). Yet this cannot be simply maintained, for Aristotle later argues
that "the end of every activity is that which corresponds to the
habit [disposition]" (iii. 7. 1115b 20-21). If every virtuous activity
has an end, it is difficult to see how any virtuous activity can *be* an
end. But in distinguishing between making (art) and doing (the
sphere of moral action), he states that "while making has an end
other than itself, action cannot; for good action itself is its end"
(vi. 5. 1140b 4-5; see vi. 2. 1139a 32-b 5). It might be suggested
that there is a distinction between activity (*energeia*) and action
(*praxis*). Aristotle appears to distinguish activity from sleep or
complete quiescence; wakeful awareness or contemplation might
be an activity without being action. After all, he does say that
contemplation is the highest *activity*. Action, strictly speaking,
might then be construed as the efficient cause or necessary
precondition of virtue but not as virtue itself. Yet it is the activity
of virtue, and not virtuous action, that is said to be a means or
concerned with means.

The end is to choose means rightly in all matters. But the
rightness of means seems relative to the ends. If the object of
strategy is victory, then any successful stratagem is "right." Or are
successful means themselves divided into two groups—the permitted (virtuous) and the forbidden? And if one is faced with a
choice between permissible means that are doomed to failure and
impermissible means that will succeed...? It will scarcely do to
suggest that the absence of virtuous means proves that the end is

bad. Suppose (to take a much less horrendous example than some that could easily be found) a man, poor through no fault of his own, and without prospects, suddenly has the possibility through a single immoral act of providing superior training and broad opportunities for his obviously talented and promising young son, that is, of giving him the hope of becoming morally virtuous in at least the surface Aristotelian sense.

Precisely this problem emerges with particular clarity in Aristotle's discussion of deliberation. Deliberation is about means and not ends. In every case deliberation assumes the end and considers the means. At the end of analysis, "if we come on an impossibility, we give up the search, e.g., if we need money and this cannot be got; but if a thing appears possible we try to do it. By possible things I mean things that might be brought about through our own efforts ..." (iii. 3. 1112b 25-28). But this definition of possibility appears to exclude virtue as a consideration; it may be possible but unjust to obtain the needed money. Besides, one is compelled to consider the worth of the ends assumed. Aristotle gives three examples. The doctor assumes that he should heal. In his capacity as doctor this may be true; but his patient may be healed only in the sense of being enabled to continue a mindless, purely animal existence (e.g., through radical brain surgery), or the patient may be a brutal and oppressive tyrant. The orator assumes that he should persuade, but he may induce foolishness or worse. The statesman assumes that he should produce lawful order, but this does not even seem definite enough to serve as an end without prior inquiry. In general, the deliberation appears to rest on an additional inquiry into the end; as Aristotle remarks enigmatically in the passage under consideration, "Not all investigation appears to be deliberation" (iii. 3. 1112b 22). Further, the distinction between ends and means is not strict. If there is a hierarchy of arts, then what is an end for a subordinate art is merely a means for a higher. Moreover, the higher art provides the horizon within which the lower is able to assume its end. We may say that if something appears to be both end and means, it cannot be the highest end or an end in itself; it may be manipulated in the name of what stands above it. But moral virtue appears to have this dual character; one can therefore deliberate transmorally about it. Finally, each of the arts has an end, a product beyond its own action that guides the action and in light of which action must be judged. Similarly, the search for knowledge has an end (not necessarily a product) by which it is guided and judged. But what beyond virtue provides its standard so that it is not merely conventional and arbitrary?

In order to grasp the ground of Aristotle's procedure, one must start from the facts that according to him the highest end of man by nature is theoretical understanding or philosophy and this perfection does not require moral virtue as moral virtue, *i.e.,* just and noble deeds as choiceworthy for their own sake. It goes without saying that man's highest end cannot be achieved without actions resembling moral actions proper, but the actions in question are intended by the philosopher as mere means toward his end. . . . The moral virtues are more directly related to man's second natural end, his social life; one could therefore think that the moral virtues are intelligible as being essentially in the service of the city. For instance, magnanimity is praiseworthy because the city needs men who are born to command and who know that they are born to command. But it suffices to read Aristotle's description of magnanimity in order to see that the full phenomenon of magnanimity cannot be understood in that way. The moral virtues cannot be understood as being for the sake of the city since the city must be understood as being for the sake of the practice of moral virtue. Moral virtue is then not intelligible as a means for the only two natural ends which could be thought to be its end. Therefore, it seems, it must be regarded as an "absolute" [Strauss, 1964, pp. 26–27].

It may be objected that this reasoning unduly circumscribes our view by emphasizing the relation of moral virtue to particular ways of life or perfections. Is the explicit theme of the *Ethics* not happiness, and is the exercise of virtue not the indispensable core of happiness? Therefore (it might be argued), we should de-emphasize the view that moral virtue must be choiceworthy for its own sake. After all, the life of the virtuous is truly blessed, for

their life is also in itself pleasant . . . the lovers of what is noble find pleasant the things that are by nature pleasant; and virtuous actions are such, so that these are pleasant for such men as well as in their own nature. Their life, therefore, has no further need of pleasure as a sort of adventitious charm, but has its pleasure in itself . . . the man who does not rejoice in noble actions is not even good. . .[*Ethics* i. 8. 1099a 12–20].

Unfortunately, this attractive harmony of the noble and the

pleasant collapses when confronted with courage, the first individual virtue that Aristotle examines.

It is for facing what is painful . . . that men are called brave. Hence . . .
courage involves pain, and is justly praised; for it is harder to face what is
painful than to abstain from what is pleasant. Yet the end which courage
sets before it would seem to be pleasant, but to be concealed by the
attending circumstances, as happens also in athletic contests; for the end
at which boxers aim is pleasant—the crown and the honors—but the
blows they take are distressing to flesh and blood, and painful, and so
their whole exertion; and because the blows and the exertions are many,
the end, which is but small, appears to have nothing pleasant in it [iii. 8.
1117a 33-b 7].

The difficulty with this analogy is that the pleasure (reward and
honor) is extrinsic to the athletic activity, and Aristotle has rejected
those apparently brave acts that stem from desire for civic honor or
fear of disgrace as flawed or imperfect; to say nothing of other
reasons, fear of disgrace is shame, and "shame should not be
described as a virtue" (iv. 8. 1128b 10). Courage must be weighed
without reference to extrinsic rewards and punishments. Thus,

death and wounds will be painful to the brave man and against his will,
but he will face them because it is noble to do so or because it is base not
to do so. And the more possessed he is of virtue in its entirety and the
happier he is, the more he will be pained at the thought of death; for life
is best worth living for such a man, and he is knowingly losing the
greatest goods, and this is painful. But he is none the less brave, and
perhaps all the more so, because he chooses noble deeds of war at that
cost. It is not the case, then, with all the virtues that the exercise of them
is pleasurable . . . [iii. 9. 1117b 7–17].

To put it most generally: courage is explicitly defined with
reference to wartime situations in which death is a real danger; even
if the courageous man does not fear death in a particular situation,
he must constantly be aware of its possibility, and the very
thought of death is painful to him above all men. Pain is
intrinsic to courage while pleasure is at least in part accidental, for
what is perhaps the greatest pleasure, the recollection of performing noble deeds, presupposes that the courageous man will survive
the danger, and this is subject to chance.

Thus, in the crucial case, the noble and the pleasant must be
distinguished; but happiness is one of the pleasant things, in fact

"the most pleasant thing" (i. 8. 1099a 24). The noble conduces
to happiness accidentally, or not always; but it is essentially and
always choiceworthy. Its goodness must be grounded in another
manner altogether.

The difficulty posed by the heterogeneity of the noble and the
pleasant is exacerbated by Aristotle's strong defense of pleasure
and happiness. He begins from the most emphatic endorsement of
"common sense" to be found in the *Ethics.* Discussing Eudoxus'
argument that pleasure is the good because all beings appear to
seek it, Aristotle comments that "those who object that that at
which all things aim is not necessarily good are, we may surmise,
talking nonsense. For we say that that which everyone thinks,
really is so; and the man who attacks this belief will hardly have
anything more credible to maintain instead" (x. 2. 1172b 35-
1173a 1). He proceeds to offer a theoretical analysis that supports
the dignity of pleasure.

For Aristotle, pleasure is not a movement directed toward an
end but rather is complete in itself; it results from the senses or
from thought and is most perfect when the organ of sense or
thought is "well-conditioned" and united to "the worthiest of its
objects" (x. 4. 1174b 19). A pleasure is the completion of the
activity in the same sense that health is the cause of a man's being
healthy; it is a formal cause. Yet it seems that pleasure is separable
from activity, in conception and in fact, to a greater degree than
health from being healthy; the formal cause of activity ought to be
the state constituted by the perfect copresence of organ and activity
rather than pleasure, which seems to be external to the specific
form of the activity. Thus, Aquinas notes that "formal perfection
is twofold. One is intrinsic constituting a thing's essence, but the
other is added to a thing already constituted in its species ...
pleasure perfects activity not as a habit that is inherent, i.e., not as
a form intrinsic to the essence of the thing, but as a kind of end or
supervenient perfection ..." (Aquinas, 1964, pp. 886-87,
¶ 2030-31). Pleasure is a sort of addition or grace of nature. Since
pleasures are correlated to activities, the rank of the pleasures is
determined by the rank of activities; pleasure is not homogeneous,
changing only quantitatively, but varies qualitatively according to
the diversity of activities. It is incorrect to approve or condemn

pleasure as a whole: the completion of good or virtuous activities is good, since it promotes or intensifies them, while it is worse that bad activities be pleasurable rather than painful (in the sense that the good conscience of vice is worse than the repentance of incontinence). Pleasure is not bodily, though in many cases it may be correlated with body; it is "of the soul" (*Ethics* i. 8. 1099a 8). Pleasure cannot be identified with the replenishment of natural or bodily needs. In the first place, it is not the body that feels pleasure from the satisfaction of need. Second, need or lack implies pain, but there are some pleasures, both sensual and intellectual, that are not preceded by and do not presuppose pain.

The moral virtues, which are particularly concerned with pleasures and pains, must "belong to our composite nature" (i.e., union of body and soul) and seem "even to arise from the body" or to be "bound up with the passions" (x. 7. 1178a 14-16). It seems then that pleasure is a mode of being affected that cannot exist without the body. Aristotle denies this. First, there is in principle a distinction between sense perception and thought:

the actuation of sense-operations is from without; namely, from the visible, the audible, and so on for the other senses. The cause [of the difference] is that sensation . . . is of particulars, whereas scientific knowledge is of universals. For the latter are, in a way, within the soul itself; hence the act of the intellect is interior and at will; whereas sensation is not from within the soul, and requires that a sense-object be presented [*De Anima* ii. 5. 417b 19-25].

This implies that whereas the pleasures of the senses come into being through the effect of some external object, intellectual pleasures are purely inward, generated by an activity that results from choice alone without reference to external causation. Without entering into the complexities of Aristotle's teaching concerning the intellect, we may say that although soul is intrinsically connected to body, and sensation and thought are both aspects of soul, nevertheless the intellect lacks the close relation to bodily organs that the senses presuppose: "Whereas the sensitive faculty is not found apart from the body, the intellect is separate" (iii. 4. 429b 4-5). The self-generation of the intellectual pleasures, their existence as the completion of an activity that is in

no sense "passive," must be traced to the nonbodily pleasures.
But since purely active, nonbodily intellect is not confined to men,
it is possible (and indeed necessary, since there are no interruptions
or contingent hindrances to divine activity) to ascribe pleasure to
God. In the *Ethics,* Aristotle states that "God always enjoys a
single and simple pleasure"; in the *Metaphysics,* the activity of
God, eternal self-contemplation, is said to be "most pleasant"
(*Ethics* vii. 14. 1154b 26; *Metaphysics* xii. 7. 1072b 24).

Aristotle identifies happiness with the highest good, the
complete and perfect end of desire; it alone is desired for its own
sake and never for anything else. The man who is happy wishes for
nothing further. Aristotle rejects the equation of happiness with
virtue; a virtuous man living with the greatest suffering and
misfortunes "no one would call happy, unless he were maintaining a thesis at all costs" (*Ethics* i. 5. 1096a 2). He accepts a
portion of Polus' argument against Socrates in the *Gorgias:* "Those
who say that the victim in the rack . . . is happy if he is good are,
whether they mean to or not, talking nonsense" (vii. 13. 1153b
19–21). Happiness includes both virtue and pleasure: it is a noble
or enviable contentedness. Virtuous acts may be inherently
pleasurable, but adverse consequences or external circumstances
may more than negate this pleasure: virtue is fully compatible
with great suffering. Happiness depends on circumstances and
"equipment" that are not for the most part within man's power;
it requires prosperity or good fortune. The difficulty is that good
fortune does not appear to be granted in proportion to virtue.
Aristotle discusses two possible sources—the gods and chance.
While arguing that it would be reasonable for happiness to be
god-given, he dismisses this question with the remark that it
would be more appropriate to another inquiry; i.e., he excludes
the problem of particular providence from the domain of ethics.
Yet the problem of the just distribution of good fortune cannot be
ignored; whether happiness can be secured through human effort
or at least in proportion to worthiness must affect our view of
nature or the cosmos.

If it is better to be happy thus than by chance, it is reasonable that the
facts should be so, since everything that depends on the action of nature

is by nature as good as it can be, and similarly everything that depends on art or any cause, and especially if it depends on the best. To entrust to chance what is greatest and most noble would be a very defective arrangement [i. 9. 1099b 20-25].

However, one cannot avoid the impression that the problem of chance is never overcome in the *Ethics*. To be sure, there is a movement from the extensive equipment and good fortune required by the virtuous man in Book 1 (requirements that reflect Aristotle's point of departure in the common opinion of the gentleman) to the much more limited equipment in Book 10, where the virtuous life is recast in the image of the contemplative life. But, to say nothing of the problems posed by the diversity of natural endowments, the philosophic happiness with which the *Ethics* concludes requires a long or complete life no less than the popular happiness with which it begins.* Happiness is a combination of chance and virtue that, when fully developed, is a sort of cause that excludes variation or chance. "Cause" is said to be of higher rank or dignity than chance; yet happiness, a combination of cause and chance, is higher than virtue, since it is in a way the end or final cause of virtue. In short, when something lower than virtue is added to virtue, something higher than virtue results. To explain this difficulty, Aristotle suggests a comparison between the virtuous man and the artisan. Circumstances or fortune are the "material" that the virtuous man uses; happiness is higher than virtue in the same way that the product of the artisan is superior to his activity.† Let us examine this premise.

Aristotle argues that "a certain difference is observed among ends; some are activities, others are products apart from the activities that produce them. Where there are ends apart from the actions, it is in the nature of the products to be better than the activities." (i. 1. 1094a 4-7). This is not self-evident. The architect may well derive a satisfaction from the exercise of his ability in pure thought; whether or not the building is erected seems dependent on chance and somehow secondary. Besides, which is more serious, an accident that destroys a building or a stroke that destroys the architectural ability of the man who designed it? The

*Compare i. 7. 1098a 18, i. 9. 1100a 5, i. 10. 1101a 17 with x. 7. 1177b 25.
†Compare i. 1. 1094a 7 with i. 10. 1100b 22-1101a 8.

architect provides the design or form in accordance with which the material is shaped and arranged; but is the combination of form and matter higher in rank than the pure form? It may be argued that the design is solicited and guided by the structure of human needs; activity is subordinate to product and product to need. But surely this depends on the particular need; an architect may be required to design latrines or public temples and monuments that express the proudest memories and essential spirit of a city. It is not implausible to argue that the activity is higher in rank than a product that serves a low though necessary end. Again, a government may provide the means whereby artisans or experts may exercise their skills even though the products are totally "unnecessary"; or rather, since it is judged better for skilled men to work than lie fallow, the making of the product is made possible (and hence necessary) for the sake of the activity. If happiness is the end or good, and if happiness is an activity, it would seem that the activity of the artisan is more akin to the good than is his product.

Yet, there is a diversity of products. To take Aristotle's explicit examples: it is, as we have seen, difficult to say unequivocally that the ship is more valuable than the shipbuilder, but is more plausible to subordinate medicine to health. The end of strategy is surely victory; but a great strategist may be defeated by an inferior opponent because of entirely unforeseeable circumstances. Is a chance victory more valuable than the art or knowledge of the defeated general? We may summarize this line of reasoning as follows: activities are human whereas their products are nonhuman, seemingly of lower dignity, for if there are nonhuman things more valuable than man, they are not made by man; the most perfect activity can be frustrated by chance, the absence of appropriate material. At most we may say that, given perfect conditions, the product is what is best, for the fully actualized conception is better even than perfect possibility. At all other times the product is in some way unworthy of its producing activity.

Even if perfect actuality is what is most wished for, the proper object of praise or admiration is the ability to produce perfection given the appropriate conditions, even if these never come about. Moral virtue is properly the object of praise (unlike happiness). It is therefore essential to distinguish the praiseworthy activity from the conditions that are subject to chance or otherwise outside human control. In so doing, it is hard to avoid the conclusion that, in addition to bodily and external goods, many traits of intellect, of natural temperament, and of sensibility are to a large extent given as conditions. One response to this difficulty has been formulated as follows:

In passing moral judgments—in praising good men or good actions and in blaming bad men or bad actions—we presuppose that a man's actions, and hence also his being a good or bad man, are in his power. We presuppose therefore that prior to the exercise of their wills, or by nature, all men are equal with respect to the possibility of becoming good or bad men, i.e., in what seems to be the highest respect. Yet a man's upbringing or the conditions in which he lives would seem to affect greatly, if not decisively, his potentiality of becoming good or bad. To maintain a man's moral responsibility in the face of the unfavorable conditions which moulded him, one seems compelled to make him responsible for those conditions: he himself must have willed the conditions which as it were compel him to act badly. More generally, the apparent inequality among men in respect to the possibility of being good must be due to human fault [Strauss, 1964, pp. 38-39].

This conclusion, a *reductio ad absurdum* of the initial premise, points toward two alternatives: the close connection between morality and the sphere of the voluntary may be severed, or the sphere of morality must be redefined to include only that which is in the power of every man as man. The former has the consequence that the distinction between the praiseworthy and the enviable becomes difficult to maintain; virtue is merged into the general category of the good, and the specifically moral sphere is lost, at least for all theoretical purposes. Fidelity to the phenomenon of morality appears then to require the second course, which moreover allows us to maintain a great number of reasonable moral assertions.

We do not praise a man for being tall or intelligent, nor do we praise him for his strength or learning if he is compelled to exercise (e.g., by military training) or to study. Yet we may wish for, admire, or envy these natural gifts and their development. We do not praise a man's ability to walk. But if a man is struck by devastating paralysis, from which he struggles successfully to regain the normal use of his limbs, we praise him for his will or

self-discipline if in his situation other men less determined would
not have persevered but rather would have resigned themselves to
what they thought to be their fate. But if it is certain that the
paralysis cannot be overcome, we tend to praise the man who
accepts this fact and works to use well what remains to him rather
than the man who chooses and strives for an end that is clearly
vain. In the same way, we admire a man who is even-tempered and
equitable; but we would not praise him for these unless we knew
or suspected that they had required considerable self-discipline.
Generally, what a man begins with and the early training he
receives appear equally to be the gifts of fortune; we wish for good
fortune but do not praise it. If moral virtue is among the
praiseworthy things, its core must be that which every man,
regardless of natural disposition or upbringing, has within his
power. But if moral virtue depends for the performance of specific
acts upon prudence, and if prudence is related to intelligence that
is unequally distributed by nature, then the core of moral virtue
must be distinguished from moral acts. Moreover, it cannot be
assumed that the fixed intention to overcome passion or lust will
succeed. It seems that men must be praised for an intention, for
the translation of intention into act may well be beyond will or
choice.

This conclusion is strengthened by the phenomenon of incontinence—the disruption of knowledge of moral virtue by passion—
for men are unequal by nature in the strength of their passions.
Aristotle distinguishes between temperance and continence.
Temperance is a virtue in the strict sense; it is correct intention
coupled with correct desire, and the acts it engenders are
pleasurable in themselves. Continence is correct intention that is
strong and determined enough to overcome excessive or disordered
desire; continent acts do not seem to be pleasurable in themselves.
Aristotle ranks temperance higher than continence, but it is not
clear why this is so. In the first place, "continence involves having
strong and bad appetites"; it is admirable precisely because of the
strength of soul required to overcome them (*Ethics* vii. 2. 1146a
10–17). Such appetites result from either nature, defective early
training, or conscious self-indulgence as an adult. With regard to
the first, there are men born with fortunate natures—moderate

desires that are in accord with or surrender easily to reason and training. If these men are well raised, their virtue is graceful, effortless, without struggle. They may be enjoyable and upright companions, but it is difficult to see why their actions should be deemed praiseworthy. Such men in a sense do not participate in becoming virtuous; it was never in their power not to be virtuous, but virtue is said to be "in our own power" (iii. 4. 1113b 6). It may be objected that this implies that only men with "difficult" natures have the possibility of being virtuous. The answer is that the praiseworthy element would seem to consist in the ability to overcome the adversity of a difficult nature, whether or not that nature is actually present. The right reason or principle of an effortlessly temperate man might well not be as strong as that of a continent man. The same reasoning would seem to apply to the man who is poorly trained or formerly self-indulgent; the self-overcoming, the repentance that goes beyond mere regret, is what is truly remarkable and praiseworthy. In such a man, even the perception of knowledge of what virtue is seems to be self-developed through effort, since *ex hypothesi* it was not engendered through habituation. Aristotle alludes to this self-willed strength when he notes that "the continent man abides by his resolutions more ... than most men can"; there is no parallel characterization of the temperate man (vii. 10. 1152a 26). Or, to draw out the implication of an analogy suggested by Aristotle, the temperate man might be compared to a ruler keeping order among a gentle and reasonable people, while the continent man must contend with an unruly and incorrigible mob. Surely he wishes for tranquillity, but that the mob is deaf to reason is not necessarily his fault. He does not lack the ability to persuade, but he must also have fear-inspiring authority and force. As a ruler, then, he may well be more fully developed and knowledgeable than the ruler of the gentle. This conclusion is in agreement with Aristotle's remark that a general is judged by his ability to command, not by the character of his troops or the circumstances in which he finds himself: "A good general makes the best military use of the army at his command ..." (i. 10. 1101a 3). The continent man may be compared to the general who regularly wins victories with very inferior troops.

Since Aristotle himself claims that continence is a kind of conquering and repeatedly characterizes victory as one of the good things, it is remarkable that in the discussion whose central focus is pleasure and pain he does not even allude to the pleasure of continent victory, of self-mastery. In a deeper sense, however, this omission is not unreasonable. The continent man wins victory after victory, but the capture and destruction of the enemy is beyond his grasp. He must be vigilant and wary; his life is composed of grim tension rather than repose. He cannot but compare himself to the temperate man and wish for his peaceful and relaxed grace, even while thinking himself his equal or superior. The knowledge that, through no fault of his own, his condition is less enviable than that to which his merit entitles him must be painful. But virtue is the praiseworthy rather than the enviable, and the core of the praiseworthy is the authority of right reason over the desires, whatever the character of the desires. The exercise of this authority is pleasurable, not essentially, but through an accidental and infrequent good fortune. It is difficult therefore to see how Aristotle can argue that an act cannot be said to proceed from a virtuous dispostion unless it is pleasurable. An indication of this difficulty is that while the temperate man is said to "delight" in his abstinence, the courageous man who stands his ground against things that are terrible "delights in this or *at least is not pained* ..." (ii. 2. 1104b 7-8; my emphasis).

The central problem of ethics is the relation of virtue to reward and punishment, desire or happiness. Virtue is thought to be good, yet happiness, the sum or aim of the desires, is thought to be the highest and most comprehensive good. The goodness of virtue cannot be derived from its utility in the pursuit of happiness, for it is universally observed that virtuous men frequently suffer and that non-virtuous men seem to be enjoying their ill-gotten gains. It may be argued that happiness is enviable contentedness and that only the virtuous are truly enviable. But, in the first place, it is undeniable that the contentedness of the virtuous and of the nonvirtuous have something important in common; if virtue and vice are alternate means of reaching the same or similar ends, one may suspect that all men would prefer to be virtuous but that in certain situations virtue is not conducive to happiness and must be abandoned. The man who is both virtuous and happy is enviable because his good fortune has allowed him to fulfill his desires through the most preferable means; but is the less fortunate man to be commended only if he abandons what he truly desires and adheres to a limited range of means, come what may? It may be argued in the second place that virtue draws the line between permissible and impermissible desires, i.e., that it is concerned with the character of the end as well as of the means. Even if this is so, the problem remains that virtuous ends and virtuous means frequently conflict—for instance, in certain circumstances, a decent man who possesses extraordinary gifts of political leadership can rise merely by peacefully exercising his abilities and gradually winning the admiration of his fellow citizens, while in other cases he may be faced with a choice between living a life of virtuous obscurity and bloodily hacking his way to the top. (The problem is compounded if, as appears to be the case in the *Ethics,* the exercise of certain high virtues is not wholly unrelated to political rank and opportunities.) But, more fundamentally, the distinction made by virtue between good and bad desires cannot simply be derived from an analysis of the desires; a conception of the good precedes the desires and rules them. Goodness and happiness are heterogeneous and can be united only accidentally or through cosmic beneficence. Yet happiness seems also to be "good." The goodness of virtue and of happiness must have something in common, some standard to which both can be referred without falsely and abstractly obliterating the gulf that divides them.

Let us briefly consider two famous cases that pose this problem in all its starkness. In the course of his discussion with Polus in the *Gorgias,* Socrates states that the noble and good man is happy and the unjust and base man wretched. Polus counters with an account of the crimes that a man named Archelaus, born in slavery, committed in order to attain tyrannical power and affirms that Archelaus would have remained a slave without these deeds. Polus implicitly argues that a ruler is enviable whereas a slave cannot be and therefore that the ruler at least has an opportunity to be happy; the desire for rule, even tyrannical rule, reflects the principle that only the noble is enviable. The discussion is

incomplete at two points. First, it is not clear whether Archelaus'
great ambition is matched by his ability to rule, i.e., whether the
position that is clearly a usurpation from the standpoint of positive
right might not be justly his through natural right. Second, the
question whether the commission of unjust acts necessarily renders
Archelaus thoroughly unjust is blurred, since Polus, oblivious to
the issue, agrees when Socrates calls him unjust even though Polus
had related merely unjust acts.

But let us make the assumptions most favorable for Polus'
argument: of all the citizens Archelaus is best suited to rule, and
his crimes, far from proceeding from bloodthirstiness, are limited
to the means required to obtain and retain his authority. Socrates
insists that Archelaus is completely unhappy and that he would
have been better off had he been prevented from carrying out his
plot and punished. Polus counters with a detailed description of
the tortures, culminating in the most agonizing of deaths, that the
unsuccessful plotter undergoes and compares his lot to the successful plotter who will "become a tyrant and ruler in his state and
continue throughout life doing whatever he liked, envied and
congratulated by both citizens and foreigners..." (Plato *Gorgias*
473b).

Socrates' reaffirmation that the tortured man is more enviable
than the successful tyrant evokes Polus' laughter, as well it should,
for it is in a very real sense ridiculous. Men rightly prefer life to
death and pleasure to pain; pain and death may sometimes be
necessary but never enviable. In addition, the assertion that
punishment is better than escaping scot-free rests on the argument
that punishment cures (or is intended to cure) the soul of injustice
in the same way that surgery or medicine cures the body of disease;
but purely vengeful punishment such as torture, castration, and
death can hardly be construed as curative. Finally, the ambition of
the aspiring tyrant, the greatness and scope of his concerns, must
to a certain extent excite our admiration. If the only alternatives
are abject slavery or the reach for tyrannical power, one would wish
for the strength to choose tyranny and to contemn the slave in
direct proportion to his contentedness with his lot. In a way Polus
is right; the tyrant may be beset with cares and enemies, even
remorse, but he is capable of great acts and a certain degree of

satisfaction in the exercise of his abilities. If his abilities are commensurate with his rank, his satisfaction may in fact be enviable, whatever the character of the acts by which he obtains and maintains his position.

One might also note that Socrates and Polus carry on their discussion within the horizon of a very conventional notion of justice and criminality. One might well argue that no regime whose laws sanction the enslavement of able men can claim any status for those laws. As Rousseau puts it, "the uprising that ends by strangling or dethroning a sultan is as lawful an act as those by which he disposed, the day before, of the lives and goods of his subjects. Force alone maintained him, force alone overthrows him" (*Inequality,* p. 177 [III: 191]). The situation created by unjust laws may make it impossible for a man to obtain what is rightfully his, or to be happy, without the employment of means that are not only illegal but also morally reprehensible; it is, to say the least, not self-evident either that men are obliged to avoid such means or that they will be more unhappy if they employ them.

The problematic relation of justice and happiness is most forcefully expounded in the memorable speech of Glaucon that opens Book 2 of the *Republic.* According to Glaucon, if justice is good, it is choiceworthy for its own sake, without reference to its consequences. To judge the worth of justice, it must be stripped of all merely external rewards and attractions. Misfortunes are heaped on the just man: he gains the greatest reputation for injustice, and eventually he is whipped, tortured, and crucified. The unjust man, on the other hand, is compared to a perfect artisan; he attempts only that injustice that he knows will succeed, and if by chance he runs into trouble he will know how to extricate himself. He has mastered the art of appearing just; he rules the city, enters into successful partnerships and contests, and accumulates wealth that enables him to benefit his friends and harm his enemies as well as to offer up magnificent sacrifices to the gods (*Republic,* 361a–62e).

Glaucon's just and unjust men are radically fictitious: it is impossible in the nature of human affairs to fool everyone all the time, and men of exemplary justice, however persecuted, almost invariably have friends, defenders, or disciples. But the

solid core of Glaucon's myth is that in many particular situations
unjust acts are instrumental in the pursuit of well-being. What
does or should prevent a man from committing these acts? The
answer cannot be the force of law or public opinion for, in addition
to being conventional and variable, they can be circumvented
through rhetoric or guile. Justice must be a standard that guides
each man as he confronts himself in the privacy of his own
thought; it must be a private and incorruptible tribunal. Justice
restrains the desire for unlimited sexuality, excessive acquisition,
vengeful punishment, and political usurpation by fiat or authority
alone.

Glaucon does not even speak of a satisfaction or inner sense of
worth provided by just acts in themselves, though his account does
not rule out such satisfaction; at any rate, the painful vicissitudes
the just man undergoes far outweigh any inner rewards, and his
life is happy only infrequently and accidentally. It might be said
that for Glaucon the problem is exacerbated by the attractiveness
of the gratifications that justice restricts; he appears to rule out the
possibility that the desires can or should be restrained noncoer-
cively, through education. This rests on the premise that the full
satisfaction of all desires is natural and even commendable.

The just man, then, is neither an artisan nor a natural man. The
goodness of justice cannot be deduced from any analysis of the
desires or of happiness; since justice is not invariably instrumental
for any end except itself or the goodness of which it is a part, it
must be praised with reference only to itself. It must be its own
ground, a kind of absolute.

Perhaps the most striking feature of the *Republic* is Socrates'
failure to comply with Glaucon's demand. To say nothing of the
manner in which the question of the goodness of justice is begged
during the definition at the end of Book 4, the dialogue ends with
a description of the earthly rewards of justice that in its denial of
any misfortunes befalling the just man is as radically fictitious as
Glaucon's speech. The problem may be posed as follows. The
argument of the *Republic* discloses that there is a natural or
self-willed basis for that limitation of desire that justice requires.
This basis, the philosophic life, achieves success by deprecating the
common objects of desire, the sources of political strife, in the

light of a higher object of desire. Philosophic justice is not self-compulsion or restraint but rather a genuine indifference or even aversion. But this justice is possible only for a very few men, and justice is preeminently a political problem concerning all men. Political justice cannot eliminate unjust desires and must accordingly make some use of compulsion and rewards. Socrates returns to the mode of praising justice forbidden by Glaucon "because the dialogue has not sufficiently demonstrated that citizen virtue is choiceworthy for itself...."*

Summary

This inquiry, admittedly incomplete, leads to the following tentative conclusion: the difficulties to which Aristotle's account of moral virtue leads may be traced to the problematic relations between virtue on the one hand, and happiness, philosophy, and politics on the other. We briefly summarize the main points under these three headings.

1. As the highest good, the ultimate end of desire and striving, happiness is said to have a definite content, i.e., is not a matter of opinion or relative to the individual. As Aquinas makes clear, this assertion rests on the debatable premises that human desire cannot be infinite and vain (hence ultimately on a cosmological principle of the First Mover) and that human nature is a "unity." Further, it seems to depend on the existence of an ordered hierarchy among human activities, but in practice this is difficult to establish because of changing circumstances and the fact that the "products" of the virtues and of the arts seem ambiguously related, perhaps even incommensurable. If happiness is the highest good and a sort of pleasure and if the soul is higher than the body, the status of happiness requires the defense of pleasure as at least potentially nonbodily, hence suited to be the highest. This leads to various difficulties: (a) the highest pleasure is the pleasure of thought, but Aristotle seems to be compelled both to affirm and deny that thought requires body; (b) pleasure is neither deducible from nor necessary for the existence of the various activities, and its source is mysterious; (c) if, as Aristotle claims, pleasure is a formal

*See Allan Bloom, "Interpretive Essay, " in *Republic*, p. 435.

cause of activity, it seems difficult to say that happiness is a final cause; (d) pleasure must be ascribed to God's activity. Finally, if happiness is the highest good, it is higher than moral virtue, but this seems questionable. (a) According to Aristotle, happiness is subject to chance and chance is lower than "cause," but virtue is a sort of cause. (b) Even if happiness is a "product" or end of virtuous activity, the general assertion that the product is nobler or better that the producing activity is questionable. (c) The praise and blame necessarily correlated to the sphere of morality imply that the praiseworthy things are within the individual's power; virtue must consist primarily in intention rather than in accomplishment or effect. The heterogeneity of the object of praise and the object of desire does not mean that the latter is more valuable merely because it satisfies.

2. Aristotle's primarily descriptive and dialectical procedure appears to presuppose that the general content of moral virtue will be the subject of agreement (at least among the virtuous). On these grounds it is difficult to explain or choose among the divergent moral views that arise among sincere partisans of virtue—e.g., the dispute between Aristotle and Christianity over magnanimity and continence. More generally, although the *Ethics* clearly presupposes that virtue has a content that is not merely variable and subject to opinion but that in a sense is the object of coherent reflection or knowledge, on Aristotle's premises it is very difficult to give a noncontradictory account of how virtue receives a determinate content or is known. Virtue requires a "right reason," but it appears that prudence and right desire depend on one another circularly for the content of this reason. Aristotle rejects in advance Aquinas' conclusion that the rule must be provided by nature in the form of innate principles, or conscience. To add to the perplexity, Aristotle's assertion that virtue is not a mode of theoretical knowledge (i.e., is not an object of prudence) seems to be contradicted by the conclusion of the *Ethics* in which the notion of a "science" of legislation coextensive with moral virtue is propounded. The most general problem may be formulated as follows. It seems equally impossible to assert either that moral virtue is an end or that it is concerned with a certain quality of means. If it is an end, it must be the highest thing, but it is not: as

Aristotle says, "Everything we choose we choose for the sake of something else—except happiness, which is an end" (*Ethics* x. 6. 1176b 30-32). If it is a means or concerned with means, it must be understood in the light of some end; but it cannot be fully understood as serving the only ends to which it might plausibly be subordinated—politics, contemplation, or happiness. Finally, if, as Aristotle seems to suggest, moral virtue must somehow be understood as choiceworthy for its own sake as well as in relation to happiness, and if philosophy or contemplation does not require the whole of virtue as ordinarily understood, then there is a tension between the choiceworthiness of moral virtue and the notion that contemplation, the completion of the quest for wisdom, is perfect happiness. The *Ethics* points toward two possible resolutions. (a) Aristotle deliberately blurs the distinction between philosophy (as quest for wisdom) and contemplation. The possibility of contemplation ultimately rests on the assertion that the human and divine intellects are identical and that man is lower than God only because his body restricts the uninterrupted operation of intellect. This assertion is weakened by the claim, advanced in the *Metaphysics*, that divine intellect is a source of motion in a manner that human intellect is not. If, as one strand of Aristotle's argument suggests, human intellect must be seen as in itself lower, human knowledge of God is not equivalent to divine self-knowledge; metaphysics may know of the existence of God but not of his essence. It might well be that human existence is the highest thing of which full knowledge is possible, that the object of morality is therefore the same as the highest attainable object of theory. But then the moral knowledge of man gained through virtuous action may surpass the theoretical knowledge of man in profundity and rank. (b) If the relation between morality and desire or happiness is severed, the relation between happiness and philosophy becomes morally irrelevant. Moreover, this preserves morality if in principle the quest for wisdom cannot reach its end or if wisdom reveals the whole to be ugly and unworthy for, as Aquinas notes, enviable pleasure, hence happiness, requires the unity of desire and the worthiest of its objects.

3. The surface of Aristotle's presentation suggests a fundamentally harmonious relation between moral virtue and politics;

as the architectonic science or art, politics is necessarily directed to
the highest end, happiness, to which all human activities are
ordered and subordinated. Happiness presupposes virtue, which,
generally speaking, is best fostered by a carefully planned system
of laws regulating every aspect of the political community. However, some ambiguities emerge. (a) The end of the city and of the
individual do not seem in all cases to be wholly congruent. Law can
not fully govern the existence, content, or use of theoretical
science, but such science (or its pursuit) is the highest happiness for
some individuals. When law does attempt to regulate inquiry, the
result is often its perversion or repression. Further, to the extent
that the end of politics, the happiness of the community as a
whole, is more than a metaphor, it may well demand sacrifices that
are incompatible with the happiness of large numbers of individual citizens. It may even be the case that the happiness of the
community is equivalent to its unity, which is greatest at times
of maximum civil peril. (b) The harmony between Aristotelian
ethics and politics is achieved through the flexibility of ethics: no
acts are absolutely forbidden, for anything may be legitimated by
circumstance. However, the distinction between morally "normal" and "extreme" situations, which cannot be made on the
basis of any rule or principle, leads to serious difficulties. (i) It is
not clear why the preservation of every political community
legitimates departures from ordinary morality. Unless one denies
or ignores the distinction between good and bad regimes, the
urgency of preservation ought to be relative to the worth of what is
being defended; but in practice no regime will disapprove of
itself. The notion of the extreme situation seems to legitimate all
acts of a despicable regime so long as they are defensive. (ii) If
morality is choiceworthy for its own sake or for some higher end, it
cannot be deduced from the requirements of group self-preservation. Can otherwise impermissible acts in the service of preservation be consistently described as anything other than immoral, no
matter how necessary? To put it another way, the moral man is not
permitted to distinguish between normal and extreme situations;
virtue will sometimes require the sacrifice of one's life. If the
political community rejects this necessity, it ceases to behave
morally. (iii) There seems to be no common principle on the basis

of which the actions necessitated by both normal and extreme situations can be called just. It seems truer to the facts to acknowledge a disjunction between morality that, as Aristotle says, deals with our "composite" nature, and politics, which must first concern itself with life (i.e., the body), and to admit that harmony between these imperatives is always temporary and the product of rare good fortune. As a consequence, there is a tension between laws that seek to promote morality directly through instruction or discipline and those that work toward the convergence of morals and politics through the elimination of the extreme situations (e.g., war and scarcity) that necessitate immorality. (c) The orientation of law to moral virtue requires injustice to the many who through no fault of their own (e.g., heredity or poverty) are not capable of virtue in the full sense and who are punished or used as mere means for the realization of the capacities of the fortunate few. The existence of the many cannot be construed as against nature in the same sense as monstrosities or deformities; in examining a species, the proper starting point for the determination of the natural is the usual, what occurs for the most part. If the existence of the many is just as natural as the orientation of the few to virtue, then not merely expediency but justice would require that law take its bearings from the legitimate claims of both groups. Conversely, if politics is to remain coextensive with morality, then morality must be within the reach of every man as man.

The Kantian Response

Kant's moral philosophy may be described as the attempt to satisfy, in an adequate and fully grounded manner, the demand of Glaucon, repeated and endorsed by Aristotle, that virtue be understood as choiceworthy for its own sake without regard to external rewards. Justice, the central theme of the *Republic*, is particularly vulnerable and obscure. Courage and wisdom are from Glaucon's standpoint unquestionably desirable, as is moderation to the extent that self-indulgence renders a man weak or unmanly. These three virtues can be justified with reference to a view of individual perfection to which all men of ability and good breeding implicitly subscribe. Justice is much less obviously an element of individual perfection and seems rather to be preeminently social; to be just is to devote oneself to the common good, to sacrifice one's own good for the good of others or to care for others. To show that justice is choiceworthy for itself is to prove that there is some nonmercenary basis for preferring others to oneself or for treating oneself precisely as one treats others. Justice in this sense is the core of Kantian virtue. This fact emerges clearly at the beginning of the First Section of the *Foundations of the Metaphysics of Morals*. There Kant argues that the various things thought by the classics to be unconditionally good are good only in a qualified sense, with reference to the higher principle of the good will. Among the virtues so subordinated he lists intelligence, courage, and moderation but omits justice. How far this is from being accidental is shown as the argument proceeds. For Kant, virtue cannot even be defined without reference to all men or all rational beings; it is intrinsically social.* Moreover, the distinctive character of virtue cannot be grasped if the attempt is made to refer it to anything other than itself. "To behold virtue in her proper form is nothing else than to exhibit morality stripped of all admixture of sensuous things and of every spurious adornment of reward or self-love. How much she then eclipses everything which appears charming to the senses can easily be seen by everyone with the least effort of his reason ..." (*Foundations,* p. 44 n. [IV: 426 n.]). Kant seeks to answer Glaucon's question without abandoning the source of his perplexity—the disjunction between morality and the satisfaction of desire.

*See Hassner, 1972, p. 565. For this reason, the argument advanced by Goldmann, 1971, p. 216, that Kant's moral-political thought was limited by the bourgeois "individualist conception of the world, which recognizes only the *I* and not the *we*" must be qualified. Kant's rational being cannot act without considering the totality of rational beings. Every man acts alone, but for all men. In general, the ethics of bourgeois individualism is achieved through the extreme socialization or politicization of the concept of man. But this politicization (which is present as much in Kant's reduction of morality to justice as in Hobbes' to peaceableness) cannot obscure the fact that man is partly for himself against all others, afflicted with an inescapable particularity. For Kant, this particularity is linked to the existence of separate human *bodies* that never can be merged and are the source of opposition to morality. The political or moral community is therefore always partial and imperfect. Goldmann (pp. 223-25) simultaneously states and obscures the limitations Kant imposes on the concepts of community and earthly progress and accordingly obscures the assumptions that Hegel and Marx are compelled to question.

The general structure of Kantian morality is well enough known
that we may dispense with a lengthy or systematic exposition.
Before proceeding to an analysis of its relation to classical morality,
we merely list its most important and characteristic premises.

In agreement with Aristotle, Kant emphasizes the "factual" or
self-evident character of morality; however, while Aristotle argues
that a certain breeding or education that not all men can receive is
required for morality to become fully visible, Kant claims that it is
known to all men as men.* Again in agreement with Aristotle (and
against the Stoics), Kant distinguishes between happiness and the
self-contentment that stems from the consciousness of virtue;
happiness requires a fortunate ordering of external conditions.†
Against both the classics and Christianity, he argues that morality
must be emancipated from prior determination by either nature or
God; to reason from nature or God to the content of morality is to
presuppose their goodness, but this must be *established*. "Even
the Holy One of the Gospel must be compared with our ideal of
moral perfection before he is recognized as such."‡ The content of
the good must be developed out of the pure concept of goodness,
i.e., it must be entirely self-grounded. The core of goodness is the
good will: "Nothing in the world—indeed nothing even beyond
the world—can possibly be conceived which could be called good
without qualification except a *good will*" (*Foundations*, p. 9 [IV:
393]). This establishes the absolute primacy of intention over

Foundations, pp. 7, 20–21 (IV: 391, 404); *Practical Reason*, pp. 31, 57 (V:
31, 55).

†*Foundations*, pp. 12–13, 80 (IV: 396, 460); *Practical Reason*, pp. 122–24 (V:
117–19); *Religion*, p. 69 n. (VI: 74–75 n.).

‡*Foundations*, p. 25 (IV: 408). Consider also *Perpetual Peace*, p. 93 n. (VIII:
350 n.): "In what concerns my freedom, I have no obligation with respect to
divine law, which can be acknowledged by my reason alone, except in so far as I
could have given my consent to it. Indeed, it is only through the law of freedom
of my own reason that I frame a concept of the divine will."

For these and related reasons, Krüger's emphasis on the "Christian origin" of
Kantian morality, and his assertions that for Kant *obedience* to God is ultimately
necessary and that autonomy requires traditional "theological metaphysics,"
seems curiously misplaced. See Krüger, 1961, pp. 198, 237, 264, 267–68. To put
the same point another way: Krüger states that Kant learned from Rousseau the
distinction between "progress of culture" and "progress of *morality*" (p. 85).
But Krüger seems to deny by implication that Kant's views of the *content* or
character of morality were significantly influenced by Rousseau. See Hassner,
1972, pp. 559, 561.

action or accomplishment: "The good will is not good because of
what it effects or accomplishes or because of its adequacy to achieve
some proposed end; it is good only because of its willing,
i.e., it is good of itself" (*Foundations*, p. 10; see also pp. 16–18
[IV: 394, 399–402]). If the good will is the same for all men and if
its content must be determined without reference to the diversity
of external phenomena—actions, desires, or sensations—then it
must consist in pure universality. If it is to be binding, a ground of
obligation, it must be seen as necessary law, that which cannot be
otherwise. Morality therefore takes the form of universal law.* But
in excluding all externality, morality is defined without reference
to the particularity of any individual man or to that of human
nature in general. It is merely reason insofar as it is applied to will;
it is therefore common to all "rational beings" (including God)
insofar as they are regarded as willing.† Aristotle had insisted that
the domain of morality was the sphere of our composite nature,
the interpenetration of body, soul, and mind; man is divine, or
resembles the divine, only through theoretical or contemplative
reason. Accordingly, he argued that the gods are above the moral
virtues, even justice. For Kant, the domain of morality extends to
God Himself; indeed, only God is characterized by morality in the
fullest sense. Human morality is identical to divine morality except
insofar as the human will is subject to influences arising from the
body. The human will moves toward divinity by resisting these
influences, to which God is not subjected. Thus, as was suggested
in the "Conjectural Beginning," through morality man enters
into a relation of moral equality with God, and God is morally
obligated to treat the beings that He has created as equals insofar
as they are "rational."‡ It follows, finally, that no human being
can ever be fully moral:

Foundations, pp. 5, 29, 37, 65 (IV: 389, 412–13, 420, 446–47); *Practical
Reason*, p. 37 (V: 36).

†*Foundations*, pp. 5, 24–25, 27 n., 30, 43, 49, 56–58, 61 (IV: 389, 408, 410 n.,
413–14, 425, 431, 437–39, 442); *Practical Reason*, pp. 17, 19, 24, 32, 35, 37 (V:
19, 20, 25, 32, 34, 36).

‡*Foundations*, p. 54 (IV: 435–36); *Practical Reason*, pp. 32, 90, 136 (V: 32,
87, 131–32). Kroner, 1956, quite properly emphasizes the distinction between
the divine will, for which willing and acting are identical, and the human will,
which, even when determined by a moral intention, is all too often impotent to
act or to transform the world. But Kroner's insistence (pp. 82–83, 118) that for

If a rational creature could ever reach the stage of thoroughly liking to do all moral laws, it would mean that there was no possibility of there being in him a desire which could tempt him to deviate from them, for overcoming such a desire always costs the subject some sacrifice and requires self-compulsion, i.e., an inner constraint to do that which one does not quite like to do. To such a level of moral disposition no creature can ever attain. For since he is a creature, and consequently is always dependent with respect to what he needs for complete satisfaction with his condition, he can never be wholly free from desires and inclinations which, because they rest on physical causes, do not of themselves agree with the moral law, which has an entirely different source [*Practical Reason*, p. 86 (V: 83-84)].

Thus, the highest possible moral condition for a human being is "virtue, i.e., moral disposition in conflict, and not holiness in the supposed possession of perfect purity of the intentions of the will" (p. 87; see pp. 131, 132 n. [V: 84, 126-27, 128 n.]). Kant therefore denies that Aristotle's moderate man can exist; for man, there is no true moderation—at best, continence. Kantian morality is akin to justice in its principle, which emphasizes the relation of the moral actor to other rational beings, and to courage in its activity, for, as Aristotle concedes, the tension between the demands of courage and of human desire cannot be resolved, even (or especially) by the most virtuous man. Through the analogy of moral with martial struggle, Kant restores and emphasizes the etymological connection between virtue and strength: "The power and deliberate resolve to withstand a strong but unjust opponent is fortitude ... and fortitude in relation to the forces opposing a moral attitude of will in us is virtue ..." (*Virtue*, p. 38 [VI: 380]).

Kantian morality may in part be seen as a response to the difficulties implicit in Aristotle's teaching. As we have seen, these difficulties stem from the ambiguous relations of morality to happiness, human inequality, theoretical inquiry (contemplation or philosophy), and politics. Let us briefly consider Kant's teaching in light of these problems.

1. The critique of "hedonism" is perhaps the most massive tendency of Kantian morality, which insists that morality cannot take its bearings or content from happiness. Kant emphasizes, in

Kant as for orthodox biblical thought the "mystery of God" cannot be fathomed obscures the radical core of Kant's moral (and religious) teaching.

the first place, the extreme variety of heterogeneity of human satisfaction. What pleases one man will not please another, and even individuals change their minds incessantly in response to their particular situations. Happiness requires total contentment, but human life consists in an infinite and unpredictable succession in which the pleasant cannot be the object of foresight. Since happiness is not correlated with any particular activity but rather consists in a relation between human activity and an evershifting environment, it cannot be known and therefore cannot in practice furnish a concrete end for human striving: "Happiness is an ideal not of reason but of imagination...."* Further, the body cannot be the highest thing, but happiness is a sort of pleasure, and pleasure is of the body or at least not without body. There is no pleasure of pure thought or will; even the purely moral feeling of contentment of self-respect is strictly correlated to the overcoming of obstacles presented by the demands of the body (*Practical Reason*, pp. 122-23 [V: 117-18]). A holy will (God) manifests itself in unimpeded purity without the possibility of constraint and cannot therefore be characterized by pleasure.† Since human pleasure is in no way a reflection of a divine attribute, it and its correlated desires cannot be seen as oriented to or elicited by divinity. Aristotle had derived the concept of happiness as the highest good from the ordering of activities and the desires and pleasures that accompany them. But this is impossible: there is a disjunction between moral and nonmoral activities, and all nonmoral activities are on the same plane. The hierarchy of the arts is morally irrelevant. There is, therefore, no hierarchy among the pleasures, which do not differ in kind, in goodness or badness, but only "in degree."‡ Happiness is good only if conjoined to a good will. But the highest good is that which cannot be made better by any addition. Therefore happiness is not the highest good (*Foundations*, p. 9 [IV: 393]). (Underlying this argument is the anti-Aristotelian premise that virtue and happi-

---

Foundations, p. 36 (see also pp. 35, 46; IV: 418, 427-28); *Practical Reason*, pp. 24-25 (V: 25-26); *Judgment*, p. 280, § 83 (V: 430).

†*Foundations*, p. 30 (IV: 414); *Practical Reason*, pp. 20-26, 62 (V: 22-26, 60); *Judgment*, p. 43, § 5 (V: 209).

‡*Foundations*, p. 36 (IV: 418); *Practical Reason*, pp. 21-24 (V: 22-25).

ness are so heterogeneous that a nonvirtuous man may be happy.) There is, moreover, an argument from teleology. No organ is provided for a purpose by nature that is not the fittest and best for that purpose. But animal instinct is best for promoting happiness. Therefore man does not exist for happiness (p. 11 [IV: 395]). This argument presupposes that human and animal pleasure or contentment are identical, that there is no constituent of happiness that is distinctively human. This assumption is made explicit in another argument. If happiness is the end of man, then the human end is the same as the end of animals. Reason is then a means to a purely animal end and man is distinguished from animals only by a different equipment of means. But it is impossible to view reason as purely instrumental, assigned its task in advance by purely animal givens. The experience of every man proves that reason is more than a tool; it proposes aims and tasks of its own.* Moreover, the orientation of morality to happiness seems to undercut the grounds of all moral judgment. If happiness is that at which all men aim, then it must be the goal of virtuous and vicious men alike. But all acts must be judged with reference to the intention of the actor. It follows that virtue and vice can only be distinguished as different means to the same end. If only virtue leads to happiness, then vice must be viewed simply as bad calculation (ignorance). But if vice may sometimes lead to or lay the basis for happiness, then there seems no basis for condemning it. In short, virtue and vice are judgments about permissible and forbidden means, but this distinction cannot be arrived at simply through an examination of their efficacy in promoting the happiness of the actor.†

Finally, Kant offers some practical or worldly arguments. Happiness requires harmony or absence of conflict. But there are only two possibilities. Differing conceptions of happiness lead to different objects of desire, hence conflict, particularly when men find themselves in groups that must act according to a common purpose. Similar conceptions of happiness lead to identical objects of desire, but valued objects are invariably scarce, and competition

---

* *Practical Reason,* p. 63 (V: 61); see *Foundations,* p. 11 (IV: 395); *Religion,* p. 41 n. (VI: 45–46 n.).

† *Foundations,* p. 61 (IV: 442); *Practical Reason,* pp. 36–38 (V: 35–37).

arises (*Practical Reason,* p. 27 [V: 28]). Nature is hostile to man, afflicting him with disease and disaster as much as any other animal. Human restlessness makes it impossible to be contented, and

the inconsistency of [man's] own natural disposition drives him into self-devised torments and also reduces others of his own race to misery, by the oppression of lordship, the barbarism of war, and so forth; he himself, as far as in him lies, works for the destruction of his own race, so that, even with the most beneficent external nature, its purpose, if it were directed to the happiness of our species, would not be attained in an earthly system, because our nature is not susceptible of it [*Judgment,* p. 280, §83 (V: 430)].

Kant is not wholly unconcerned, however, with the claims happiness makes. He criticizes the Stoics for equating happiness with the consciousness of virtue: "The voice of their own nature could have sufficiently refuted this" (*Practical Reason,* p. 132 [V: 127]). He argues that all finite beings necessarily desire happiness, and that the conjunction of virtue (the worthiness to be happy) and happiness constitutes the *summum bonum.** Virtue is the "supreme" good but not the "complete" good. For good to be complete,

happiness is also required, and indeed not merely in the partial eyes of a person who makes himself his own end but even in the judgment of an impartial reason, which impartially regards persons in the world as ends-in-themselves. For to be in need of happiness and also worthy of it and yet not to partake of it could not be in accordance with the complete volition of an omnipotent rational being ... [*Practical Reason,* pp. 114-15 (V: 110)].

However, virtue and happiness are heterogeneous: the pursuit of happiness undermines virtue, while there is no necessary connection between happiness and "the most meticulous observance of the moral law" (p. 118, [V: 113]). Human beings desire the highest good; they must *intend* and *act* purely according to morality and *hope* that happiness will be added unto them. The search for the ground or possibility of this hope leads to the existence of God as a "postulate" of practical reason.†

Foundations, p. 33 (IV: 415); *Practical Reason,* pp. 24, 114 (V: 25, 110).

†Pp. 128-36 (V: 124-32); see *Pure Reason,* pp. 638-44 (A 809-19, B 837-47); *Judgment,* p. 304, §88 (V: 453). For a discussion of the difficulties of this position see below, pp. 251-56.

2. In Aristotle's account there was a tension between moral praise and blame, which appeared to rest on the ascription of moral responsibility to all men, and the unequal capacities and opportunities of men for being moral. Kant resolves this tension by denying the inequality of moral capacities. In the first place, he denies the moral relevance of intellectual inequality by severing the connection between morality and prudence. In every circumstance the right moral course of action can be known by all men: "Human reason, even in the commonest mind, can easily be brought to a high degree of correctness and completeness in moral matters . . . the most remarkable thing about ordinary reason in its practical [moral] concern is that it may have as much hope as any philosopher of hitting the mark" (*Foundations,* pp. 7, 21 [IV: 391, 404]). Second, not only is knowledge available to all, but also the possibility of moral intention and deed. All men are ends-in-themselves, have worth and dignity, are worthy of respect because each has the capacity to prescribe the moral law to himself and to obey (pp. 47, 52, 54 [IV: 429, 433, 435]). In blaming a man for evil deeds we continue to suppose his moral capacity: "Humanity itself is dignity. . . . I cannot deny all respect which belongs to him in his quality as a man, even though by his deed he makes himself unworthy of his humanity" (*Virtue,* pp. 132-33 [VI: 463]). Accordingly, Kant denies that any men are "born villains"; we must assume that what appears to have nature as its ground is in fact the product of choice (*Practical Reason,* p. 103 [V: 99-100]).

3. Kant's reformulation of morality provides a coherent principle on the basis of which the content and status of morality can be understood. First, the ambiguous character of Aristotelian morality as both end and means is resolved. Morality is an end, in fact *the* end, which is chosen exclusively for its own sake and not for the sake of anything higher. It is coextensive with the good will, the one object of infinite worth. As we have seen, this assertion is rendered plausible by Kant's depreciation of happiness; it is strengthened by his subordination of theoretical wisdom to morality. Theoretical (scientific) knowledge deals with objects as they can be known through the categories. It views them as conditioned by prior events or causes and necessarily arrives at a general conception of the "unconditioned," that which stands at the beginning of a causal

sequence and behind which no regress is possible; but in principle it cannot provide any determinate content for this requirement of reason. Morality provides content by furnishing an undeniable and concrete example of unconditioned causality. It is the sole avenue of insight into the ultimate questions posed by scientific inquiry (pp. 48–51 [V: 47–50]). In fact, the moral experience becomes the sole basis for exploring the traditional questions of metaphysics and theology—God, freedom, and the immortality of the soul (pp. 128–36 [V: 124–32]). Kant goes so far as to argue that theoretical ignorance of the highest questions is a precondition of morality. If God and immortality could be known purely theoretically, the certain knowledge of commands and punishments would bring about actions that conformed to duty but whose nature was non-moral: "Most actions conforming to the law would be done from fear, few would be done from hope, none from duty."* Full dedication to the moral law is possible only if morality precedes and grounds the concepts that in turn support it. Finally, Kant insists that "every interest is ultimately practical, even that of speculative reason being only conditional and reaching perfection only in practical use" (*Practical Reason*, p. 126 [V: 121]). All scientific inquiry is necessarily preceded by the question "Why science?", which is a moral question and cannot be answered unless the conditional activity of knowing can be referred to an activity that has unconditional or absolute worth.

The status of Aristotelian virtue was further complicated by the problem of common opinion or agreement. The virtues were not deduced, but rather enumerated and described. Since there was no common principle in light of which the virtues could all be known as "virtue" or "good" (an omission not accidental but structural, as is shown by Aristotle's critique of Plato's Idea of the Good), there arose the need for an appeal to self-evidence. But virtue was self-evident only in the opinion of those who were themselves virtuous. Moreover, sincere partisans of virtue disagree about its nature. Kant appeals to the experience of all men concerning the *fact* of morality, but the *content* of morality is deduced from the

---

*P. 152 (V: 147). For the identical reasoning see the statement of Jacob Burckhardt quoted by Arnold Brecht in Forkosch, 1954, p. 152. See also Kroner, 1956, pp. 24, 45, 74.

fact without any further reference to opinion. He provides a unifying ground and principle of virtue that claims to render it precise and rigorous, to reveal the required moral action in each case without complexity or ambiguity. Once the principle is elucidated, it moves on a plane entirely independent of opinion. Aristotle had argued that "those who object that that at which all things aim [happiness] is not necessarily good are, we may surmise, talking nonsense. For we say that that which every one thinks really is so; and the man who attacks this belief will hardly have anything more credible to maintain instead" (*Ethics* x. 2. 1172b 35-1173a 1). Kant responds that even if human beings were "unanimous in the kinds of objects their feelings of pleasure and pain had, and even in the means of obtaining the former and preventing the latter . . . they could not set up the principle of self-love [happiness] as a practical law, for the unanimity itself would be merely contingent." Morality must have "objective necessity arising from a priori grounds," i.e., it must be deduced in order to be binding.*

Finally, Kant resolves the difficulty engendered by the circular relation of prudence and moral virtue, a difficulty rooted in Aristotle's denial that any part of the intellect is capable of apprehending virtue. Thus, although virtue is said to be the end for which prudence finds the means, it is, as Aquinas points out, a matter of utmost perplexity how the end of action can be known. His solution, that the end is given by nature, is rejected by Aristotle. Kant takes a middle way. With Aristotle, he denies that nature is the source of moral principles. But, in agreement with

---

Practical Reason, p. 25 (V: 26). For this reason, as well as others noted previously (above, pp. 180-83), Goldmann's argument that the heterogeneity of virtue and happiness is a reflection of the "fundamental limitation of man in bourgeois individualist society" (Goldmann, 1971, p. 198) must be rejected. Rather, it reflects the fundamental limitations of man *as such*—as a being who participates in a material world that is indifferent to human purpose and whose will, even when morally well-disposed, is almost completely impotent to reshape the world in accordance with its intention. As Kant makes clear, the issue is only secondarily that of individualistic egoism, the clash of discordant *conceptions* of happiness; even universal agreement does not alter its submoral status. Similarly, Kant's separation of thought and action is not, as Goldmann would have it, a reflection of the "life of present-day individualist man," to be overcome through political change (p. 195), but rather a permanent feature of the human condition.

Aquinas, he denies that men are merely disposed to receive virtue
and argues that it is in some sense innate, present in all men:
"The consciousness of this fundamental law [of morality] may be
called a fact of reason, since one cannot ferret it out from
antecedent data of reason ... and since it forces itself upon
us..." (*Practical Reason,* pp. 31, 48 [V: 31, 47]). In so doing, the
moral experience of every man suffices for the knowledge not only
of the fact but of the content of morality, for from the simple
experience of resisting self-aggrandizing impulses that are unjust
to others or of resisting the lure of pleasure that demeans oneself
without harming another, from the call of conscience and the
mysterious inner sense of absolute obligation, the whole of
morality can be developed.

4. Kant resolves the tension between morality and politics by
strictly subordinating politics to morality:

> True politics can never take a step without rendering homage to morality.
> Though politics by itself is a difficult art, its union with morality is no art
> at all, for this union cuts the knot which politics could not untie when
> they were in conflict. . . . One cannot compromise here and seek the
> middle course of a pragmatic conditional law between the morally right
> and the expedient. All politics must bend its knee before the right
> [*Perpetual Peace,* p. 128 (VIII: 380)].

Thus there are no extreme situations that justify the departure
from ordinary morality. Kant cites with approval the maxim *Fiat
iustitia, pereat mundus.* He appears to assume that the central
difficulty lies in the reluctance of good men to act in accordance
with strict morality if such a course would mean pain or death for
those who are not good. To this he replies that morality must be
served "regardless of what the physical consequences may be. The
world will by no means perish by a diminution in the number of
evil men" (p. 127 [VIII: 379]).

However, the true difficulty would seem to lie in the opposite
direction, when by following the dictates of morality (e.g.,
refusing to prosecute a war with the immoral tactics that an
unscrupulous and brutal enemy makes necessary) just men and
nations give themselves over to destruction. Kant offers two

general lines of argument. First, there are "permissive laws of reason" deduced from the fact that entering into and maintaining the existence of civil society is itself a dictate of morality (pp. 120, 126 [VIII: 372, 379]). Thus all acts (e.g., violent reforms for which a given society or community of nations is not prepared) that have the potential for destroying society and creating an "anarchic condition" are forbidden (p. 120 n. [VIII: 373 n.]). The principle of the necessity of change in a morally desirable direction must be adhered to, but in a manner compatible with the maintenance of the legal order of society that is the ground of all justice. Second, there is a sort of hidden convergence between the demands of morality and the practical requirements of political life:

. . . it is the peculiarity of morals, especially with respect to its principles of public law and hence in relation to a politics known a priori, that the less it makes conduct depend on the proposed end, i.e., the intended material or moral advantage, the more it agrees with it in general. This is because it is the universal will given a priori (in a nation or in the relations among different nations) which determines the law among men, and if practice consistently follows it, this will can, by the mechanism of nature, cause the desired result and make the concept of law effective [pp. 125-26 (VIII: 378)].

Just as in the case of individuals, morality is performed for its own sake and happiness may be justly received only if it is not directly sought, so in the case of politics it may be said, "Seek ye first the kingdom of pure practical reason and its righteousness, and your end (the blessing of perpetual peace) will necessarily follow" (p. 125 [VIII: 378]). Yet the difficulty remains. We may grant that moral politics as Kant outlines it is not logically impossible, that it could emerge and persist if followed "consistently." But if one nation seeks to be moral while all others seek to aggrandize themselves, will the moral nation not quickly come to grief?

The Problem of Natural Science

The foregoing analysis should not be interpreted as demonstrating the superiority of Kantian ethics to those of Aristotle, but only as indicating how the former might be regarded as a resolution of the tensions within the latter. Without going into details here, it may be said that Kant's attempt to resolve Aristotle's contradictions gives rise to new contradictions that are no less fundamental. On the purely moral plane, the resolution of the controversy seems to be a matter of individual choice guided by prior intuitions as to the relative moral status of pride and humility, or the possibility or impossibility of perfect human virtue. But even a superficial reading reveals that Kant's argument does not emerge from moral considerations alone. It can be shown, in fact, that the hard core of Kant's rejection of classical ethics is the rejection of classical physics and metaphysics—a rejection founded on the conviction that the procedures and postulates of modern natural science are unqualifiedly superior for the investigation of nature.

The most enduring thread of Kant's thought, starting with one of his earliest works, *Universal Natural History and Theory of the Heavens,* is the belief that Newton was correct in positing the homogeneity of all matter, analyzing material motion without reference to final purpose, and describing that motion in dynamical mathematical formulas. Kant's famous description of his subsequent moral "conversion" is often cited:

By inclination I am an inquirer. I feel a consuming thirst for knowledge, the unrest which goes with a desire to progress in it, and satisfaction in every advance in it. There was a time when I believed this constituted the honor of humanity, and I despised the common man, who knows nothing. Rousseau corrected me in this. This blinding prejudice disappeared, and I learned to honor men. I would consider myself more useless than the common laborer if I did not believe that this attitude of mine as an inquirer can give worth to all others in establishing the rights of mankind [quoted in Cassirer, 1963, p. 1].

But it must be noted that this transformation affects only the use or rank of speculative knowledge, not its content. It may be that scientific activity can ultimately be justified only with reference to morality; but science proceeds according to rules and procedures that are entirely self-derived. Kant insists repeatedly on the sort of primacy that science enjoys vis-à-vis morality: what science justifiably denies, morality cannot affirm.* To be sure, Kant, like

*See Kelly, 1969, pp. 98-99. Kant's position has been expounded with particular emphasis by Krüger: "Unlike Plato [Kant] has against him the force of a highly developed exact science. He is a prisoner of the work of Newton" (Krüger, 1961, p. 30; my translation; see also p. 269).

Rousseau, begins with two unquestioned poles of experience, morality and mathematical nature, which must be grounded and reconciled, and his view of morality is deeply influenced by Rousseau's description and formulation.* But the most fundamental stratum of his thought is the response to the question: What must nature and human mind be so as to make possible the necessary truth of mathematical natural science? The manner in which he appropriated and used Rousseauian morality was entirely determined by the requirement that morality in no way contradict those characteristics of mind and nature on which the truth of science rests.

For Kant, as for Rousseau, the essential beginning point is Cartesian—the distinction between nature (pure lifeless extension) and human mind. Though it may have been speculative or hypothetical when Descartes first enunciated it, it is now, Kant argues, fully grounded and justified; Newton's achievement proves that the Cartesian insight has made possible an endlessly progressive insight into nature that replaces the sterile quarrel of competing doctrines. But nature so conceived is entirely devoid of life or purpose; it is the sum of events or conditions, purely passive. Aristotle's description is reversed: nature is precisely that which does *not* have an internal principle of motion. Nature is entirely other than human; there is an unbridgeable discontinuity between nature and human subjectivity or inwardness—man as he knows himself, accepting ideas freely on the basis of truth, formulating decisions, and initiating actions. Accordingly, man is adrift in the natural world, unique and entirely alone; nature provides no guidance for human action. To be sure, man participates in the natural world to the extent that he "has" a body; but the body must be viewed as entirely nonhuman, in no way different from any other material thing in its essence or mode of motion. The body cannot be seen as a standard; its pleasures and desires must be considered purely external, standing in an accidental relation to the mind that perceives them. Moreover, all bodily motions are produced by external or material causes, and can as little be called "human" as the motion of the planets.

*See Kroner, 1956, pp. 1-5, 62-65, 85; Hassner, 1972, p. 555; Beck, 1965, pp. 12, 17.

There is no human action; the human is confined to the domain of pure inwardness, that which can never be, or be manifested as, extension.

Science achieves its success by restricting itself to the domain of extension—those objects that can be seen as caused or conditioned. In so doing, science has revealed the cause of interminable philosophical argumentation: only material objects can be the object of theoretical investigation, and any attempt to "transcend" them leads to concepts that are empty, cannot be verified, and therefore contradict each other without hope of resolution. Yet, in the first place, the very description of the scientific domain as the "caused" or "conditioned" logically entails the conception of beings that are somehow prior, standing at the origin of sequences of conditions and spontaneously giving rise to the effects that we observe in the world of sense. Science is grounded on, or points beyond itself toward, a higher reality that it can in no way know. Second, since humanity itself is the nonextended, it cannot be scientifically known. The essence of man, in the first instance, must be defined purely negatively as the unconditioned, that which is not determined by material causes and can itself be a cause. In short, the disjunction between man and nature that underlies the success of mathematical natural science required that the core of humanity be seen as "freedom." Since freedom is not extension, it cannot be described in terms of the categories employed in the understanding of the external world. In particular, freedom is not subject to determination of quantity; insofar as freedom exists, it does not allow of greater and lesser but must be seen as homogeneous and identical in every manifestation. It is impossible to say that humanity = freedom without conceding that all men are equally characterized by freedom.

The ground of science is causality, which requires that certain events (or, in the twentieth-century view, a certain range of events) be seen as necessarily conjoined to others. But, as Hume demonstrated, if the mind is seen as a *tabula rasa,* then no valid conception of necessary cause is possible; the indefinite repetition of similar events does not provide any basis for concluding that they will necessarily repeat themselves in the future. To ground the necessity of scientific laws, Kant was compelled to develop a

doctrine of mental activity or "spontaneity." All necessity proceeds from the human mind, is imposed through the categories on
the natural phenomena:

... reason has insight only into that which it produces after a plan of its
own ... physics, therefore, owes the beneficent revolution in its point of
view entirely to the happy thought, that while reason must seek in
nature, not fictitiously ascribe to it, whatever as not being knowable
through reason's own resources has to be learnt, if learnt at all, only from
nature, it must adopt as its guide, in so seeking, that which it has itself
put into nature [*Pure Reason*, p. 20 (B xiii)].

This implies that laws of nature are a combination of necessitation
and contingency; i.e., theoretical knowledge is a combination in
its form of human spontaneity (categories) and, in its content, that
which is given by external nature and cannot be deduced from
mind—for instance, the particular values assigned to the "con-
stants" in equations relating force to mass, mass to energy, and so
on. Science necessarily seeks comprehensive knowledge, the proof
that the cosmos is purely necessary, cannot be other than what it is,
but must transcend its proper bounds in order to achieve it. (As we
shall see, Kant elaborates the doctrine of natural teleology in an
attempt to eliminate the arbitrariness or opacity of the merely
given, but this effort remains fundamentally hypothetical.)

The discovery that all necessity emanates from man has a
profound consequence for morality. As we have seen, Kant and
Aristotle agree that the integrity of the moral sphere cannot be
preserved unless morality is seen as choiceworthy for its own sake,
self-grounded, the source of its own necessity and binding force.
Given Kant's theoretical premises, it follows that morality must
proceed purely from human inwardness and cannot be delimited
by any external given without being rendered, to a certain extent,
arbitrary or contingent. But human inwardness is freedom. It
follows that freedom and morality are coextensive and imply each
other reciprocally: the content of morality must be deduced from
the formal character of freedom, and the reality of freedom is
grounded on the undeniable fact of morality. Two further consequences emerge. First, if morality is to be a ground of obligation,
it must take the form of a universally valid law, for if there are
exceptions to moral maxims they must be legitimated in light of

some higher principle. An infinite regress ensues, rendering morality impossible, unless there is some ultimate principle that grounds all exceptions but itself admits of no exception. Thus, freedom cannot be viewed as lawless or arbitrary since, as coextensive with morality, it constitutes the ground for universal principles. Second, science pointed to the negative concept of the unconditioned but could not provide any positive content for it. If the moral experience enables us to arrive at a concrete characterization of the unconditioned as freedom, then it is the sole way of access to the highest things, the traditional objects of metaphysical inquiry. The classical subordination of morality to contemplation must be reversed on precisely the classical grounds: the ranking of all activities must correspond to the rank of the objects of the activities. The peculiar character of morality, to be an end in itself, receives its ultimate justification: it is the highest activity and therefore choiceworthy for its own sake, the ground and justification of all other activities.

It is thus through the mediation of modern natural science that the most fundamental tenets of Kantian morality—the elimination of all natural guidance, the radical deprecation of desire and pleasure, the exclusive emphasis on intention as opposed to action, the identification of morality with freedom and law, the primacy of the moral experience over theoretical inquiry or contemplation—receive their firmest justification. It is in the light of the success of modern science that Kantian morality ceases to be an arbitrary choice, or a merely plausible replacement, guided by Christian insight, for classical morality. The line of descent from Kantian morality to historicism and existentialism is unbroken. In fact, Kant himself has formulated the existentialist problem. In the words of Löwith, "he realizes the impossibility of establishing the inner necessity of the whole creation. To establish it we would have to know that there is an ultimate principle of existence which exists necessarily or essentially. But we cannot conceive of any existence, not even that of God, as necessary" (Löwith, 1966, p. 26). Thus, says Kant,

Unconditioned necessity, which we so indispensably require as the last bearer of all things, is for human reason the veritable abyss. . . . We cannot put aside, and yet also cannot endure the thought, that a being, which we represent to ourselves as supreme amongst all possible beings, should, as it were, say to itself: "I am from eternity to eternity, and outside me there is nothing save what is through my will, *but whence then am I?*" All support here fails us; and the *greatest* perfection, no less than the *least* perfection, is insubstantial and baseless for the merely speculative reason, which makes not the least effort to retain either the one or the other, and feels indeed no loss in allowing them to vanish entirely [*Pure Reason,* pp. 513-14 (A 613, B 641)].

In short, there ensues Heidegger's question—"Why are there beings rather than nothing?"—that results from the denial of the classical doctrine of the eternity of the world and the rejection of the Christian answer to the question that results from this denial (see Heidegger, 1961, pp. 1-42). Both denials are the outcome of the new view of theoretical reason that the success of science appears to make necessary. Thus, it is unquestionably true to say, with Löwith, that

the exclusive emphasis on our human existence and on the world as a historical one has a concomitant in the lack of a sense for that which is natural. This denaturation of human life to a historical existence did not, however, arise with modern historicism and existentialism, but with modern natural science. It is against the background of nature as conceived by modern natural science that existentialism itself comes into existence, for its basic experience is not the historicity but the contingency of human existence within the whole of the natural world [Löwith, 1966, p. 24].

It follows that the impasse of modern moral and political thought "cannot be overcome without questioning its older counterpart, modern natural science" (p. 20).

The historical question, whether the modern moral and political orientation precedes or follows the modern theoretical orientation, is irrelevant, for modern politics is merely arbitrary in both its moral premises and its material presuppositions, unless it is seen to be grounded in a theoretical position that can plausibly claim to be superior in essential respects to that which underlies the political thought of antiquity. The conquest of Fortuna or nature would be a vain hope, even the dream of a madman, if nature were not such that it can be conquered to a certain extent, as modern science shows it to be. And the political orientation toward freedom and equality merely would be one choice among many, as it was in antiquity, if modern science did not compel us either to abandon all qualitative distinctions between the human and the nonhuman

or to view the essence of humanity as freedom and all inequality as
only apparent or inessential in that it is produced by natural forces
that cannot be ascribed to human fault and do not impinge on
that freedom that all men share equally. We must therefore locate
the core of modernity in natural science rather than in the arbitrary
rejection of the orientation by virtue, motivated by antitheological
ire engendered by the political misfortunes of applied Christianity.* Accordingly, the essential character of our theoretical
situation is that there is no important moral or political problem
that can be fully resolved within the domain of the social sciences.

Kant's Political Orientation

Viewed externally, Kantian morality may appear to presuppose a
certain political horizon that belies its claim to be a priori and
self-grounded or to "give the rule" to politics. There is, first, the
obvious kinship between the concept of universal law and Rousseau's general will, which is derived from certain empirical
conditions; if Kantian morality is, as has been alleged, a depoliti-
cized form of the general will, can it be completely free of the
factual or "natural" basis of Rousseau's doctrine? Second, as we
have seen, Kantian morality tends to merge with justice, the
preeminently political virtue; but the reduction of virtue to
political virtue has a long prehistory stretching back to Hobbes and
Machiavelli. Relatedly, the formulation of morality as law and the
identification of the moral actor as a "legislator" who is both
subject and sovereign in the "realm of ends" seems to betray an
inherently political orientation. Finally, as Hassner remarks, there
is a hidden relation between moral formalism and civil society
whose ends are essentially Hobbesian—the prevention of conflict
and the elimination of danger to the individual:

It is precisely to the extent that political theory tends to limit itself to a
universal juridical order, abstracting from empirical circumstances, the
practice of statesmen and the spiritual state of the citizens, that it tends
to be no more than a theory of war and peace. Certainly no political
philosophy can avoid facing these concepts and this problem. But to the

*For an expression of the view being questioned see Strauss, 1959, p. 44. At
the very least, a distinction must be drawn between the *genesis* of a body of
thought and the arguments that constitute its philosophical *claim*.

extent that philosophy accepts the concrete goods which actually-existing communities give themselves or proposes others for them (power, wealth, happiness, virtue, etc.) war and peace can according to the particular case have a primary or subordinate importance to the extent that they are means or obstacles with respect to these ends. But if the essential question is to provide in some negative way for the coexistence of the free wills of various individuals, following one law of liberty, if one refuses to determine the content of this liberty but contents oneself with requiring it to allow the free development of inclinations and eventually of morality, then the essential and, in some ways, sole political problem is to prevent war and guarantee peace. To the extent therefore that it is a priori, universal and purely formal, the end of politics can only be negative: it is to prevent war ... and guarantee peace, i.e., to guarantee to every man the security which will permit him to follow freely his individual destiny. *

In short, one might ask, is it not more than accidental that Kantian morality issues in liberal politics? A partial answer has been provided through the exposition of the relation between science and Kantian morality that, if valid, does provide a nonpolitical foundation for morality and, therefore, at least the possibility of a moral foundation for liberal politics. But the possibility also remains that the republican liberalism alleged to be the logical consequence of Kantian morality in fact represents an admixture of strict morality and certain nonmoral or even immoral elements taken over from the liberal tradition that cannot be derived from the moral teaching. To determine the validity of Kant's claim that his a priori morality can serve as the new theoretical ground of liberalism, we must briefly examine the systematic presentation of his political thought.

The content of Kant's political thought is well known: on the national level, it is a doctrine of republicanism; on the international, of world peace through world law and the organization of nations (Hassner, 1972, pp. 554-55). In both cases its character is preeminently legal; *Perpetual peace* takes the form of "preliminary" and "definitive" articles of a treaty of peace among nations. In addition to *Perpetual Peace,* Kant's political thought appears thematically in the essay "Theory and Practice" and in Part 1 of *The Metaphysics of Morals,* entitled *The Metaphysical Elements of Justice.* Both *Perpetual Peace* and "Theory and Practice" begin

*Hassner, 1961, pp. 644-45; my translation. See also Hassner, 1972, pp. 556-58.

from the premise that republicanism and peace constitute the core
of justice and for the most part merely elaborate the detailed
internal structure of these ends and refute the claim of the
"realists" that their realization is impossible. But, unlike Hobbes,
Kant does not merely assume or assert that peace is the peak or
ground of justice; he attempts to deduce its desirability from higher
principles. The whole of his political thought is misunderstood if its
claim to be derived purely formally from the concept of morality is
not taken seriously.* This deduction appears only in the *Metaphysical Elements of Justice*. We summarize its main points before
proceeding to analysis and criticism.

1. Moral law consists of two elements: "first, a law that
objectively represents that action that is to be done as necessary,
that is, that makes the action a duty; second, an incentive that
subjectively links the ground determining will to this action with
the representation of the law . . . [i.e.,] that the law makes duty
the incentive" (*Justice*, pp. 18-19 [VI: 218]). If both conditions are
fulfilled, the action is ethical; the mere agreement of action with
the moral law without the motive of duty is "legality." Legislation
indifferent to the motive is "juridical"; it deals with "external
duties" (actions occurring in space-time) and can make use of
nonmoral motivations or "incentives." In fact, it cannot use moral
motivation: the performance of duty for its own sake is an intention
that arises purely internally through the moral struggle of the
individual and cannot be engendered by any laws that do not
proceed fully from the individual.

2. Justice, the criterion by which correct and incorrect external
legislation can be distinguished, has the same form as the general
principle of morality, with the condition that it is restricted to
external actions: "Act externally in such a way that the free use
of your will is compatible with the freedom of everyone according to
a universal law" (p. 35 [VI: 231]). This principle implies that there
is "only one innate right . . . the sole and original right that
belongs to every human being by virtue of his humanity[:] freedom
(independence from the constraint of another's will), insofar as it is
compatible with the freedom of everyone else in acordance with the
universal law. . . ." This right contains the concepts of: (a)

*See the excellent discussion in Kelly, 1969, pp. 103-4, 125, 149.

"innate equality, that is independence from being bound by others
to do more than one can also reciprocally bind them to do" and (b)
"the authorization to do anything to others that does not by
itself detract from what is theirs ..." (pp. 43-44 [VI: 237-38]).

3. If a particular action violates the freedom of others, then the
use of coercion to counteract it is "the prevention of a hindrance to
freedom [and] is consistent with freedom...," i.e., is just (p. 36
[VI: 231]). In fact, since justice is purely external and cannot invoke
the concept of duty (consciousness of obligation), it necessarily relies
on "the principle of the possibility of external coercion that is
compatible with the freedom of everyone ..." (p. 37 [VI: 232]).

4. An external object is a "possession" if the possessor is so bound
to it that anyone using it without his consent thereby injures him.
Possession *de jure* must be distinguished from physical possession,
for whereas physical possession by definition ceases when there is a
spatial separation between subject and object, it is of the essence of
possession *de jure* to be "intelligible," i.e., indifferent to this
spatial relation. Wherever the subject may be, the possession *de jure*
remains "his." The juridical postulate of practical reason asserts
that "it is possible to have any and every external object of my will as
property ... a maxim according to which ... an object of
will would have to be in itself (objectively) ownerless ... conflicts
with ... justice (p. 52 [VI: 246]). Although such an object would
restrict the freedom of everyone to the same degree, it conflicts with
the general character of practical reason, which as purely formal
abstracts from all characteristics of external objects except their
existence as objects of the will. From a moral point of view, to speak
of an intrinsically ownerless object is simultaneously to affirm and
deny its existence. This postulate "confers on us an authorization
that we cannot derive from mere concepts of justice in general ...
to impose an obligation on all others—an obligation they otherwise
would not have had—to refrain from using certain objects of our
will because we were the first to take possession of them (p. 53 [VI:
247]). The postulate implies that "it is a duty of justice to act toward
others so that external objects ... can also become someone's
[property]," which in turn requires that every man must act to
recognize the possession *de jure* of external objects by all others.
This means, from the standpoint of law or right, that this recogni-

tion must be extended to all objects (in particular, those merely taken from nature by the first possessor) where possession does not conflict with the freedom of everyone. But further, every man must act to *guarantee* the *de jure* possessions of all others; "I am not bound to leave what is another's untouched if everyone else does not in turn guarantee to me with regard to what is mine that he will act in accordance with exactly the same principle" (p. 64 [VI: 256]). The state of nature (the noncivil situation) is not necessarily one of violence and injustice, but it is one in which justice is absent, in which no judge exists to settle controversies about property and, therefore, in which every man will have the right to do what seems just to him. Under these conditions, property is merely "provisional"; it is justly held but not justly guaranteed (through public coercion). Property can be fully guaranteed ("preemptory") only in civil society. If property were created rather than merely guaranteed by civil society, then in the precivil state there would be no property, hence no duties of justice, hence no command to leave the precivil state (p. 77 [VI: 312]). In short, the moral obligation to enter civil society derives from the fact that possession *de jure*, an a priori moral right of the individual, is fully possible only in civil society. Thus, the fundamental postulate of public law: "If you are so situated as to be unavoidably side by side with others, you ought to abandon the state of nature and enter, with all others, a juridical state of affairs [civil society]" (p. 71 [VI: 307]).

5. If civil society is to guarantee property, to render final decisions in cases of controversy, it must contain a supreme authority from which there is no appeal.

It is the people's duty to endure even the most intolerable abuse of supreme authority . . . resistance to the supreme legislator can itself only be unlawful; indeed it must be conceived as destroying the entire lawful constitution, because in order for it to be authorized, there would have to be a public law that would permit the resistance. That is, the supreme legislation would have to contain a stipulation that it is not supreme . . . [p. 86 (VI: 320)].

6. The republic is "the one and only legitimate constitution," the only one "which makes freedom its principle and, indeed, the condition of every use of coercion . . . [which condition] is required for a juridical constitution of the state in the proper and true

sense. . . ." It is "the only enduring political constitution in which the law is autonomous and is not annexed by any particular person . . . and the only condition under which each person receives his due peremptorily . . ." (p. 113 [VI: 340–41]).

7. Because the earth is not unlimited, nations inevitably come into conflict; they stand in the same relation to each other as men in the state of nature. Until the establishment of a universal union of states under public law that will make authoritative decisions in cases of controversy, all the rights and property of nations are merely provisional: the internal guarantee of property provided even by the just nation is not fully secure until the nation as a whole has been made secure in its rights vis-à-vis all other nations. The kinds of public law are municipal law, law of nations, and world law: "If just one of these possible forms of juridical condition lacks a principle circumscribing external freedom through law, then the structure of all the others will unavoidably be undermined and must finally collapse" (p. 76 [VI: 311]). Hence, "the establishment of a universal and enduring peace is not just a part, but rather constitutes the whole, of the ultimate purpose of law within the bounds of pure reason. When a number of men live together in the same vicinity, a state of peace is the only condition under which the security of property is guaranteed by laws, that is, when they live together under a constitution" (pp. 128–29 [VI: 355]).

The precise analysis of this deduction would be the subject of another study. For present purposes we need note four major difficulties.

1. The sphere of justice or of civil society is said to be that of "external freedom"—the reciprocal limitation of actions without reference to intention. Kant argues that a will determined only by inclination (internal or external material causation) is "animal"; human will is affected but not necessarily determined by impulses; it is free insofar as it is independent of "determination by sensible impulses" (p. 13 [VI: 213]). However, "as regards juridical legislation, it is easily seen that the incentive [motive for action] . . ., being different from the Idea of duty, must be derived from pathological grounds determining will, that is, from inclinations and disinclinations . . ." (p. 19 [VI: 219]). Thus, the entire sphere of external freedom consists in actions that are in principle unfree, materially

determined, although they are actions that the subject would
perform if he were acting freely. However, as Kant emphasizes in
the *Foundations,* the crucial measure of action is intention, for any
external motion can be produced by nonmoral causes. It thus
becomes very difficult to see how any unequivocal moral meaning
can be attached to pure externality or indeed in what respect
"external freedom" is free, for freedom is, according to Kant, only
attributable to *will* determined in a particular manner. This
dilemma is precisely equivalent to the Rousseauian dualism of
natural and moral freedom and the difficulty of determining a
general concept that includes both.

   2. The ambiguity of external freedom manifests itself in a tension
between strict morality and justice. According to Kant's initial
presentation, the universal principle of justice, which has the form
of the categorical imperative, necessitates or allows no actions that
do not also flow from morality; it merely refrains from making the
moral intention obligatory. However, precisely because justice
universalizes actions rather than intentions, it emerges that certain
actions can be both immoral and just. For instance, morality forbids
lying, but justice forbids only those lies that are "immediately
prejudical to the right of another"—in particular, lies concerning
property (p. 44 n. [VI: 238 n.]). In general, justice is far more
permissive than morality. This difficulty arises because the categorical imperative rests, as we have seen, on the sharpest possible
separation between action and intention; its very form reflects the
primacy of will and the strict subordination of action as an "effect"
that by itself can have no moral meaning, cannot be an object of
respect. In universalizing actions, the principle of justice contradicts
its allegedly moral foundation, and the discontinuity between
action and intention betrays itself in the contradiction between
moral commands and requirements of justice.

   3. Justice culminates in the idea of world peace and depends on
the possibility of such peace. But Kant seems unsure whether it is
possible (see Hassner, 1972, p. 566). At the conclusion of the
Metaphysical Elements of Justice Kant tries to show that since the
impossibility of peace cannot be demonstrated we are free (and
therefore morally impelled) to act as though it can be realized. Yet
only a few pages earlier he had declared that "perpetual peace . . .

is, of course, an Idea that cannot be realized'' (*Justice*, p. 124 [VI: 350]). As Hassner has shown, this ambiguity is not confined to the *Metaphysical Elements of Justice* but runs throughout Kant's discussion of the question. But one must endorse Hassner's conclusion: Kant, to be sure, hesitates on important points— ''whether perpetual peace would be precarious and provisional or definitive and even whether it constitutes a foreseeable fact or an inaccessible ideal. But ... these doubts ... never shake for a second his conviction concerning the principle ... and the necessity of working for its realization'' (Hassner, 1961, p. 651).

4. Kant's extremely strict principle of legitimacy suggests that all nonrepublican regimes use coercion in a manner that contradicts external freedom and therefore that their legislation does not constitute a system of justice. On this basis it becomes difficult to distinguish between illegitimate regimes and the state of nature that all men have a moral obligation to leave; yet Kant insists that all resistance to illegitimate authority is unjust (with the possible exception of disobeying laws that command immoral acts—e.g., perjury). Kant's implicit argument is that in every existing civil society there is to a greater or lesser degree a tension between the private will of the sovereign and the generality of the law. To the extent that even the most corrupt and repressive regime must use laws (and in fact must not infrequently promulgate laws that, if executed, would be just), civil society by its very existence tends toward justice in a way that anarchy in principle cannot. Yet even if this is so, it remains the case that morality demands a certain political order but forbids us to use the means apparently necessary to bring this order into being. As we saw in the Introduction, this creates a paradox wherein the ''moral spectator'' of a republican revolution both condemns and applauds it and the revolutionary consciously makes himself a martyr to immorality so that those who come after may enjoy justice. This paradox is only sharpened by Kant's admission that the justice or even the authority of a regime has nothing whatever to do with its origin. Once the republic has come into being, it is irrelevant whether it was achieved through revolution or legal reform. In fact, every citizen is prohibited even from inquiring publicly into this question.*

*For a discussion see Kelly, 1969, pp. 153-58.

Politics and History

Kant's moral reformulation and deepening of liberalism seems at
this point to have led us back circuitously to the major practical
conclusion of classical thought—the actualization of the best regime
is subject to chance and must in almost all cases be the object of wish
or prayer rather than direct action. Yet Kant cannot leave it at this.
His denial of the classical premise of the superiority of contemplation to the sphere of morality or politics means that the actualization
of the good regime, the disappearance of the tension between
positive law and justice, is far more crucial for him than it was for
Plato and Aristotle. If, as his thought requires, internal justice and
universal peace are regarded as possible, then it must be possible to
describe a path leading from the present toward the ideal—a path
that shows how the more perfect can arise out of the less without
invoking any uncaused or miraculous disappearance of the obstacles
to the good. Classical thought could content itself with describing
the preconditions of the good because its various elements were
present in actually existing regimes: some were prosperous and
well-endowed with natural resources, others were relatively isolated,
some were blessed with a spirited population jealous of its freedom,
others open to civilization and the arts. The good might then arise
from the chance coexistence of favorable preconditions, given order
and direction by a wise legislator, of whom many examples existed.
The "parts" were given by nature: chance governed only the
coming-into-being of the whole. In particular, although no existing
regime had ever been permanently at peace, the best regime did not
require a miracle because it was not thought to require perpetual
peace.

It is because the parts as well as the whole of Kantian justice are
unprecedented or wholly novel and the requirement of its perpetuity so exacting that its possibility appears so questionable and
the description of the path to it so necessary. The philosophy of
history comes into being as a response to this demand. It seeks to
render plausible the idea of a universal, perpetual peace and to
mediate between morally desirable national or international goals
and the morally impermissible means they appear to require. Most
important, taking men and things as they are, it tries to show how

the good can, indeed must, develop out of the evil that seems man's eternal lot. Kant bases this attempt on a principle that, converted into ontological or material terms, will remain equally fundamental for subsequent historical philosophy: "Moral evil has by nature the inherent quality of being self-destructive and self-contradictory in its aims (especially in relations between persons of a like mind), so that it makes way for the moral principle of goodness."*

*Perpetual Peace, p. 127 (VIII: 379). For an interpretation see Kelly, 1969, pp. 141-42.

Kant's Philosophy of History: *System and Critique*

"Idea for a Universal History from a Cosmopolitan Point of View"

The short essay entitled "Idea for a Universal History from a Cosmopolitan Point of View" contains Kant's most systematic and profound examination of the problem of history. But its brevity stems in part from the fact that crucial concepts and premises are left unexamined, sometimes even unstated. To comprehend Kant's doctrine of history and its relation to the general structure of his thought, we are compelled to engage in an extended exegesis.* Let us begin with the title.

The Concept of "Idea" †

The term "idea" is not synonymous with sketch or thought; it is a precise, almost technical concept that Kant takes over from Plato in radically altered form. According to Kant, Plato observed that reason naturally rises to cognitions that transcend all experience but that must be recognized as having their own reality. In some cases, these cognitions are the only possible grounds for judgments and decisions we must make. The idea of virtue or the good is not

---

*For what is, to my knowledge, the only other comprehensive analysis see Weyand, 1963, pp. 49–107.

†For additional discussions see Beck, 1960, p. 183; Kelly, 1969, pp. 126–33; Heidegger, 1969, pp. 59–79; Vlachos, 1962, pp. 111–17; Delbos, 1926, pp. 270–72.

derived from experience; to maintain that it is would be to say that virtue changes according to time and circumstances, that what virtue is must be circumscribed by how virtuous men in fact are. Rather, our judgments of virtue and vice, good and evil, must be traced back to a preceding idea that is the law or measure of the world and that, however dimly perceived, is the ground or constitutive principle of every moral experience. This idea "serves as an indispensable foundation for every approach to moral perfection— however the obstacles in human nature, to the degree of which there are no assignable limits, may keep us far removed from its complete achievement" (*Pure Reason,* p. 311 [A 315, B 372]). In politics, moreover, we are "required to abstract from the actually existing hindrances, which, it may be, do not arise unavoidably out of human nature, but rather are due to a quite remediable cause, the neglect of the pure ideas in the making of the laws" (p. 312 [A 316, B 373]). The "experience" to which cynical or despairing statesmen and philosophers refer in forming adverse judgments concerning the practical possibility of utopias may be a very partial experience, fundamentally constituted and circumscribed by an unwarranted a priori judgment that utopian thought is useless. Even if the perfect state may never come into being, the idea serves to bring the political organization of mankind to its highest possible perfection.

For what the highest degree may be at which mankind may have to come to a stand, and how great a gulf may still have to be left between the idea and its realization, are questions which no one can, or ought to, answer. For the issue depends on freedom; and it is in the power of freedom to pass beyond any and every specified limit [p. 312 (A 317, B 374)].

Plato correctly extends the ideas beyond man to nature and the ordering of the cosmos; but it is in regard to the principle of morality, legislation, and religion that the experience itself, not merely its explanation, is grounded on the ideas.

For whereas, so far as nature is concerned, experience supplies the rules and is the source of truth, in respect of the moral laws it is, alas, the mother of illusion! Nothing is more reprehensible than to derive the laws prescribing what *ought to be done* from what *is done,* or to impose upon them the limits by which the latter is circumscribed [p. 313 (A 319, B 375)].

It would be a different (and greater) task to determine the adequacy of Kant's interpretation of Plato, although it may well be asserted that his identification of virtue and freedom, and the distinction between freedom and nature that underlies it, is wholly non-Platonic. For present purposes we must confine ourselves to the following points. First, the relation between the idea and existing reality is mediated by three factors that on the surface do not appear entirely congruent: "idealism," human nature, and freedom. Idealism, the belief in the possibility of utopia, can actualize the idea to the extent that the obstacle to its realization is the belief that the idea is impracticable. Human nature creates "obstacles" to its realization but has no assignable limits that can be known in any particular instance. Freedom, the spontaneous cause that seeks to move from the real to the ideal, has the power to move beyond any limit. Given the formal similarity of these characterizations of human nature and freedom, one must wonder whether human nature constitutes any obstacle at all, whether it ever justifies the assertion that a particular goal is desirable but beyond human reach. If human nature is not hypostatized, is not the ground of practical wisdom or precepts, then it is difficult to see why it is "nature" in any sense. The apparent collapse, at least for all practical purposes, of the distinction between human nature and human freedom implies that the optimistic premise of the idealist can never be refuted.

Second, Kant argues that experience is the source of rules in the realm of nature; if the idea of the best political order is to retain its force as a guide for action, the entire political domain must be excluded from nature, i.e., must be totally assimilated to the realm of freedom. The status of political legislation and moral laws must be the same. To put it another way, Kant speaks of the idea of the best political order as "a constitution allowing the *greatest possible human freedom* in accordance with laws by which *the freedom of each is made to be consistent with that of all others*" (p. 312 [A 316, B 373]). If the discouraging experience of the abuse of freedom and even the wisest laws is to be disregarded, political or "human" freedom must be fundamentally identical to the transcendental freedom that underlies the moral law. It follows, moreover, that the relation between the idea of history and experience must depend on whether the domain (subject matter) of history is more closely akin to nature or to morality.

We tend (abstracting from the question of whether particular facts or instances can be grasped in isolation from opinions, categories, or "conceptual frameworks") to think of history as the sum of all occurrences each of which was experienced by human actors and which, *mutatis mutandis,* can be imaginatively reexperienced by an assiduously scientific historian. Kant appears to deny the adequacy of this view. In the same way that virtue is not the sum of virtuous deeds but rather is identical to the idea of virtue, history *is* the idea of history. It is a concept of reason that "does not allow of being confined within experience, since it concerns a knowledge of which any empirical knowledge (perhaps even the whole of possible experience or of its empirical synthesis) is only a part. No actual experience has ever been completely adequate to it, yet to it every actual experience belongs" (p. 308 [A 310, B 367]). It is concerned with something "to which all experience is subordinate, but which is never itself an object of experience—something to which reason leads in its inferences from experience . . . but which is never itself a member of the empirical synthesis" (p. 309 [A 311, B 367]). History is not a category required for the observation of individual occurrences but rather an "inference" from experience that reason cannot help making and that moves naturally to synthesize all particular experiences into an absolute whole. But, according to Kant, this inference can never produce certainty; the proposition that arises out of it is not "constitutive"—a universal premise that can be used syllogistically to derive properties of particular instances—but rather "regulative"—a heuristic guide for the investigation of particulars and a reminder of the profoundest longing or goal of reason. Thus, history is not merely the inquiry into, or what is written about, human events; though not an object in the everyday or Kantian sense, it is a demarcated and self-subsisting realm, an aspect of reason that can be subjected to philosophical analysis.

The Universality of History

Kant announces that his history is "universal" (*allgemein*). One of his earliest works is entitled *Universal Natural History and Theory of the Heavens;* it deals with the origin and structure of the universe. One might expect that the "Idea for a Universal History" would be equally comprehensive, but the most perfunctory reading shows that it deals almost exclusively with the earth. Although history purports to be an idea of reason, it is somehow correlated very closely with the particular constitution of earthly human life in a way that "natural history" is not. At the same time, it deals with all earthly humanity, with "mankind"; no portion of the globe is irrelevant or excluded, for mankind has a single fate that indeed cannot be seen for what it is unless it is seen as a unity. Yet man is not yet mankind, for the cosmopolitan unification is merely an "intention." History must be viewed as a process of ever-greater unification, with the massive political divisions, nation-states, as the highest stage yet reached and the vehicle of further change.

If history is the idea of the unity of human events, the problem arises that such events occur incessantly and apparently limitlessly; it seems impossible to circumscribe the totality of particular instances that reason seeks to unify, to conceive of history as a "whole," even purely abstractly. There are two possible solutions. The first is to draw an analogy between history and nature. There is potentially an infinity of natural occurrences, but each occurrence may be seen as belonging to a previously known case or as a combination of known variables. The homogeneity or unity of natural occurrences is expressed in the form of laws that themselves tend toward a comprehensive unification. In principle, there is nothing new but only the perpetual recombination of what already is. The passage of time is in no sense an unfolding or revelation because the lawful character of nature permits prediction, the perfect comprehension (and thereby the abolition), of the future. Two difficulties arise. (1) The homogeneity or lawful unity of nature cannot be separated from its determined character, the exclusion of spontaneity, but it is questionable whether the distinctiveness of human history can be preserved if human action is so conceived, i.e., if the realms of nature and history are simply coextensive. (2) Far from denying change, Kant appears to hold out the possibility of a decisively new mode of human existence; humanity is not yet cosmopolitan but will become so. The question is whether cosmopolitanism can be seen as a merely epiphenomenal alteration or recombination of previously existing aspects of human life, or rather must be considered a qualitative transformation.

The second solution is to assert that genuine historical change is possible but that at some point (the "end of history") change will cease and, further, that knowledge of the content as well as the formal properties of the end is available. History is movement of a particular kind: not the endlessly recurring revolution of the planets but motion guided by a goal that is steadily approached. Or, if one prefers, it resembles a plant that, reaching full growth, bears fruit in perpetuity. The "wholeness" of history is the unity provided by a single purpose or intention. The difficulty is to determine how the character of this novel goal can be known in advance and how it can be distinguished from a dream or wish imposed on a disordered and directionless human existence.

The Problem of History

The "Idea for a Universal History" is divided into nine theses or propositions (*Sätze*) preceded by a brief introduction in which Kant seeks to clarify the status of his project. The central problem is somehow to situate history within or alongside of the apparently exhaustive distinction between nature and freedom. Whatever one's beliefs, Kant begins, concerning freedom of the will, human actions, the appearances or manifestations of the will in the world of experience, are determined by universal natural laws like every other event. The natural causes of these actions are complex and concealed; although the science of human action is a part of physics, it may never be possible to arrive at a comprehensive causal explanation.

But history does not seek to provide a causal explanation of individual events, for two reasons. First, there is a distinction between explanation and description: history "narrates" or "gives an account of" events. It seeks to provide the appropriate divisions and categories, to discover patterns. It is a phenomenology that, articulating the surface of human affairs, contributes to but necessarily precedes causal questions. Second, it is concerned not with particular events but with collections or aggregates, events "on a large scale." It may be possible on the basis of this approach to abstract from the specific character of each event. For instance, natural science furnishes descriptions of the behavior of gases and of the disintegration of radioactive nuclei. It is, in principle, possible to explain the motion of each individual gas molecule whereas it may not be possible to explain ultimately the behavior of any individual nucleus, yet the quantitative accuracy of description and prediction is not affected by this distinction. Kant adduces the example of the weather, in which unpredictable daily variations occur within a stable pattern of seasonal change, and compares it to the statistics of marriages, births, suicides, and deaths. Individual suicides cannot be predicted, but in the aggregate the total number of suicides is likely to fall within a relatively narrow range. Yet it may be argued that the behavior of the aggregate is equally subject to variation. The cycle of the seasons occurs within the context of changes in general climatic conditions (alterations in the composition of the atmosphere, position of the poles, etc.); births and deaths respond to war, stress, economic conditions, public policy.

In fact, Kant wishes to describe, not a steady state or immutable order, but an overall change in the condition of mankind, not things as they are but rather "movement." The individual may be seen as a part of the human race, which is undergoing a "steady and progressive though slow development of its original capacities" ("Idea," p. 11 [VIII: 17]). A child performs a great variety of apparently random and chaotic acts, but as a whole they can be understood as solicited by and contributing to his developing capacities. An observer from another planet who did not understand the relation betwen child and adult would be unable to comprehend the meaning and consequence of the child's awkward striving. Moreover, the child is, to a certain extent, free to help or hinder his own development, but he is not free to divest himself of his capacities. His strength, desires, and thought expand and deepen; he is drawn along irresistibly, whatever he may wish or intend. The growth of the child can only be understood as a tension between what he is and what he can be. His freedom is bounded by the fact of being a creature of a particular kind; he is free when he grasps and affirms his highest potentiality and strives toward it. But the child could not develop at all if the consequences of his acts and choices were not somehow cumulative— every exercise building on the strength and agility produced by preceding exercises, every thought beginning from the wisdom of previous experience. If the implied analogy between childhood and the present status of man is to be valid, then mankind must be a unified whole and the consequences of its past deeds cumulative. If a rising people or nation goes no higher than another that has declined or if each generation must in the most important respects begin anew, then there is no development and no history but only endless flux.

Now, it is obvious that mankind is not a whole in the sense that a child is, since it is divided biologically into individuals and politically into peoples and nations. Moreover, men are not united by a single intention, devotion to the common good; "...each, according to his own inclination, follows his own purpose, often in opposition to others" (ibid.). If one man's gain is merely another's loss, then opposition does not develop the world or mankind but only redistributes the good things sought by men. Kant must assert that universal struggle is not incompatible with universal progress. "Each individual and people, as if following some guiding thread, goes toward a natural but to each of them unknown goal; all work toward furthering it, even if they would set little store by it if they did know it" (p. 12 [VIII: 17]). This clearly resembles the situation of Adam Smith's individual who, eager to secure his own advantage, is "led by an invisible hand to promote an end which was no part of his intention" (Smith, 1937, p. 423). Yet Smith appears to suggest only that the struggle of each for himself produces salutary changes in the external world— increased quantities of desired goods and services. Men themselves are not fundamentally changed in the course of their striving; their desires are fulfilled rather than transmuted and neither move nor point beyond themselves. Human nature is immutable and fully developed as manifested in the striving for gain and security. Kant, on the other hand, indicates that, not only is the world changed, but also mankind; struggle develops new human capacities and possibilities. Although *The Wealth of Nations* abounds in historical examples, it lacks any thematic treatment of history, which comes into sight as a crucial phenomenon only when a new end or hope, the qualitative transformation of humanity, is fused onto the vehicle provided by the liberal dialectic of selfishness.

In fact, Kant argues, the peculiar character of human existence dictates that history be a superimposed order or force. There are two sorts of predictable lawful regularity: the purely instinctive behavior of animals, governed by laws of nature; and behavior fully governed by rationality, which issues in universal agreement. Human action is characterized by the wild, unpredictable inter-penetration of instinct and reason that issues in destructive vices unknown to animals. Accordingly, the course of human affairs is "distasteful" and "idiotic" to the philosophic spectator; wisdom is the exception, folly prevails in and constitutes the whole. But precisely this whole is the subject matter of history. The philos-opher must contrast the actual situation of man with his gifts and overweening species-pride. Only two responses are possible: despair (misanthropy coupled with skepticism concerning the benev-olence or intelligibility of those forces that produce human existence); or the hope that vice and folly are merely transitory. But folly cannot be expected to understand either its own self-overcoming or the end that it serves. History is "a definite natural plan for creatures who have no plan of their own" ("Idea," p. 12 [VIII: 18]).

Kant concludes the introduction with an analogy that clarifies the status and intention of his history. Kepler, confronted with an enormous quantity of seemingly disordered observations of plane-tary motion and position, at length found simple patterns into which the data could be fitted. The planets, no longer eccentric wanderers, were seen to follow paths that could be mathematically characterized and predicted. But Kepler's feat in a sense remained on the surface; it offered a description of planetary motion but not an explanation. The reason why the paths were elliptical, a reason that had to be deduced from the character of heavenly bodies themselves, was lacking. Newton rectified this shortcoming. His theory of universal gravitation demystified the heavenly bodies, abolished the distinction between them and all other matter.*

---

*See especially Newton, 1960, pp. 3–5.

Beginning from the descriptions of celestial phenomena provided
by Kepler, he rose to a universal characterization of matter from
which all motion could be deduced, this principle serving therefore as the "force" or "cause" (i.e., explanation) of observed
motion (Newton, 1960, pp. 9–11).

Kant implicitly compares himself to Kepler. He will attempt to
bring order out of the apparent chaos of human action, to reveal
the path along which humanity is traveling. But he will treat
humanity as a special case, i.e., will not attempt to show the
continuity between man and the rest of the cosmos or to deduce
human history from universal principles. He realizes clearly that
the effort to discover order is not a task that, once begun, can be
terminated arbitrarily. If human history is rational or lawful, a
proper object of philosophical speculation, then it must be swept
up in the inherent propensity of reason to search for absolute
unity; if an idea, it is only *one* idea that reason seeks to unite with
all the others. Kant will inquire whether it is reasonable to assume
a purposiveness in all the parts of nature and deny it to the whole.
But either human history is the whole, or merely a part that, in
addition to its own internal purposiveness, must be seen as
directed to something beyond itself. However this may be, it is
clear that the "Newton" of human history whom Kant foresees in
the future must inquire into the connection between the historical
character of human existence and the general character of reality—
in Kantian terms, between human history and transcendental logic.

Nevertheless, the fundamental difference between Kant's and
Kepler's projects should not be overlooked. Although the phenomena with which Kepler dealt were in a sense disordered,
they possessed an overall order—the repetition of cycles. Since
each cycle was complete, a microcosm of the indefinite duration of
celestial motion, it could not be doubted that there was a unity or
whole, a rational order to be explained. Thus, from the very
earliest times the order of the heavens was a topic of speculation
and inquiry; only the content of the explanation was contested.
Concerning human history no such agreement existed. Kant
therefore must attempt to prove that history *is* a whole as well as
that its unity is of a particular character. This task is greatly
complicated by his account of the whole. In classical thought the

order of human events was formally similar to that of the cosmos—the eternal repetition of cycles (not, however, of fixed or uniform movement but of the successive alternation of progress and catastrophe). In Kant's view there is only one cycle, a steady movement from beginning to consummation. But we are in the midst of the cycle, which has not yet been completed. The whole has never been observed or experienced; at present it is merely an inference or projection from incomplete data. Kant must indicate what gives reason the warrant and ability to move out beyond experience in this manner, not only interpreting events but also positing events without which all interpretation is impossible. This difficulty, the peculiarly projected or constructed character of history, contributes to Kant's hesitation and reserve: he speaks only of the possibility or hope that rationality may exist in the course of events.*

Natural and Historical Teleology

The First Proposition states that all natural capacities of a creature are destined to evolve completely to their natural end. This assertion explicitly rests on the teleological theory of nature, which Kant does not here seek to justify; he merely observes that without teleology nature is no longer lawful or rational but rather aimless and subject to blind chance. This is somewhat surprising, for Kant has just alluded to Newtonian cosmology that is lawful and rational without being in the least teleological. But whereas Newton dealt with planets, the present discussion concerns animals or "creatures." Mechanical laws, it seems, are somehow insufficient to explain living beings. This is very far from being self-evident; if we wish to understand the status and intention of history, we must turn to the explicit discussion of teleology in the *Critique of Judgment.*

Kant distinguishes between external and inner purposiveness of

---

*It is worth noting that this problem cannot be completely avoided by positing that the end of history has come, that the whole is present to view. Setting aside the problem of identifying the end, the term is ambiguous. It must be asserted that the end (= final cause) is the end in the temporal sense as well: once actualized, it will never suffer decline and will endure forever. If this cannot be known, the possibility of destruction or cyclical repetition cannot be denied. Any doctrine of the end of history requires an indefinite projection—i.e., a characterization of eternity— with all its attendant philosophical difficulties.

nature. External purposiveness would require not only that a given material or organism contribute to the existence or well-being of another but that the cause of its existence is precisely this contribution. The sea creates tracts of sandy soil peculiarly suited to the growth of pine forests. Yet it cannot be said that the soil exists for the advantage of the trees, for the existence of the trees may be completely accidental. In the highest case, man uses many things. But human rationality is capable of "arbitrary fancies"; the use of an object or organism in a particular manner does not prove that it was intended to be so used. Moreover, even nonarbitrary use proves nothing, for the very existence of the human race may be accidental, unintended. "Only, *if* we assume that men are to live upon the earth, then the means must be there without which they could not exist as animals, and even as rational animals (in however low degree of rationality); and thereupon those natural things, which are indispensable in this regard, must be considered as natural purposes" (*Judgment,* pp. 214f., §63 [V: 368]). But this assumption can never be completely justified by the contemplation of nature, and the judgment of external purposiveness remains hypothetical.

Kant does contend that the necessity of human existence can be deduced from the assumption of "the final purpose of the existence of a world, i.e., of creation itself." One must then ask, not only why beings have particular forms or interrelations, but why beings as such have come into existence. Their existence must be deduced from the existence of something that is "unconditioned," that is, whose nonexistence is impossible, which exists "necessarily, on account of its objective constitution" (p. 285, §84 [V: 435]). There is in the world only one kind of being that is purposive and in such a manner that its purposes are both unconditioned and necessary: man, considered as a free or moral being. This argument seems absurd. Man is clearly not the efficient cause either of the world or of himself. The existence of creation therefore requires a nonhuman force. Is it then possible to maintain that the existence of humanity is unconditioned? In short, if one assumes a final purpose, one arrives at a conception of God rather than of man; man cannot be the final purpose of creation if God is. It may be asserted that the creation of the material world entails the creation of man, but this merely pushes back the question one step. Kant appears to argue that man is the equal of God insofar as he is a moral being: moral man wills what God wills, in the manner in which He wills it. But man is imperfect, lower than God, not only because the material aspect of his dual nature infects his will but because human will even at its most divine is incapable of creating the whole of reality in accordance with its intention. Man is finite because nature is other than his will. God knows no Other, is the ground of the whole. Since man is not God, he does not fully participate in the necessity of His existence, and the question ''Why man?'' returns in all its unfathomable force.

Kant also describes the concept of internal or natural purpose, which arises, as it were, directly from the experience of the natural world. The primary mode of explanation is the mechanism of nature, the complex of physical laws. But although mechanical laws can explain individual occurrences, they are unable to give a full account of the organized (living) beings we encounter—in particular, of self-generative growth or development and of the relation of the various organs to each other and to the functioning of the organism as a whole. In a famous passage Kant declares:

It is indeed quite certain that we cannot adequately cognize, much less explain, organized beings and their internal possibility according to mere mechanical principles of nature, and we can say boldly it is alike certain that it is absurd for men to make any such attempt or to hope that another Newton will arise in the future who shall make comprehensible by us the production of a blade of grass according to natural laws which no design has ordered [p. 248, § 75 (V: 400)].

This does not represent a return to the Aristotelian doctrine of the eternity of the species; in fact, Kant elaborates a hypothesis of the gradual evolution from the lowest to the highest species after the coming-into-being of the earth. But he denies the possibility of ''the production of an organized [organic] being through the mechanics of crude unorganized matter'' (p. 268 n., § 80 [V: 419 n.]). The organized being is both cause and effect of itself. It is distinguished from a work of human art in that the concept that determines its form is not external to it. It is distinguished from a machine in that it has the power of repairing or reproducing itself, giving the mere matter it uses an organization that matter does not of itself possess.

The principle of natural purpose is in Kant's terminology not constitutive or determinant but merely reflective. It cannot be affirmed with certainty as the essence of living beings because "it cannot be derived from experience and . . . is not requisite for the possibility thereof"; it is rather a guide that reason prescribes for the investigation of nature (p. 245, § 74 [V: 397]). In practical scientific inquiry it leads to the maxim that no part of a living being is vain or without purpose. The activity of an organ may be described and predicted according to mechanical laws but it cannot be discovered without reference to this maxim, i.e., without asking what its function is. Natural purpose is the indispensable "heuristic principle."*

Kant vigorously denies that he is reintroducing a "supernatural" causation into physics or returning to discredited Aristotelianism. Nature is matter, and matter is inanimate. The notion of natural purpose is not constitutive because "no design [purpose] in the proper meaning of the word can possibly be ascribed to inanimate matter" (*Judgment*, p. 230, §68 [V: 383]). It is preposterous to make nature an intelligent being and presumptuous to place an intelligent Being above it as its Architect. Natural purpose signifies only "a kind of casuality of nature after the analogy of our own in the technical use of reason, in order to have before us the rule according to which certain products of nature must be investigated" (ibid; see also p. 205, §61 [V: 359]).

Yet Kant, while insisting that natural purpose pertains to cognitive acts rather than to being itself, does provide some basis for contrary inferences. At one point he speaks of organized beings as affording "objective reality" to the concept. And since the cases in which mechanical causation can fruitfully be supplemented by investigation in accordance with natural purpose can be known only through experience, it looks as though distinctions among

---

*P. 259, § 78 (V: 411). Fackenheim quite properly points to a crucial distinction between natural and historical teleology: while biological science requires the teleological as a heuristic concept, the same cannot be said for empirical history. "[T]eleology is needed in history, not in order to explain historical events, but to show that they have value" (Fackenheim, 1957, pp. 392-93 n.).

investigated objects contribute to the concept in a way that cannot be fully deduced from the general character of the faculty of judgment. To put it another way, the concept of natural purpose seems to have as its foundation the assertion that organic being (life) cannot be understood through mechanical causation. But the relation of this assertion to the concept of natural purpose is either tautological or empirical, for there is no a priori category of "life." In fact, Kant appears to appeal to the generally accepted "absurdity" of a mechanical explanation without demonstrating why it is absurd. This appeal is all the more sweeping and striking because Kant here rejects the simple dichotomy of freedom (or thought) and mechanically determined matter. He rejects, that is, the assertion of Descartes that only reason is life and that all animals are machines: rather, they are "(as living beings) of the same genus as man" (p. 316 n., §90 [V: 464 n.]). But whatever may be the case concerning the logical possibility of a mechanical explanation of man, it is clearly not self-evident that such an explanation of lower species is permanently beyond our reach. *

The idea of an ordered "whole" of nature first arises from the observation of individual ordered beings and leads to the heuristic maxim that everything in the world is in some way good for something, that nothing is vain (*Judgment,* p. 225, §67 [V: 379]). But while all men must admit that individual beings at least *seem* purposive, nature as a whole "is not given as organized," i.e., is not self-evidently an organized whole for the unity of which it is necessary to provide a description and explanation (p. 246, §75 [V: 398]). In fact, says Kant, the "ancients" in considering the arrangement and course of things in nature

met with good and evil, the purposive and the unpurposive, mingled together (at least as far as our insight goes), and could not permit themselves to assume nevertheless that wise and benevolent purposes of which they saw no proof lay hidden at the bottom, in behalf of the arbitrary idea of a supremely perfect original author . . . [p. 289, § 85 (V: 439)].

*Kelly, 1969, p. 119, rightly emphasizes the status of the concept of life as an "intermediary sphere," one of the many "mediating substance[s]" that Kant employs to moderate the difficulties of dualism, i.e., to speak from the "point of view of the world" (p. 113). But Kelly does not ask forcefully enough whether the devices Kant employs *contradict* rather than merely *supplement* his dualistic premises and, if so, what conclusions might be drawn from this contradiction. See below, pp. 265–68.

To be sure, an ordered nature can be deduced from the idea of such an author, but the use of this idea as a premise of demonstration is impermissible since it cannot be known with certainty. If it is through teleology that we rise to the notion of a perfect God, then the subsequent use of God to explain natural purposiveness is a "delusive circle" (p. 228, §68 [V: 381]). Kant clearly indicates that the first impression of honest and thoughtful men is of disorder and arbitrariness in the world, considered in its totality.

For these and other reasons, Kant's most profound and funda-mental argument for natural purpose as a necessary idea for the judgment, not only of individual organisms but of the world as a whole, arises out of the general character of human reason itself. Understanding (that aspect of reason that deals with the experience of nature) distinguishes between the possible and the actual. This distinction arises because experience has two components: con-cepts (categories) and sense perception. Concepts are abstract, universal determinations of objects that can be provided with specific content through thought alone without any guarantee that the specific object so conceived has any real existence. The gulf between possibility and actuality can be bridged only through sense perception, which furnishes the categories content corres-ponding to an existing object. But sense perception originates from the "outside"; it is neither caused nor constituted by the activity (spontaneity) of the mind, which, rather, is passive with regard to its apprehension and content. That is, sense perception reveals to us individual objects whose particularity seems absolutely contingent: we cannot explain why things are precisely what they are although we can identify general similarities within classes of objects and among all beings insofar as they are objects. Even when the enormous diversity of objects is reduced to a few fundamental constituting elements (particles, fields, etc.), these retain particular properties or mathematical interrelations that cannot be deduced from the general form of objects in general. We appear to be confronted with an irreducible diversity of contingencies, of "parts" that are not fully understandable and are in no sense a whole. But by its very nature human reason seeks a comprehensive explanation or unity: it seeks, that is, a noncontingent (absolutely

necessary) ground of all that exists and cannot rest content as long
as any aspect of experience remains unexplained. Reason requires
"unity and conformity to law in the combination of particular laws
of nature"; the otherness or opacity of nature must be overcome
in pure thought.* The pure form of the abolition of contingency is purposiveness. In asserting that a whole is more than
the sum of the parts whose effects are determined through
mechanical causation, each part becomes related to every other and
to the whole; each one loses its contingency in becoming, precisely
as what it is, necessary for the whole. But clearly the demand of
reason is not satisfied by a diversity of particular wholes the
existence of which can be regarded as accidental or unnecessary; to
be a necessary part of a contingent whole is to remain in principle
contingent. Internal purposiveness is not enough; such wholes
must point beyond themselves to "the whole of nature as a
system," the organization of which is grounded on an absolutely
necessary cause of all being.† Thus, Spinoza's conception of a
simple substance in which all diversity inheres satisfies one condition of the problem posed to us by reason—the unity of ground.
But it fails to explain, except perhaps formally, how contingent
diversity flows from this unity; rather, a unity that is merely the
sum of disordered or ontologically equal parts is either pure

---

*P. 252, § 76 (V: 404). The problem of the opacity of the given necessarily
induces a philosophy that seeks absolute certainty to elaborate a "transcendental
logic" that contains not only the *possibility* of experience but also the *content* of
experience. Fichte and Husserl are the two most significant cases. For an excellent
discussion see Quentin Lauer's introductory remarks in Husserl, 1965, pp. 21–24,
26, 32–33.

†*Judgment*, p. 258, § 77 (V: 409). For an extended discussion of this subject
see McFarland, 1970. McFarland notes the dual basis of Kant's argument for
teleology—Reason's demand for the systematic unity of empirical (scientific)
laws, and the observation of (living) organisms the mode of existence of which
cannot be explained through mechanical laws. He emphasizes the hypothetical
character of the demand for systematic unity, i.e., the fact that it does not flow
deductively from the categories of the understanding but only from the
permissible yet ungrounded hope or assumption that nature as a whole is so
ordered as to be graspable by human reason. The movement from the
purposiveness of individual organisms to that of nature as a whole is equally
hypothetical. McFarland is acutely aware of the conflict between mechanical and
teleological explanations, although his attempt to resolve this difficulty through
the distinction between mechanical *categories,* which are constitutive, and
mechanical *explanation*, which is regulative, is not successful. See pp. 13,
22ff., 41, 91, 93, 96–97, 114, 120, 137.

monism or pure diversity. At least for finite (human) reason, the One must explain the Many without explaining it away: it must preserve our original sense of the distinctions between disordered matter and organized forms and among organized forms themselves. The One that both explains and preserves diversity is simple intelligent substance whose relation to nature is that of final purpose (pp. 270-71, §80 [V: 421]).

Let us put the problem in overtly theological terms. The assertion "all beings are God" eliminates all contingency at the price of eliminating the world of diversity as it appears to men. But the assertion "All beings are from and for God" raises the question "Why are there beings rather than nothing?"; if God is self-subsisting, why Creation (nature)? If God is *the* ground, the only absolute necessity, then for Creation to be necessary it must *be* God and not only stem from Him. But if Creation is necessary, it is not creation unless God is somehow Creation. We cannot enter further into this question except to note that the assertion of a mutual relation between God and creation that is neither identity nor duality, i.e., that rejects the analogy between God and the human artisan, is characteristic of an entire theologico-metaphysical tradition, exemplified by Jacob Boehme, which rejects the Christian-Aristotelian proposition that *operatio sequitur esse* and proposes instead that *esse sequitur operationem* (see Fackenheim, 1961, pp. 28ff.). According to Kant, we must at least say that *if* nature is necessary, it can only be so for a being that is itself natural (hence influenced by nature) while possessing the absolute necessity or worth ascribed to God. This can only be man, and only in that respect that is unconditionally worthy. There are two human ends toward which nature might contribute: that which "can be satisfied by nature in its beneficence, or . . . the aptitude and skill for all kinds of purposes for which nature (external and internal) can be used by him. The first purpose of nature would be man's *happiness,* the second his *culture*" (*Judgment,* p. 279, §83 [V: 430]).

It is both empirically and theoretically impossible to maintain that the end of nature is human happiness. (We merely summarize the reasons Kant adduces.)* Happiness, merely a subjective ideal

*For a fuller discussion of Kant's treatment of happiness see above, pp. 180-83, and below, pp. 251-54.

of the imagination, is infinitely variable. It is not human nature to be contented with the possession and enjoyment of anything whatever. Man is as subject to the "destructive operations" of nature—famines, earthquakes, etc.—as all other beings. Moreover,

the inconsistency of his own *natural disposition* drives him into self-devised torments and also reduces others of his own race to misery . . . even with the most beneficent external nature, its purpose, if it were directed to the happiness of our species, would not be attained in an earthly system, because our nature is not susceptible of it.

Finally, happiness, as subjective sensation, is purely natural, existing at the whim of nature and on the same level as all other natural things. If nature is a means, the end in light of which it gains worth must be above (beyond) it. Man is beyond nature only by virtue of "the aptitude of setting purposes in general before himself and (independent of nature in his purposive determination) of using nature, conformably to the maxims of his free purposes in general, as a means." Nature contributes in two ways to the development of this aptitude (culture). First, the furtherance of purpose in general requires skill, i.e., the development of arts and sciences, which in turn requires inequality. This leads to extremes of wealth and poverty, to war and internal revolution, that spur the development of human ability and prepare the way for that cosmopolitan whole that alone allows the greatest development of capacities. Second, if human choice is to differ from simple animality, the will must be freed from "the despotism of the desires" by which we are "rendered incapable even of choosing...." This essentially negative condition of aptitude, the "culture of discipline," is furthered by nature through arts and sciences, society, and the evils, whether inflicted by nature or other men, that "summon, strengthen, and harden the powers of the soul not to submit to them, and so make us feel an aptitude for higher purposes which lies hidden in us."*

The most striking feature (indeed, the crucial premise) of Kant's procedure is the absolute denial of chance or accident. In this respect he is far more radical than the original teleological thought of classical antiquity. In the *Physics* Aristotle follows an exposition

Judgment, pp. 279-84, § 83 (V: 429-34); Fackenheim, 1957, p. 396; Kelly, 1969, pp. 142-44.

of final causes with a discussion of chance. There are, he argues, three classes of beings or events: those that are or occur invariably, usually, or occasionally. Occasional events are inherently unpredictable; they are exceptions to rules and could be predicted only if there were additional rules governing them, which is by definition impossible. No event is uncaused; but if it were possible to specify the cause of occasional events they would cease to be unpredictable. Chance is an "accidental cause" of which it is not evident that the content can be known even generally. "There is no science of accidental being [or chance] for every science is of that which is always or for the most part." Even natural beings, which are characterized by an internal principle of movement and a final cause, are subject to chance: in the same way that an artisan can err, defectively actualizing his intention, the final cause represents an end of movement or striving that nature does not always attain. Only in this way can monstrosities and freaks be explained.*

It is precisely by denying chance that Kant can affirm, in the First Proposition of the "Idea," that "all natural capacities of a creature are destined to evolve completely to their natural end," that an ordering or organ that does not achieve its purpose is a "contradiction" (*Widerspruch*) in the teleological explanation of nature. He argues that Aristotle's commonsense view is impossible, that there is no middle ground between complete lawfulness and complete disorder, between reason as the principle of the whole and "blind chance." Without entering further into this controversy, from which flow the profoundest consequences, we note only that the denial of chance is required both by Newtonian physics and Christian theology; whatever the status of human freedom, from the standpoint of Christianity there is no being, no event, of which God is not somehow the ground. And however overwhelming the difficulties that flow from this conception, it is far from clear that Aristotle successfully integrated the notion of chance as an independent cause into either his physics or his metaphysics. It is a label on a mystery, more a representation of the problem than a rationally satisfying solution.

*Physics ii. 4. 195b 30–199b 32; *Metaphysics* vi. 1–3. 1025b 1-1027b 16, xi. 8. 1064b 15-1065b 4. See also *Politics* i. 5. 1254b 32; *Ethics* iii. 3. 1112a 29.

Teleology and Human Progress

In the Second Proposition Kant proceeds to draw conclusions from this comprehensive teleological understanding of man. Human beings are endowed by nature with capacities, among which the chief is reason. Like all human capacities, reason is destined to be fully developed. But men differ from plants and animals in that the life of the individual is too short to encompass the full development of capacities, reason in particular. Evidence for this is the observed progress in the arts and sciences: no one generation has completed the task, but each has profited from the labors of all preceding generations. Thus, nature needs "a perhaps unreckonable series of generations, each of which passes its own enlightenment to its successor, in order finally to bring the seeds of enlightenment to that degree of development in our race which is completely suitable to Nature's purpose" ("Idea," p. 13 [VIII: 19]). Let us briefly enumerate the important implications of this argument.

First, the cumulative or progressive character of some aspects of reason (exemplified by the arts and in modern times by natural science) is expanded to encompass reason as a whole. Reason results in discoveries—propositions, techniques, or modes of behavior—that can be transmitted and serve as the basis for new discoveries. There is a sharp distinction between the product of reason, which can be appropriated and understood directly, and the process of reasoning, which may be compared to a scaffold discarded after a building is complete. It is unnecessary for each generation to recapitulate the process of construction; it need only improve and expand the edifice. Second, it can be known in principle, without specific investigation, that the thought of the present is superior to that of any past age; it is therefore impossible that any past doctrine can convey a teaching that is comprehensively true. Third, there are no great individuals who by sheer force of intellect can completely surmount the limitations imposed by their position within the movement of reason. The situation may be compared to that of a runner in a relay race; individual speed and endurance crucially affect the outcome, but only the sequence of runners determines who will cross the finish line. The last man may not in fact be the swiftest or most skilled but achieves his goal through the combined efforts of those who have gone before. Fourth, the baton is never dropped: no forgetting of essential insights occurs, no slackening of spirit or indifference to wisdom, no all-consuming wars or natural catastrophes. The discoveries wrested with utmost difficulty by one civilization from the phenomena are the permanent possession of all. Fifth, the development of reason will occur in all men ("our species" [*Gattung*]), if not in the process, at least at the end of history; history culminates, not in the possibility of individual greatness, but in a sort of universal rationality. If human perfection is the goal of nature, it must be the perfection of all men. The observed or apparent distinctions among the natural capacities of individuals ultimately will disappear or become irrelevant. No enduring science of man, political or otherwise, can base itself on the distinction between the few and the many. It is perhaps for this reason that reason seems to be inherently public, the product and possession of "generations," the source of "enlightenment."

Two great problems emerge. First, what is the status of the Kantian doctrine of history? Kant insists that the completion of reason is "unreckonably" distant; it would seem that the notion of history itself ought to undergo an indeterminable degree of modification. Yet, according to Kant's explicit teaching, the future brings into being a plan or project that can be fully comprehended in the present. Hegel draws the logical conclusion: if history is the movement of reason, then the total comprehension of history (and its end) must coincide with the completion of history. There is in Kant's work no systematic reflection on the relation between the individual thinker and the historical process; scattered statements emphasize the decisive role of genius and accidental (unpredictable) discovery. The *Critique of Pure Reason* is explicitly modeled on the prior Copernican-Newtonian reformation of natural science, but it is unclear whether Kant considers this temporal relation to be intrinsically necessary (although we may well judge from the outside that it is). The concluding chapter of the *Critique of Pure Reason*, entitled "The History of Pure Reason," sketches the major questions and controversies of metaphysics since its inception but describes all previous efforts as "structures . . . in ruins" (p. 666 [A 852, B 880]). No necessary dialectical relation between past error and the truth of the *Critique of Pure Reason* emerges (see Kelly, 1969, p. 90, n. 3). Nor is there even a temporal progression of errors; rather, opposing positions are portrayed as persisting fundamentally unchanged from ancient to modern times. The following is offered as a clarification rather than resolution of the difficulty.

It is well known that there are two aspects of "reason" in Kantian thought—theoretical (scientific) and practical (moral). In the realm of theoretical reason, genuine progress is possible. The *Critique of Pure Reason* constitutes a foundation, blueprint, or "treatise on the method" that can be established for all time, but the specific content of theoretical science is the work of future generations. The distinction between the nonprogressive and progressive portions of science mirrors the disjunction between the universal categorical lawfulness of nature and its indefinite particularity. The case of practical reason is more complex. As we have seen, the "Conjectural Beginning of Human History" suggests that men were at first incapable of comprehending or obeying the moral law. But in this condition men were indistinguishable from the other animals. The transition from animality to humanity corresponds precisely to becoming an addressee of the moral law. For man as man, sound moral judgment was and is always possible. As Kant declares, he provides only the general principle that underlies and unites the diverse moral judgments men have always made (*Practical Reason*, p. 8 n. [V: 8 n.]). If moral progress is possible, it must consist in a steady increase of the extent to which universal moral judgments (manifest in even thoroughly degraded men as "conscience") are translated into moral action. But to what extent is this progress an affair of "reason"?

To investigate this question, it must first be observed that in the Second Proposition Kant employs a peculiarly equivocal and negative definition of reason. It is "a faculty of widening the rules and purposes of the use of all its [i.e., creature's] powers far beyond natural instinct," i.e., liberation from nature. Reason in this formulation seems clearly allied with, in fact indistinguishable from, freedom. Kant goes so far as to say that it "acknowledges no limits to its projects" ("Idea," p. 13 [VIII: 18]). Yet reason is not merely a tool (instrumental rationality); arriving at insight, the awareness of rules and purposes stemming not from nature but from reason itself, it guides the use of all human powers. Reason's purposes are obstructed by nature, human and nonhuman. If reason is liberation from nature, it must be concerned with the conditions of actions as well as knowledge. In moral terms, the extrusion of nature's influence on the content of what is willed must be matched by the subjugation of nature in the service of the will. The full development of reason implies bringing into being those conditions under which reason fully rules. In political terms (abstracting from the recalcitrance of external nature), even the good and wise man cannot be fully rational unless all men are good and wise or at least behave as if they were. How can this apparently absurd conclusion be defended? We recur to a problem discussed previously.

The existence of evil men or nations intent on getting their way forces good men to choose in the extreme case between virtue and life; i.e., a case in which to be unwilling to return evil for evil is to condemn oneself to die. There is no rational principle on the basis of which this choice can be made. Only the living can be virtuous; the virtuous deed annihilates virtue (in principle, all virtue, since the virtuous man is implicitly making a universal judgment about the proper course for all men in his situation). Perhaps no one deed is decisive: the good man can do evil and remain good. But in remaining good, he has harmed others, and there is no guarantee that the recipients of the injury will coincide with those who "drove" the good man to the injurious deed. And if it is doubtful that the good man is permitted to harm even the bad, then a fortiori he must refrain from harming those who may well be as good as he is.

The core of the problem may be expressed as follows. Kant asserts that "the only object of respect is the law, and indeed only the law which we impose on ourselves and yet recognize as necessary in itself. . . . All respect for a person is only respect for the law . . . of which the person provides an example" (*Foundations*, p. 18 n. [IV: 401 n.]). Individual life has worth only with reference to a universal (law = freedom = practical reason) that transcends the individual, in fact all individuals as a totality. Yet morality and reason are not fully self-subsistent; they inhere essentially in man and, therefore, in individual men. The destruction of the human race would mean the destruction of morality and reason on earth. Reason cares and does not care about mankind; the mutual dependence of the universal and human particularity is incomprehensible, even absurd. Yet, if this dependence is the unavoidable human situation, then any situation that forces us to choose between morality and individual existence (even one's own) condemns us to essentially absurd or irrational alternatives. But such situations are brought about largely by the existence of evil men. Rational action is possible for the good man only if all men are good, or act rightly. More broadly, only in a fully rational world can individual action be rational and the profound inner contradiction of being human overcome. Reason is not merely thought or will; it consists in a certain relation between thought and will, as they must be, and the world. Thus it is possible for human reason to grasp the true and the good in a manner valid for all time, but it is also possible for reason to progress in the sense that the world is progressively transformed in accordance with the demands of human reason.

It may be argued that the initial premise of the foregoing argument is faulty: there is no contradiction between the finite and the infinite because Kantian morality leads to the postulate of the immortality of the soul and proceeds in utter disregard of the worldly consequences of moral action. But it will be shown that Kant adumbrates the philosophy of history as an explicit alternative to despairing otherworldliness; it is an attempt to provide a ground for the possibility of justice or happiness in this world without reference to eternal rewards and punishments (see Strauss, 1965a, p. 15). It may be that the philosophy of history and morality are not ultimately compatible, but since morality leads up to the postulate of a just God, Kant can hardly avoid inquiring into the rationality of God's Creation, which men to a certain extent are compelled to take seriously, and attempting to harmonize it with divine justice.

The second great problem is raised explicitly by Kant but left unresolved. The full development of reason is human perfection and happiness insofar as it is possible on earth. It is the "goal" or "ideal" of all human striving, whether or not individuals are aware of it. But the enjoyment of this reward is contingent, not on an individual's goodness or wisdom, but on his position within the historical process. Men at the end of history are no more meritorious than their forebears, yet they enter into earthly heaven. As Kant remarks, it is "strange that the earlier generations appear to carry through their toilsome labor for the sake of the later, to prepare for them a foundation on which the later generations could erect the higher edifice which was Nature's goal, and yet that only the latest of the generations should have the good fortune to inhabit the building on which a long line of their ancestors had (unintentionally) labored without being permitted to partake of the fortune they had prepared" ("Idea," p. 14 [VIII: 20]). He accurately notes that this "puzzling" conclusion is the unavoidable consequence of the premise that the species of mortal men is destined to develop to perfection. The difficulty, of course, disappears if mankind is taken as a single developing entity or totality, but Kant is unwilling to do this. The basic unit of moral action and of happiness is the individual, who is therefore worthy of unlimited solicitude and respect. Morality commands that every man be treated "always as an end and never as a means only" (*Foundations,* p. 47 [IV: 429]). The concept of a unified totality reduces individuals to mere means that receive only a pale reflected dignity from the truly respectable entity—"humanity." Yet the notion of the sequence of generations, each laboring for the last, appears to reduce men to means with equal thoroughness.

The basic problem may be formulated as follows. History is the attempt to show that the world is just and benevolently ordered. Without human mortality and imperfection there would be no history or need for the idea of it; God is in no way historical. However, it seems impossible to explain why men are mortal and why they are condemned to labor toward perfection rather than being created perfect. It is not enough to refer to God's mystery or the inscrutability of Providence in the manner of orthodox theologians, for, according to Kant, God's Will consists in perfect execution of the moral laws by which men are so imperfectly constrained. The distinction between divine and human justice is one of actualization, not content. Divine justice can be known because the principles of human justice are known.* But although God's Will is pure Law, is not arbitrary or unbounded, there is no force that resists His Will in the actualization of Law. It must then be possible to interpret all of Creation, mortality and imperfection included, as conforming to moral law. There is, it seems, only one (barely intelligible) possibility. It may be that analysis of the concept of perfection shows that it consists in activity of a very particular kind. If perfection means "making oneself perfect," then the notion of creating perfection is self-contradictory unless it is interpreted to mean the creation of beings who perfect themselves. In a way perfection is the goal or end of striving, but it is somehow inherently related to the act of striving. The consequences of viewing Divine Perfection in this light have been discussed previously (see above, p. 222).

Progress and Perfection

The Third Proposition, of which the "Conjectural Beginning of Human History" is an amplification, depends crucially on precisely this conception of perfection. The perfection of the world is shown by the dispensation that man should "partake of no other happiness or perfection than that which he himself, independently of instinct, has created by his own reason" ("Idea," p. 13 [VIII: 19]). Nature has given man reason and freedom, i.e., has denied him ready-made knowledge and instinctual guidance. He is therefore compelled to develop insight and goodness through his own efforts. This is proof of the perfection of nature's order, for man alone has credit for the existence of everything human, has only himself to thank. If nature had been guided by the end of maximizing human happiness, man would have been created wise and good. But the prime goal is rather man's "rational self-esteem."

The crucial assertion is that nothing that is merely given to man can be an object of esteem or unconditional worth. As we have seen in chapter 4, this premise is not wholly inharmonious with

*P. 25 (IV: 408); *Practical Reason*, pp. 90, 136 (V: 87, 131).

ordinary moral judgment. A man may be envied or admired for his talent and good fortune, but he is praised for the use that he makes of them. The waste of great gifts is reprehensible, even if one might (on purely hedonistic grounds) prefer a life of talented profligacy to that of patient and earnest development of modest abilities. A man born wise and good would be beyond praise. For this reason, however, the relative rank of praise (esteem) and admiration is questionable. God is the object of admiration but not praise. His Perfection is without labor, cannot be other than what it is; the Holiness of His Will is eternally unhindered. Whichever way one turns, it seems, the contrast between finite and infinite, the mystery of the finite issuing from the infinite, cannot be avoided. But within the sphere of finite beings, the perfection of whose existence is separable from existence simply, perfection is a goal, is strictly correlative to striving.

Two problems emerge. First, man is not simply a *causa sui*. Even Kant's account, which emphasizes the "parsimony" of nature, acknowledges that nature is the source of the most fundamental aspects of humanity—reason and freedom. Although man at the outset may appear indistinguishable from other animals, he is already essentially (albeit potentially) radically different. It is for this reason that Kant describes man's beginnings as "the lowest barbarity" rather than animality simply. Furthermore, perfection, the goal of human history, is immanent in the beginning. It is not a free or arbitrary project of reason and will but rather derives from the essential structure of these powers, a structure that is *given* and is in no way subject to human choice. Moreover, there is nothing human, no inner moving principle, besides reason and will; they are not instruments whose use is guided by an external intention, nor are they inert objects moved by an external force. If the development of humanity is a purely human process, then reason and will must be self-directed and self-moved. In short, to employ the traditional terminology, nature provides the formal, material, efficient, and final causes of humanity. It is difficult to see how this conclusion can be avoided as long as the necessity of the historical development is affirmed.

There is, however, an even more fundamental difficulty. Rational self-esteem would seem to require actions that are consciously intended. The man who, intending to do harm to another or only to serve his self-interest in the narrowest sense, unintentionally betters himself or another is lucky but hardly praiseworthy. Yet Kant begins this essay by distinguishing between natural purpose and individual human purposes and asserting, not only that men are unconscious of the function that their acts serve in furthering the development of humanity, but that if they were aware of this great end they would be indifferent or perhaps even hostile to it. At the end of history, man surveys the nearly unrelieved panorama of war, crime, vice, and vanity and realizes retrospectively that it all contributed to his present good fortune. But it is difficult to see why this "last man" should esteem either himself or his forebears. He is lucky, they were unlucky. His perfection is a gift or grace; their contribution to it was essential but unintended. Both are in the grip of an external force that uses humanity as a means. It becomes then extremely difficult to distinguish on moral grounds between immediate, spontaneous Grace that creates man perfect and the nature whose order makes them perfect from without (and the distinction that does remain hardly redounds to the credit of human history). The temporal sequence of generations that nature requires is of moral or ontological significance only if it is a sequence of purposeful human striving, but *ex hypothesi* it cannot be so.

Progress and Social Antagonism

In the Fourth Proposition, Kant describes concretely the force that impels men to unconscious self-development. Man begins with talents and capacities, but there is no immanent impulse toward their development. Left to his own devices as pure possibility, man would never advance; living as the "Arcadian shepherd" in contentment and mutual affection, man would remain an amiable beast. However, the simple pleasure of human association contains the seeds of its own transcendence. The original simplicity, which is harmless and unthinking selfishness, divides into two contradictory desires. Associating with other men is pleasurable because it provides a sense of fullness, of increased strength and worth. But each man also wishes that everything be regulated in accordance with his own interests and desires. Human beings constantly tend toward and away from each other; their lives are defined by the inescapable tension of this "unsocial sociability." Each man expects to be opposed by all other men because through introspection he knows that he is inclined to oppose everyone when his self-interest is threatened. This antagonism, mutual threat of opposition, makes each man fearful and energetic; there is no security or satisfaction without achieving a position of preeminence over all others. Awakened, all human powers are pressed into the service of this goal, of which the constitutive elements are vanity, lust for power, and avarice. Through this struggle, barbarism gradually gives way to culture: talents, taste, and enlightenment develop, and the foundations are laid for a "way of thought which *can* in time convert the coarse, natural disposition for moral discrimination into definite practical principles, and thereby change a society of men driven together by their natural feeling into a moral whole."* Thus, the "incompatibility ... heartless competitive vanity ... the insatiable desire to possess and to rule," which are usually thought to be the greatest of human misfortunes, even the work of an "evil spirit, who bungled in his great work or spoiled it out of envy," are instead the visible testimony to the wisdom of Providence (p. 16 [VIII: 22]).

This analysis is obviously heavily indebted to the tradition of liberalism and to Rousseau, but certain distinguishing features should be briefly noted. First, whereas Hobbes condemns vanity unconditionally as the root of all the evils of the human situation, Kant comes close to praising it as the most salutary passion. He is perfectly well aware of what Hobbes emphasizes, that the competition engendered by vanity can easily transform itself into a life-and-death struggle. His devotion to peace is, if anything, more comprehensive than that of Hobbes. But, for Kant, peace is merely a means; self-preservation cannot be the end, the ground of human obligation, because human life has no absolute worth if it

---

*"Idea," p. 15 (VIII: 21; emphasis added). It is noteworthy that Kant does not assign the same necessity to the development of morality among men as to the development of human capacities; morality appears merely as a possibility. We shall return to this problem.

is circumscribed by desires that men share with animals. As Rousseau indicates, Hobbes sees no essential difference between natural man and man in civil society; the change is only in the situation or configuration of unaltered units. Vanity poses the constant threat of regression to the state of war without holding out in the least the prospect of human improvement. Kant's praise of vanity is strictly correlated to the argument that the temporal sequence of human acts changes not only man's situation but also his innermost being. Yet, in the second place, this argument, while necessary, is scarcely sufficient. Rousseau emphasizes the great gulf between natural and civil man and identifies vanity (*amour-propre*) as the passion most responsible for effecting this transformation, but his condemnation of vanity is hardly less vigorous than that of Hobbes. This, of course, stems from his profound ambivalence as to the desirability of the transformation that humanity has undergone. Kant can approve of vanity because of his greater conviction that the change is salutary. He does not completely disagree with Rousseau's assertion that the present situation of man is inferior to his savage beginnings, nor with his moral judgment that, in themselves, men driven by vanity are dangerous and somewhat pitiable. But the end of history both requires and justifies the sins of the present. The difficulty, one may say, is that human history is a game played for very high stakes, and even according to Kant the goodness of the end is somewhat hypothetical whereas the evil of the present is real and palpable. Our hopes for the future may lead us to condone or even applaud the evil that surrounds us when we might have exerted ourselves to mitigate it. If our hopes are wishful and illusory, does not human suffering stain our hands?

Moreover, however certain the end may be, the dilemma discussed briefly in the Introduction cannot be avoided. The antagonisms conducive to progress arise from the "selfish pretensions" of each man, but Kant is the architect of the doctrine that morality consists in the antithesis of selfishness—in resisting the temptation to make an exception of one's own case and in broadening the implicit justification of every act to include equal consideration for all men. History is a sequence of immoral acts. One therefore applauds the consequences of acts that one would not oneself choose to commit, in fact would be publicly compelled to counsel all others not to commit. A disjunction emerges between the moral man who retards and the immoral man who advances the course of history; the moral man is more than likely to be swept aside by onrushing events. This theme becomes especially pronounced in the writings of Hegel.

The most fundamental difficulty emerges through an apparent contradiction that rather reflects Kant's sensitivity to diverse aspects of the question. In the "Conjectural Beginning" the first movement away from animality is caused, not by opposition among men, but by "restless reason," which is self-developing. In fact, prior to any significant sociality, this solitary progress eventuates in the most essential constituent of humanity—man's self-awareness as a moral being of infinite worth, on a level of equality even with God. Yet in the "Idea," reason is quiescent, has no immanent principle of development, must be dragged along, as it were, in the wake of the passions. This latter description emphasizes the uniqueness of man. All other organized (teleological) beings achieve their end directly: the final cause is at the same time the efficient cause. Only in man is development mediated by a cause that is seemingly distinct. This mediation is related, in a manner that Kant does not make explicit, to the other distinctive feature of human development, its temporal mediation, for in all other organized beings, each member of the species has equal potential for full development and, with the exception of a limited number of natural miscarriages, each achieves its end.

The difficulty may be expressed as follows. The hypothesis that reason is self-moving emphasizes the distinction between human history and the laws of mechanical motion; it gives dignity and worth to history, makes of it a process for which man is responsible and which could be the basis for rational self-esteem. But, as we have noted, history in fact consists of acts for which reason cannot be responsible because they cannot be willed by (practical) reason. They must therefore be the product of an external cause—the passions. However, the passions are in Kant's terminology "heteronomous," strictly subject to mechanical laws. Acts so caused have no human component. By abstracting from human intention, this hypothesis lifts the moral burden of evil from men's shoulders, but at the cost of depriving man of any responsibility for his own history.

Hegel overcomes this antinomy on the level of description. Vanity is fundamentally desire for recognition or prestige, i.e., the desire for something that is not merely material nature and may not, in the onset of the desire, even exist. The desire for recognition is active, seeking to bring about the condition of being desired or esteemed by another. But this activity does not arise out of the necessities of mere animal existence, in fact threatens that existence; it is free, essentially human. Moreover, desire is the ground of self-consciousness; but man is self-consciousness, i.e., consciousness of his own dignity. The desire for recognition is therefore the ground of reason, for in revealing man the subject to himself, it first reveals the world as "object" opposed to man, to be known and used by him. Vanity (= desire for recognition) and reason are not essentially distinguishable (see Kojève, 1969, pp. 3-30). This account is perhaps superior to the Kantian analysis in that it preserves the phenomenon of vanity as peculiarly human, but it achieves the reconciliation of vanity and reason at the cost of abstracting from the problem that engendered Kant's difficulty— the immorality of all acts stemming from vanity.

Whatever the proper analysis of vanity and, more generally, of opposition among men, important theoretical consequences flow from its new centrality. If mankind is necessarily tending toward its natural perfection and if struggle is the vehicle of this movement, then man is not even thinkable as a solitary being or individual. Human association can no longer be regarded as simply artificial or contrived but rather becomes an ordering or form that in some ways is higher than the individuals that it comprises. Although it does not come into being through deliberate choice, it is what men would choose if they were fully rational or self-conscious. Yet, struggle is "abstract"; it is difficult to see how one can distinguish between struggles of isolated pairs, of families, tribes, nations, or indeed of mankind as a whole. That is, struggle leads to the necessity of society without, it seems, leading to the vindication of any particular mode of sociality. Politics is not a separate domain of inquiry subject to a science, since society is merely the pure form of human association or multiplicity, while political science rests, as was seen at its very inception, on the distinction between family and political association, and between political association and empire or mankind. (The abstractness of struggle becomes most manifest in the writings of Hegel, whose social science is able to take its bearings from the archetypical struggle of an isolated pair of men.)

Yet the concept of struggle does have concrete and highly important implications for Kant and his successors. First, it is necessarily universal. Vanity can never be satisfied with the honor and recognition of one or a few men, for every man who goes his own way or refuses to honor the vain man is a direct threat to his self-esteem. Vanity feeds on, indeed requires, new conquests, for in a curious way the men who bow down cease to be taken seriously, their esteem ceases to be esteemed. The vain man thus looks for larger and larger worlds to conquer and ends up by desiring universal recognition. The desire for power or rank undergoes the same development. The ruler of a small group may wish to remain content with his limited authority but cannot, for the men surrounding him may intend to usurp his position. Merely to assure his situation he must attempt to control or eliminate political opposition. If successful, this expands his domain and confronts him with even larger external threats. There is an unbroken continuum stretching from personal to civil strife to warfare among nations, whether the war is "aggressive" (stemming from the desire of rulers to be universally honored) or defensive-preventive, stemming from the desire to remain secure. Thus, even international wars must be seen as working toward the same end as all antagonism among men—the development of the capacities of mankind.

The difficulty is that war cannot lead directly to the desired end. It spurs the development of arts and sciences, of ingenuity and the theoretical faculties. But human perfection is preeminently a moral condition, and war is almost completely immoral. It leads men to extremes of misery, animality, and selfishness and forces them to treat others as mere means (as natural or material objects) rather than as beings of infinite worth and dignity. Moreover, war and the constant preparation for war divert resources from the education and moral improvement of the citizens; and even if wealth exists, it is impossible for moral improvement to occur in times of war. The cessation of war is the precondition for the complete development of humanity but does not coincide with it. Yet struggle remains the chief, perhaps the only, force for progress. The solution is a form of association that preserves "mutual opposition among the members" but strips it of its dangerous potential for violence. Domestically this is achieved through "the most exact definition of freedom and fixing of its limits so that it may be consistent with the freedom of others" ("Idea," p. 16 [VIII: 22]). This requires laws backed with irresistible power, a "perfectly just civic constitution." But no solution within an individual political community can be comprehensive, for the harsh necessities imposed by war or threat of war can nullify the effect and intention of even the most just regime. Thus, Kant concludes in the Seventh Proposition, "the problem of establishing a perfect civic constitution is dependent upon the problem of a lawful external relation among states and cannot be solved without a solution of the latter problem."* This solution is the "cosmopolitan condition," a federal union of states or league of nations. Just as the war of all against all forces men in the state of nature to do what reason and duty prescribe, so the warring nations will ultimately be forced to enter into some transnational agreement when they have been devastated, bankrupted, and exhausted by endless hostilities.

Kant's concept of history cannot be understood unless one sees that in his view the cosmopolitan condition of universal and perpetual peace is not the goal or end of history. Rather, peace is the "halfway mark in the development of mankind" ("Idea," p. 21 [VIII: 26]), the "womb wherein all the original capacities of the human race can develop" (p. 23 [VIII: 28]). It is the condition or political institution most in accord with morality, but it is not a moral condition because it is not the result of a moral intention. It is forced upon men by unwilled circumstance, maintains itself "automatically," and is perfectly compatible with the nonviolent but immoral social antagonism among men. This is possible because war is not only immoral but irrational as well: if selfish

---

*P. 18 (VIII: 24). For the ambiguities in Kant's account of this "solution" see Hassner, 1972, pp. 579–83, 585–87.

men are brought to understand the preconditions for the satisfaction of their desires, they will seek peace. Thus, in a famous passage in *Perpetual Peace,* Kant declares:

Many say that a republic [and a fortiori a world republic] would have to be a nation of angels, because men with their selfish inclinations are not capable of a constitution of such sublime form. But precisely with these inclinations nature comes to the aid of the general will established on reason, which is revered even though impotent in practice. Thus it is only a question of a good organization of the state (which does lie in man's power), whereby the powers of each selfish inclination are so arranged in opposition that one moderates or destroys the ruinous effect of the other. The consequence for reason is the same as if none of them existed, and man is forced to be a good citizen even if not a morally good person.

The problem of organizing a state, however hard it may seem, can be solved even for a race of devils, if only they are intelligent [*Perpetual Peace,* p. 112 (VIII: 366)].

In the "Idea," Kant makes the imperfection of this condition perfectly clear: "The ideal of morality belongs to culture; its use for some simulacrum of morality . . . constitutes mere civilization. . . . Everything good that is not based on a morally good disposition . . . is nothing but pretense and glittering misery" ("Idea," p. 21 [VIII: 26]). There is, in short, a gulf between institutional progress and moral progress, between legality (doing what the moral law prescribes) and morality (acting in the right spirit or for the right reasons). Institutional progress goes hand in hand with scientific and technical enlightenment but at its completion results only in a situation that is necessary but not sufficient for moral progress.

The Ambiguity of "Progress"

At this point two related difficulties arise. First, Kant's perfect civil constitution, which effects the maximization of human freedom under laws backed by irresistible authority, is formally identical to the objective of traditional liberal theory. But liberalism encounters the problem that laws, no matter how magnificently impartial and just, are not self-executing; the authority that backs them is composed of men who are constantly inclined to pervert the law for their private advantage. The "systematics" of liberalism is a series of attempts to deflect selfishness into modes compatible with law-abidingness and to subject the irreducibly public and dangerous residue of selfishness to the constraint of other wills. However, this project can never be fully successful because some aspects of politics resist being reduced to the vector sum of competing wills; even if all decisions can be arrived at in this manner, their execution seems inescapably hierarchal. Thus, the flywheel or automatic governor that channels private selfishness into public benefit works only in certain respects and within certain limits. The political compact is always in principle vulnerable to clashes of belief and overweening ambition.

Kant devotes the Sixth Proposition to this difficulty. There must be a "master" to enforce the laws, but this master is a man, hence somewhat unjust. In *Perpetual Peace* Kant goes so far as to argue that even the Platonic solution, the rule of the philosopher, would not resolve the problem because "the possession of power inevitably corrupts the untrammeled judgment of reason" (*Perpetual Peace*, p. 116 [VIII: 369]). In the "Idea" he appears to reject this simple antithesis and to hold out the hope that this obstacle can be overcome. But he is therefore compelled to maintain that "a good will ready to accept [the just] constitution," a will shared, it would appear, by all the citizens, not just the master, is the indispensable condition for its actualization ("Idea," p. 18 [VIII: 23]). But the "good will" is nothing other than the moral disposition itself that, as we have seen, Kant repeatedly argues will arise only after the perfect constitution comes into being.* Clearly morality cannot be both the precondition and the product of the good political order (see Hassner, 1972, pp. 588–89).

This contradiction points to the second and larger difficulty, Kant's failure to clarify the source of moral progress per se. His analysis implies that the enlightenment that produces institutional progress and eventually peace actually leads to moral regression: primitive men may be selfish, but they are not shrewd and "devilish." He offers two possible sources of moral progress: social antagonism and moral education. The operation of the former is compared to the development of trees: trees that are isolated branch randomly and grow stunted and twisted, while those

---

*In addition to the passages in the "Idea" already discussed see *Perpetual Peace*, pp. 112–13 (VIII: 366): "A good constitution is not to be expected from morality, but, conversely, a good moral condition of a people is to be expected only under a good constitution."

together in a forest, forced to compete with one another for air and sun, grow straight and tall. Antagonism militates against lawless freedom and compels a kind of restraint or self-discipline. However, Kant sufficiently indicates the difficulty by characterizing the results of this process as "culture, art which adorns mankind, and the finest social order," for even the best constitution can be composed of immoral citizens, and Kant distinguishes sharply between art (or culture generally) and genuine morality ("Idea," p. 17 [VIII: 22]). Further, if human struggle, like that of trees, is directed solely to life and growth, it is never-ending; acts undertaken for such reasons are not and can never become moral. It is almost impossible to see how the dialectic of antagonism can transcend itself or realize the object of history, to "change a society of men driven together by their natural feelings into a moral whole" (p. 15 [VIII: 21]).

As for moral education, there are both practical and theoretical objections. Kant notes in his treatise on education that the two main sources, parental guidance and public instruction, are both badly flawed. If parents are not themselves moral, then even if they care for their children it is only in the hope that the children will "make their way in the world" (*Education,* p. 15 [IX: 448]). Public instruction is even worse. The sovereign, whether one man or a multitude, is not moral; it views the citizens as raw material to be shaped in accordance with its own purposes. The sovereign will favor the type of instruction that maximizes its own power and legitimacy: artistic and scientific training may be fostered, but moral training, the attempt to form truly free and independent men, is likely to be politically dangerous in direct proportion to its effectiveness. The only alternative with any chance of success is that of education supervised by "the most enlightened experts" (p. 17 [IX: 449]). But such schools require resources, which must come from the sovereign and will not be granted without some form of political control, and freedom of action, which will be granted only insofar as the training is not considered seditious. But let us suppose these practical problems to be overcome, as they can be to a certain extent in a republican regime whose guiding principle is the maximization of freedom. The real difficulty is that education is inherently coercive while morality is noncoercive.

Acts, which are merely legal, can be compelled, but morality consists in the free choice of an intention that is the product or reflection of freedom. It would be a "contradiction," Kant remarks in *Religion within the Limits of Reason Alone,*

for the political commonwealth to compel its citizens to enter into an ethical commonwealth [i.e., universal obedience to moral laws], since the very concept of the latter involves freedom from coercion . . . woe to the legislator who wishes to establish through force a polity directed to ethical ends.*

More generally, the question of education occasions one of the major disjunctions, both practical and theoretical, between classical and Kantian thought. Since Aristotle held that moral virtue is the perfection of our dual nature, the peculiarly human interpenetration of mind and body, he was able to concede that it must have a bodily (sub-rational and involuntary) component, habit, which has to be formed by means other than rational argument. Thus, moral education is a mixture of hortatory speeches, disciplined repetitions, and rewards and punishments. For Kant the essence of morality is freedom, and since freedom is in principle both indifferent to the external or phenomenal world and vitiated by coercion, moral education becomes questionable not only practically but morally. Further, such education presupposes a certain inequality among men: those who are moral seek to improve those who are not. But whereas for Aristotle moral inequality is possible because morality depends on the capacity for reason and control of the body, which is unequally distributed among men, for Kant it is in a sense a contradiction in terms, because morality presupposes only freedom, with which all men are equally endowed.

The principle of moral equality is not altogether easy to maintain. In the *Foundations of the Metaphysics of Morals* Kant insists that morality is compatible with innocence and simplicity as long as it is not threatened by corrupting theories and asserts that even young children judge rightly in moral matters (*Foundations,* p. 27 n. [IV: 411 n.]). But in the treatise on education, Kant acknowledges that certain acts must simply be presented to children as duties because they are "not . . . able to see the

Religion, p. 87 (VI: 95–96). See Hassner, 1972, pp. 589, 592.

reason" (*Education,* p. 87 [IX: 482]). Voluntary obedience, i.e., submission to what the children themselves feel is a "good and reasonable will," is most desirable but is not possible under all circumstances. Especially in cases of direct conflict between the child's desire and his duty, involuntary ("absolute") obedience to commands is necessary for, among other things, it "prepares the child for the fulfillment of laws that he will have to obey later . . . even though he may not like them" (p. 86 [IX: 482]). This description applies not only to civil laws but to moral laws as well. The difficulty, of course, is that if the difference between child and adult in the development of reason is morally relevant and sufficient to justify a relation of mastery and servitude, it becomes possible to ask whether equivalent intellectual differences exist among adults and what their moral-political consequences might be. If some adults remain childlike either in their incapacity for reason or in their refractory selfishness, education is no longer possible but some form of coercive discipline would seem necessary. In short, the inequality between child and adult, which Kant does not dare to deny completely, is the entering wedge for a theoretical critique of moral egalitarianism and leads to a practical critique if significant intellectual inequalities are in fact observed among men.

A similar difficulty arises from Kant's ambiguous account of the basis on which men ought to be respected. The question may be formulated very simply: does human dignity and worth result from moral action or rather from the capacity to act morally, whether or not it is ever exercised? No ethics can fail to distinguish between morality and immorality, to praise one and blame the other, and to instruct and exhort men to follow the moral path; it is almost unthinkable that this could be reconciled with equal respect for the moral and the immoral. On the other hand, blame presupposes that the immoral man was and is responsible for his deeds: it is a form of respect accorded to the faculty of choice as such, and it is never extended (except by conscious analogy) to animals and mere matter.* But consistency requires Kant to maintain that there is no "bad will." Insofar as man truly wills, he

---

*For a discussion see Hassner, 1972, pp. 562–63.

is free and moral; all other acts are heteronomous, induced by purely material causes. The realms of nature and morality are exhaustive; there is, strictly speaking, no immorality. The respect accorded to men cannot be deduced from blame, for man does not will not to will, i.e., to subject himself to the laws of nature. All men are equally worthy of respect, for insofar as man is man, he cannot but be moral; the will is always good.* But, as all acts take place in the natural world, it becomes almost impossible to explain the relation between act and will. It cannot be specified what determines whether in a particular instance nature will triumph over the moral intention to produce an immoral act. In fact, the will itself becomes invisible and ineffectual; the problem of how it can be the ground of action is rendered insoluble. Reciprocally, it is difficult to see how in principle any action or worldly event can have the slightest effect on the will.

In short, it must be said that Kant fails to indicate the path from institutional to moral perfection or even to establish a clear relation between them, in spite of the fact that the institutional progress is merely "glittering misery" unless it comes to be supplemented by morality. This failure is grounded in the Rousseauian assertion that intellectual and moral perfection are governed by different laws and histories, and it is virtually necessitated by Kant's radical separation of morality (*qua* pure intention) from the world of human desiring and striving. As Kant himself once said,

If . . . man is to become not merely *legally*, but *morally*, good . . . , this cannot be brought about through gradual *reformation* so long as the basis of the maxims remains impure, but must be effected through a *revolution* in . . . man's disposition. He can become a new man only by a kind of rebirth, as it were a new creation . . . and a change of heart [*Religion*, p. 43 (VI: 47)].

*For explorations of this difficulty see Krüger, 1961, pp. 198-207, 245-56; Silber, "Introduction" to the English translation of *Religion*, pp. lxxx-cxxxiv; Fackenheim, 1954, pp. 339-53. In *Religion* Kant moves to the position that man possesses the capacity to choose evil as well as good. In addition to the paradoxes, emphasized by Fackenheim, that this position engenders within the purely moral sphere, it requires the abandonment of the strict dualism of nature and freedom (see Silber, pp. xcvii-ciii). But, as we have seen, this dualism is by no means arbitrary but rather is the outcome of Kant's most fundamental reflections on the character of theoretical (scientific) knowledge. The crucial problem of Kant's philosophy is the tension between his desire to remain faithful to the human world as it is experienced and apparently inescapable premises that render such fidelity impossible.

Thus, in "An Old Question" Kant asks, "What profit will progress toward the better yield humanity?" and answers "Not an ever-growing quantity of morality with regard to intention, but an increase of the products of legality in dutiful actions whatever their motives." Even the cosmopolitan society is realized "without the moral foundation in mankind having to be enlarged in the least; for that, a kind of new creation ... would be necessary."*

There is, then, in Kant's thought a radical ambiguity as to the proper limits of expectation from political life. If we hope for the universal reign of morality among men, we "fall prey with good reason to the mocking of the politician who would willingly take the hope of man as the dreaming of a distraught mind" ("An Old Question," p. 151 [VII: 92]). Kant is perfectly aware of this sorry dialectic of idealism and cynicism; yet it can hardly be denied that in the "Idea" he holds out precisely the "idealistic" hope that is elsewhere criticized in the name of the ineradicable selfishness and evil of man. This difficulty is not the product of carelessness or simple indecision but derives from the very core of Kant's thought. Man's moral imperfection can be deduced a priori from his finitude as a creature of needs; yet, Kant asserts, the necessity of his future perfection can be deduced from his very ability even to conceive of moral action, with its concomitant, the theoretically unprovable but morally necessary existence of a just God whose existence is and must be perfect. The antinomy can be abolished only if man ceases to be essentially finite or becomes God, but Kant, unlike some of his successors, was unwilling to take this step. It must be said, however, that even in speaking of a kind of "new creation" in which the moral perfection of mankind could be realized, Kant reveals the enormous difficulty inherent in maintaining that the present creation is necessarily characterized by perfection.

History as Idea
and Empirical Science

This same ambiguity manifests itself on a lower level in the

* "An Old Question," p. 151 (VII: 91-92). See Fackenheim, 1957, pp. 396-98; Hassner, 1972, pp. 587-92; Kelly, 1969, pp. 116-17.

remainder of the "Idea" (Seventh through Ninth Propositions), which is largely devoted to the attempt to find "faint indications" that the human history deduced from the demands of reason itself is actually in the course of being realized. This attempt may appear superfluous; after all, Kant never searches for empirical proof of the other ideas of reason—God, freedom, immortality—but contents himself with demonstrating that they can be thought without contradiction. In fact, he frequently speaks of history in the same manner. "We act in accordance with the Idea of such an end [of history], even if there is not the slightest theoretical probability that it is feasible, as long as its impossibility cannot be demonstrated either" (*Justice,* p. 128 [VI: 354]). The course of human events may well

give rise to endless doubts about my hopes, and if these doubts could be proved, they might persuade me to desist from an apparently futile task. But so long as they do not have the force of certainty, I cannot exchange my duty . . . for a rule of expediency. . . . However uncertain I may be and remain as to whether we can hope for anything better for mankind, this uncertainty cannot detract from the maxim I have adopted. . . ["Theory and Practice," p. 89 (VIII: 309)].

The difficulty is that Kant cannot simply maintain that history is an idea derived from reason, theoretical or practical. This emerges very clearly in the "Idea." Kant remarks that "the role of man is very artificial. How it may be with the dwellers on other planets and their nature we do not know. . . . Maybe among them each individual can perfectly attain his destiny in his own life. Among us, it is different; only the race can hope to attain it" ("Idea," p. 18 n. [VIII: 23 n.]). That is, the relation between the length of human life and the time required for full development of capacities cannot be deduced from the nature of rational beings in general or even from that of finite beings. It is an "empirical" peculiarity of the human race. Further, the completion of history rests on the assertion that the human species is "immortal," i.e., the denial of a natural catastrophe that would destroy human life or even the earth itself. But this is an empirical or scientific question having to do with the configuration of matter in the universe; it is impossible to say with certainty that there is no celestial body, as yet invisible to the most powerful telescope,

heading on an unchangeable course toward a destructive conjunction with the earth.*

Since history rests on, indeed arises from, empirical observations
and scientific postulates, it is inescapably part of the phenomenal
world, whatever relation it may have to human freedom and
morality. Kant's attempt to find empirical confirmations for the
idea of progressive history is therefore essential rather than orna-
mental. The evidence he adduces is repeatedly outlined—i.e., in
the "Idea," the "First Supplement" to *Perpetual Peace,* Section
83 of the *Critique of Judgment,* "An Old Question," "Theory
and Practice"—and may be briefly summarized. Nature has made
it possible for men to live in all parts of the world, and through
incessant war has dispersed them thither. The war of all against all
finally drives men into civil societies and first induces them
to submit to coercive legislation. The various societies remain
in a state of war, actual or potential, with one another; but
to remain strong they must encourage education, civil and religious freedom, and commerce. Uneducated societies will lack
technology, without which they will be hard pressed to win
even defensive wars against more advanced foes. Without civic
freedom, the individual citizen ceases to feel any interest in
the outcome of national affairs, "the vitality of the entire
enterprise is sapped, and therewith the powers of the whole
are diminished" ("Idea," p. 22 [VIII: 28]). Wars produce enormous national debts, which may well be self-limiting; if not so
immediately, they make necessary rapid economic expansion that
is impossible without greatly increased international commerce. As
interdependence grows, the cost of serious disruptions in international relations increases while the benefit of conquest at best
remains constant, and the risk-reward ratio steadily moves in the
direction of the peaceful adjudication of grievances. Finally,
education results in popular enlightenment and eventually in great
movements of peoples guided by abstract ideas of justice rather
than simply by the desire to revenge themselves on their erstwhile
masters. Such movements lead to governments that are republican
in inspiration if not form, but all republican regimes are essentially

---

*"An Old Question," p. 148 (VII: 89). See Hassner, 1972, p. 571.

peaceloving because, unlike monarchies and aristocracies, the people who must bear the burden of war also determine whether or not it shall be waged.*

Yet these indications, no matter how encouraging, can never furnish certainty that the progress we believe to perceive in the present will continue, because "we have only empirical data (experiences) upon which we are founding this prediction, namely, the physical cause of our actions as these actually occur as phenomena; and not the moral cause—the only one which can be established purely a priori..." ("An Old Question," p. 151 [VII: 91]). The possibility of the disappearance of the human race from the face of the earth cannot be ruled out, for "in the face of the omnipotence of nature, or rather its supreme first cause which is inaccessible to us, the human being is, in his turn, but a trifle" (p. 148 [VII: 89]). Nor is it impossible that all civilization and culture could be annihilated through the devastation of a world war; in fact, Kant remarks, "this is the fate we may well have to suffer under the rule of blind chance—which is in fact identical with lawless freedom—if there is no secret wise guidance in Nature ("Idea," p. 20 [VIII: 25]). Ultimately, the affirmation of progress is motivated not by empirical or theoretical but by moral considerations.

We observed in the "Conjectural Beginnings" that the apparent chaos of human affairs produces distress for the moral spectator. In virtually all of Kant's other historicopolitical writings the source of this distress is expounded:

It is a sight fit for a god to watch a virtuous man grappling with adversity and evil temptations and yet managing to hold out against them. But it is a sight quite unfit not so much for a god, but even for the most ordinary, though right-thinking man, to see the human race advancing over a period of time toward virtue, and then quickly relapsing the whole way back into vice and misery. It may perhaps be moving and instructive to watch such a drama for a while; but the curtain must eventually descend. For in the long run it becomes a farce. And even if the actors do not tire of it—for they are fools—the spectator does, for any single act will be enough for him if he can reasonably conclude from it that the never-ending play will go on in the same way forever ["Theory and Practice," p. 88 (VIII: 308)].

*See Hassner, 1972, pp. 583–86; Fackenheim, 1957, pp. 394–95.

This farcical alternation of good and evil "can endow our species with no greater value in the eyes of reason than that which other species possess, species which carry on this game with fewer costs and without expenditure of thought" ("An Old Question," p. 141 [VII: 82]). To assume that the hopes held out by morality for its own actualization were deceptive "would give rise to the disquieting wish to dispense with reason altogether and to conceive of ourselves and our principles as thrown together with all the other species of animals under the same mechanism of nature" (*Justice*, p. 128 [VI: 355]).

Two difficulties arise. First, the view of human affairs to which Kant ascribes such disastrous consequences does not differ in any essential from the cyclical hypothesis (discussed in chapter 1) expounded by Plato and Aristotle, yet classical thought does not appear to eventuate in nihilism. A partial explanation may be found in the formal differences between classical and Kantian teleology that, as we have seen, rest on the differing treatments accorded the question of chance. In concrete terms, classical thought was the justification of human existence in the orientation toward the good rather than its attainment, a directedness fully compatible with the probability that very few if any men will reach perfection. Moreover, in the classical view, perfection consists in the contemplative life that is necessarily private or individual and the preserve of the few; there is a disjunction between contemplation and the world of human affairs moderated only slightly by the bodily needs of the thinker and the fact that for him the human world is one (though by no means the only or even the highest) object of inquiry. In ranking morality above contemplation and in asserting that morality is equally accessible to all men, Kant necessarily increases the importance ascribed to the world of human action because morality is in principle intended to manifest itself in the actions of all men, whether or not this is possible in particular situations. Finally, classical thought, to say the least, is ambiguous concerning the problem of cosmic creation. Aristotle certainly seems to have defended the doctrine of the eternity of the world, and it is questionable whether the intention of the creation-doctrine of the *Timaeus* is not political rather than metaphysical or theological. But although Kant claims to prove in

the First Antinomy that the issue of creation versus the eternity of
the world cannot be resolved by theoretical reason, his moral
teaching leads to the postulate of an omnipotent and perfectly just
God Who is the Author of all creation. Since, as we have seen, the
principles of divine and human justice are for Kant identical and
human justice is knowable, the creation, the outcome of an
unfettered and perfectly just intention, must itself be perfectly just
and its justice intelligible to men; but the permanent existence of
evil is unjust. It is for this reason that Kant says: "If we assume
that humanity never will or can be improved, the only thing which
a theodicy seems unable to justify is creation itself, the fact that a
race of such corrupt beings ever was on the earth" (*Perpetual
Peace,* p. 128 [VIII: 380]), for "it cannot be reconciled with the
morality of a wise creator and ruler of the world if countless vices,
even with intermingled virtues, are in actual fact allowed to go on
accumulating" ("Theory and Practice," p. 88 [VIII: 308]). In
short, Kant argues, the fact that the world of human affairs is a
part of a perfectly just creation makes it absolutely necessary to take
seriously the fate of every man, to show its place within a pattern of
overall justice. (It might also be noted that the eternity of the
world and of the human species is not favorable to the idea of
progress for—ignoring the traditional paradoxes—if it has taken
an eternity to reach the present sorry state of humanity, what hope
is there that the good can be actualized?)

But, to come to the second difficulty, according to the very
principles of Kantian morality it seems neither necessary nor
possible to ascribe central significance to the sphere of events and
actions as such. Kant observes in the *Foundations* that if human
happiness were the goal and justification of human existence, then
instinct would have been sufficient to achieve it, and reason
superfluous. The pursuit of happiness leads to "misology" (hatred
of reason), the desire to lead a simply natural or animal existence
(i.e., precisely the desire that Kant, as we saw, elsewhere claims
will arise from the conclusion that moral intentions cannot be
actualized). But, he continues, this conclusion is inadmissible
because it follows from the mistaken ascription of absolute worth to
an end to be achieved through action. The only source of worth is
the moral intention, the "good will," which is

not good because of what it effects or accomplishes or because of its adequacy to achieve some proposed end . . . [but] only because of its willing. . . . Even if it should happen that, by a particularly unfortunate fate or by the niggardly provision of a stepmotherly nature, this will should be wholly lacking in power to achieve its purpose, and even if the greatest effort should not avail it to achieve anything of its end, and if there remained only the good will . . . , it would sparkle like a jewel in its own right, as something that had its full worth in itself [*Foundations,* p. 10 (IV: 394)].

In short, one can never have "respect" for the object or effect of a proposed action "precisely because it is a mere effect and not an activity of a will" (p. 16 [IV: 400]). Of course, the moral man is a finite being; as such, he desires happiness and knows that his moral intentions will not necessarily be actualized. For the moral man to be completely satisfied, nature would have to be so ordered that earthly happiness is proportionate to individual human worth and nature itself subject without fail to moral command. But the worth of the moral man, and therefore of humanity, does not depend on a benevolent ordering of the external world. Thus, at the conclusion of the *Critique of Judgment,* a work explicitly devoted to establishing some relation between the theoretically sundered realms of nature and morality, Kant declares that morality would stand even if there were no God and no hope of the eventual convergence of the two realms; only the hope of the universal actualization of morality "in the world" would have to be abandoned.*

It is impossible to deny that Kant ascribes centrality to the concept of the highest good—the coexistence of happiness and morality. In the *Critique of Pure Reason* he poses three famous questions: "What can I know?", "What ought I to do?", and "What may I hope?" The first is purely theoretical, the second purely moral. But

the third question —if I do what I ought to do, what may I then hope?— is at once practical and theoretical, in such fashion that the practical serves only as a clue that leads us to the answer to the theoretical question, and when this is followed out, to the speculative question. For all *hoping* is directed to happiness, and stands in the same relation to the practical and the law of morality as *knowing and the law of nature* to the theoretical

*_Judgment_, p. 302, § 87 (V: 451). See Fackenheim, 1957, pp. 391-92.

knowledge of things. The former arrives finally at the conclusion that *something is* (which determines the ultimate possible end) because *something ought to happen;* the latter, that *something is* (which operates as the supreme cause) because *something happens* [*Pure Reason,* p. 636 (A 805, B 833)].

The idea of God arises in response to the question: What is the necessary ground for the hope that, if a man acts morally, he will enjoy happiness as well? But this presupposes that the desire for happiness has a worth or status such that moral inquiry must take it into account. In view of Kant's attack on happiness, how can this be established?

Kant distinguishes between "ideas" and "maxims." Ideas are the basis of the "estimation of morality, in regard to its purity and consequences." Maxims are the "subjective grounds of actions," i.e., of "observance" of the moral law:

It is necessary that the whole course of our life be subject to moral maxims; but it is impossible that this should happen unless reason connects with the moral law, which is a mere idea, an operative cause which determines for such conduct as in accordance with the moral law an outcome, either in this or in another life, that is in exact conformity with our supreme ends. Thus without a God and without a world invisible to us but hoped for, the glorious ideas of morality are indeed objects of approval and admiration, but not springs of purpose and action [p. 640 (A 812, B 840)].

The hope for happiness, in short, mediates between perceiving the good and willing the good. Since willing the good is morally necessary, happiness as an essential ground of willing takes on moral necessity as well. For "since reason commands that such [moral] actions should take place, it must be possible for them to take place" (p. 637 [A 807, B 835]).

It is difficult to reconcile this argument with the view so emphatically advanced in the *Foundations* that moral action is action done for the sake of duty and that every man bows down before the purity of duty considered in isolation from all consequences. In the *Critique of Practical Reason* (in which, unlike the *Foundations,* the concept of the highest good is introduced and defended) Kant nevertheless states that when happiness is made "the determining ground of the will," the result is "the direct opposite of the principle of morality" (*Practical Reason,* p. 36

[V: 35]). But if the hope for happiness is necessary for the adoption of the moral law as a "subjective maxim," how is it possible to avoid the conclusion that it serves as a "determining ground"? In the chapter of the *Critique of Practical Reason* entitled "The Incentives of Pure Practical Reason" and devoted to a discussion of what can serve as "a subjective determining ground of a will whose reason does not by its nature conform to the objective [moral] law," Kant asserts that only the moral law and its effects on the faculty of desire can be viewed as such grounds if morality is not to be undermined. These effects are described as pain and respect, both of which are distinct from, indeed opposed to, happiness (pp. 74-92 [V: 72-90]).

The argument that Kant advances for the principle of the highest good in the *Critique of Practical Reason* is somewhat different:

since ... the furthering of the highest good, which contains this connection between happiness and virtue in its concept, is an a priori necessary object of our will and is inseparably related to the moral law, the impossibility of the highest good must prove the falsity of the moral law also. If, therefore, the highest good is impossible according to practical rules, then the moral law which commands that it be furthered must be fantastic, directed to empty imaginary ends, and consequently inherently false [p. 118 (V: 114)].

The problem is to establish that the highest good is a necessary object of the will. In chapter 2 of the Analytic, entitled "The Concept of an Object of Pure Practical Reason," Kant argues that "the sole objects of a practical reason are ... those of the good and the evil" and that since "good and evil always indicate a relation to the will so far as it is determined by the law of reason to make something its object," it follows that "good and evil are properly referred to actions and not to the sensory state of the person" (pp. 60-62 [V: 58-60]). Happiness can only be judged according to the categories of "well-being" and "woe"; as a "sensory state," it cannot be called either good or evil. Kant emphasizes that even the universality of the desire for well-being does not suffice to transform it into a genuinely moral ground of action. To be an object of practical reason, the goodness of happiness must be *deduced* from the moral law; that is, it must be proved that "happiness is worthy to be conjoined to moral action." But (1) both the moral and immoral man can be happy; happiness is morally neutral. (2) In principle, the goodness of happiness cannot be deduced from the moral law because happiness is not an activity of the will. (3) If Kant takes his stand on what all men desire, he admits a (heteronomous) principle of judgment independent of moral action and ascribes normative status to the sphere of externality that earlier he had deprived of moral significance. (4) Kant's premise that the highest good requires happiness "not merely in the partial eyes of a person who makes himself his end but even in the judgment of an impartial reason, which impartially regards persons in the world as ends-in-themselves" is merely asserted without any attempt to show that it can be deduced from the strict requirements of morality (p. 114 [V: 110]). In fact, no such deduction is possible without the fundamental revision of Kantian morality.

If these arguments are correct, there is no necessary connection between the core of Kantian morality and the postulates of God and immortality; only Kant's final position in the *Critique of Judgment* is fully compatible with the rigor of his moral doctrine.*

It seems, then, that history too, which is emphatically in and of the world, cannot be deduced simply from the requirements of morality. Yet, given the Kantian bifurcation of morality and happiness, the nonexistence of history dooms mankind to an eternity of earthly misery, the perpetual Stoic struggle against a natural environment that in human terms is not so much hostile as indifferent, i.e., completely without relation to human purpose. This is not, ipso facto, unacceptable. As Kant movingly asks in the "Idea,"

what is the good of esteeming the majesty and wisdom of Creation in the realm of brute nature and of recommending that we contemplate it, if that part of the great stage of supreme wisdom which contains the

---

*For an elegant statement of many of these points see Beck, 1960, pp. 242–45, 253–54. This argument makes possible a philosophical resolution of the conflict in Kant's thought between "ethical voluntarism" and "religious faith" that Kroner discerns. Without entering into the historical-exegetical problem of the senses in which Kant may or may not have been a believer, if a "postulated God" ceases to be a "logical consequence" of Kant's ethical views, the *philosophical* problem disappears. See Kroner, 1956, pp. 38–45.

purpose of all the others—the history of mankind—must remain an unceasing reproach to it? If we are forced to turn our eyes from it in disgust, doubting that we can find a perfectly rational purpose in it and hoping for that only in another world? ["Idea," p. 25 (VIII: 30)].

Morality, then, can find support in the hope of an afterlife that provides the possibility of indefinite progress of the immortal soul toward moral perfection, a hope that cannot be undermined by worldly occurrences. Philosophy of history is, at least at its inception, not so much a competitor of religion as a morally unnecessary supplement. In ministering to moral disgust, it is in truth the triumph of pity for suffering mankind over not only the wisdom of experience but also the strict demands of morality itself.*

The status or significance of the philosophy of history is not simply an internal problem of a now-discredited era of thought, but continues to affect our present situation. It is well known that existentialist thought originated in a revolt against Hegel; but it was a distinctly Hegelian revolt, a negation that preserved the

---

*For these reasons, the assertion that Kant's philosophy of history was subordinated to his philosophy of religion because of the "historical conditions of his time" (Goldmann, 1971, p. 181) is questionable. Goldmann correctly notes the parallel between the religious postulates of God and the immortality of the soul and the historical postulates of the hidden plan of nature and the eternity of the human species, and even concedes that the historical postulates concern "concrete reality." But then how can he maintain that these assumptions are "not a part of empirical knowledge" (pp. 216–18)? In addition, the status of the postulates of God and immortality derives from the argument (whatever its merits) that they are necessary conditions for morality, which is strictly necessary. If the status of earthly progress is lower than that of morality (i.e., not strictly necessary), then its supporting postulates are not strictly necessary either. It is a *question* for Kant whether progress has the character of strict philosophical necessity. Is man's existence "tragic" if the good cannot be realized on earth? Kant's tendency to affirm this proposition is counteracted by his theoretical and practical principles and in particular by the possibility of *religion*. A truly tragic existence is possible only when religious hope is denied. Goldmann's equation of tragedy with the nonfulfillment of earthly hopes is based on Hegelian-Marxist assumptions that obscure the ambiguity of Kant's position.
Like many other interpreters, Goldmann does not take the implications of dualism as seriously as does Kant himself. Goldmann correctly notes (p. 215 n.) that for Kant the movement of history guarantees less than the highest good. The explanation for this, however, is not Kant's lack of "confidence" but rather his strict application of the distinction between the moral and the material. Similarly, the insufficiency of human action for the realization of the highest good is not, as Goldmann alleges (p. 216), a consequence of Kant's *individualism* but rather of his *dualism*.

essence of the prior affirmation. Hegel had argued that the character of reason itself made it necessary that reason be realized in the world, that history be a lawful progress toward the perfect incarnation of the rational in the real, and therefore that the world of human acts was ultimately and essentially the only world, the sphere that had to be accorded the highest seriousness as the manifestation of the highest form of being. In theological terms— the existence of humanity (= reason or freedom) was absurd without the dominion of Providence. Nietzsche accepted this premise but denied Providence:

> To look upon nature as if it were a proof of the goodness and care of a God; to interpret history in honour of a divine reason, as a constant testimony to a moral order in the world and a moral final purpose, to explain . . . experiences . . . as if everything were a dispensation or intimation of Providence . . . : all that is now *past,* it has conscience *against* it, it is regarded by all the more acute consciences as disreputable and dishonourable. . . [Nietzsche, 1964, p. 308].

Having denied Providence, he is compelled to ask "Has existence then a significance at all?" and to conclude that the answer must be negative if one continues to view man as essentially characterized by rationality and freedom. But, to repeat, this consequence follows only on the basis of the Hegelian premise that reason itself requires the rationality of the historical process.

It should also be noted that Nietzschean atheism, the famous announcement of the death of God, is peculiarly Kantian in its logical structure: the existence of God is not disproved theoretically but rather is alleged to flow from the strict requirements of morality or "conscience." It follows, first, that Nietzschean atheism has precisely the status of Kantian theism, a "rational faith," and, second, that the plausibility of this atheism is no greater than that of the morality that supposedly engenders it: the morality may be merely a questionable *interpretation* of morality or, even if correct, atheism may follow only on the basis of a questionable minor premise.

Kant's reservations as to the centrality or even significance of history make possible a doctrine of morality and of the worth and significance of human existence that can withstand the onslaught of lifeless nature and of atheism without giving way to nihilism or irrationality. The existence and coherence of this possibility emerges clearly in the ethical thought of Sartre, which may in large part be viewed as Kantian ethics stripped of the concept of the highest good and, therefore, of belief in God or immortality. Sartre's point of departure is identical to Kant's—the critique of materialism:

This theory [existentialism] is the only one which gives man dignity, the only one which does not reduce him to an object. The effect of all materialism is to treat all men, including the one philosophizing, as objects, that is, as an ensemble of determined reactions in no way distinguished from the ensemble of qualities and phenomena which constitute a table or a chair or a stone. We definitely wish to establish the human realm as an ensemble of values distinct from the material realm [Sartre, 1957, p. 37].

Human "dignity" must therefore be viewed as the *negation* of determinism: "There is no determinism, man is free, man is freedom" (p. 23). But freedom does not imply whim, caprice, untrammeled subjectivity; freedom inheres in will or choice, it *is* willing or choosing, and "though this may seem purely formal, it is highly important for keeping fantasy and caprice within bounds" (p. 41). The analysis of pure willing reveals that choice is not the affirmation but rather the negation of self-enclosed or self-referring subjectivism:

When we say that man chooses his own self, we mean that every one of us does likewise; but we also mean by this that in making this choice he also chooses all men. In fact, in creating the man that we want to be, there is not a single one of our acts which does not at the same time create an image of man as we think he ought to be.... Certainly, many people believe that when they do something, they themselves are the only ones involved, and when someone says to them, "What if everybody acted that way?" they shrug their shoulders and answer, "Everyone doesn't act that way." But really, one should always ask him, "What would happen if everybody looked at things that way?" [pp. 17–19].

Thus, the formal analysis of will provides at least a partial basis for moral judgment. First, "if we have defined man's situation as a free choice, with no excuses and no recourse, every man who takes refuge behind the excuse of his passions, every man who sets up a determinism, is a dishonest man" (pp. 44–45). Second, we want freedom for freedom's sake and in every particular circumstance. And in wanting freedom, we discover that it depends entirely on the freedom of others, and that the freedom of others depends on ours. . . . I am obliged to want others to have freedom at the same time that I want my own freedom. I can take freedom as my goal only if I take that of others as a goal as well [p. 46].

In all these respects, as Sartre explicitly concedes, he merely restates Kantian doctrine. Yet he rejects the orientation by the "highest good" and the belief in God or immortality. To a large extent, he does so on strictly Kantian grounds. If the essence of humanity = ethics = willing = freedom, then the analysis of ethics must proceed without reference to a determinate "human nature" that presents standards for choice, and it must deny that "non-will" ultimately has any effect on the act of moral choice (pp. 14–15). Thus:

the existentialist does not believe in the power of passion. He will never agree that a sweeping passion is a ravaging torrent which fatally leads a man to certain acts and is therefore an excuse. He thinks that man is responsible for his passion [p. 23].

No passion has any effect on the will unless and until it is *chosen,* and the will is not obligated to ascribe moral significance to any particular passion. When a passion is freely chosen, it becomes the basis for a moral orientation that excludes all others. In particular, there is nothing about the desire for happiness that is either universal or of a priori moral significance. Happiness can be rejected, e.g., in the name of "human solidarity." If chosen, it excludes other choices. "One may choose anything if it is on the grounds of free involvement." For Sartre, happiness, like everything external to the will, belongs to the material realm that in itself is valueless until chosen. Happiness has no special status that necessitates reflection on the conditions of its acquisition or coexistence with moral action (pp. 47–48).

Kant argues that the traditional theoretical arguments are inherently without merit and that only the requirements of morality can legitimate the belief in God. Implicitly accepting Kant's critique of theory, Sartre argues that morality does not lead to God either. All possible arguments having been excluded, atheism is the only honest position.* But, for Kant, God is the ground of hope not only for happiness but for the efficacy of moral action in the world. Sartre accepts this premise and rejects the moral significance of efficacy:

... we shall confine ourselves to reckoning only with what depends upon our will, or on the ensemble of probabilities which makes our action possible.... The moment the possibilities I am considering are not rigorously involved by my action, I ought to disengage myself from them, because no God, no scheme can adapt the world and its possibilities to my will [p. 29].

But of course the denial of the moral significance of efficacy lies at the core of Kantian ethics as well. In agreement with Kant, Sartre contends that morality must be viewed as the striving for holiness —the attempt to escape contingency and imperfection, to become God. But, he adds, this attempt is "in vain"; the moral impulse (and, therefore, man himself insofar as the core of his being is moral choice or striving) is a "useless passion" (p. 90). Yet the ultimate futility of moral action neither deprives it of moral significance nor releases man from the necessity of engaging in it. The primordial freedom of man withstands the indifference of the universe.

In short, Sartrian ethics attempts to demonstrate the self-sufficiency of Kantian moral principles without the concept of the

---

*Sartre does not explicitly argue for atheism in this rigorous fashion, but this construction is perhaps the only way of lending philosophical depth to his position. Otherwise atheism would be merely asserted as an arbitrary choice. He states: "Existentialism isn't so atheistic that it wears itself out showing that God doesn't exist. Rather, it declares that even if God did exist, that would change nothing" (p. 51). But Sartre cannot really maintain this position. For instance, he argues that "the existentialist ... thinks it very distressing that God does not exist, because all possibility of finding values in a heaven of ideas disappears with Him.... Dostoievsky said, 'If God didn't exist, everything would be possible.' That is the very starting point of existentialism. Indeed, everything is permissible if God does not exist..." (p. 22). But if the existence of God is a matter of indifference, it follows that everything is permissible *whether or not* God exists. Not only does this eliminate the basis for the existentialist's "distress" at the disappearance of God, it is incompatible with Sartre's most fundamental argument. Absolute human freedom can be affirmed only if the moral status of human nature is denied. But "when we conceive God as the Creator, He is generally thought of as a superior sort of artisan [and thus] the individual man is the realization of a certain concept in the divine intelligence" (p. 14). The moral insignificance of human nature can be affirmed only if its relation to the Divine is denied. Sartre cannot be indifferent to God; he must deny Him.

highest good. It has been charged that this effort fails because the ethics that results cannot be distinguished from a nihilism in which everything is permitted. Sartre defends himself against this charge:

Though the content of ethics is variable, a certain form of it is universal. Kant says that freedom desires both itself and the freedom of others. Granted. But he believes that the formal and the universal are enough to constitute an ethics. We, on the other hand, think that principles which are too abstract run aground in trying to decide action.... The content is always concrete and thereby unforeseeable; there is always the element of invention. The one thing that counts is knowing whether the inventing that has been done, has been done in the name of freedom [p. 47].

In effect, Sartre argues that the formal principle of freedom provides a basis for non-nihilistic moral choice and that in this respect existentialist ethics is neither more nor less nihilistic than the Kantian—merely more conscious of the gap between the formal principle and each concrete moral situation. Nor can it be argued that the concept of God bridges this gap in Kant's thought, for Kant insists that God is the *guarantor* of morality but not its *source:* the content of morality cannot be deduced from the idea of God because the idea of God is deduced from a morality the content of which is determined in advance. In this limited respect—the relation between the general and the particular in moral choice—Sartre's contention that the existence of God is a matter of indifference would seem to be justified.

Conclusion: Kant and Hegel

The "Idea for a Universal History" is an idea not only in the technical sense discussed earlier but also in that it is an outline or foundation rather than a completed, concrete work. In the Ninth Proposition Kant sketches the material that the concrete history would have to encompass: the influence of Greek history on the Romans, of the Romans on their barbarian conquerors, and so on down to the constitution of European states, "which will probably give law, eventually, to all the others." In each civilization the political and philosophical advances must be discovered, the immanent evil that led to destruction identified, and the mechanism laid bare whereby "a germ of enlightenment was left to be further developed by this overthrow and a higher level ... thus prepared...."* This is to a remarkable degree the project that Hegel executes. In fact, the introduction to Hegel's *Philosophy of History* bears a startling (though entirely unacknowledged) resemblance to the "Idea for a Universal History."† Yet in Hegel's thought all of the Kantian hesitation, ambiguity, and perplexity has vanished; the philosophy of history does not so much complete moral and political philosophy as engulf and annihilate it. We conclude with a brief comparision of the two thinkers that will clarify the equivocal status of Kant's philosophy of history.

Let us first enumerate the points at which Hegel is fully in agreement with Kant. (1) Purposiveness is undeniably present in lower organisms and individual human lives. It is unreasonable to ascribe purpose to the matter or individual parts of human existence and deny it to the whole, i.e., to world history (*Reason in History*, p. 18 [*S.W.* XI: 42]). (2) The spectacle of a course of human events that is disordered, a "slaughterbench" with no relation between good intentions and actualized consequences, leads to sorrow and disgust, a "revolt of the good will." Morality itself is endangered, for the attempt to actualize the good is incompatible with despair of any such possibility (pp. 26-27 [*S.W.* XI: 48-49]). (3) Reason is incompatible with the existence of historical chance; it commands us to believe that "the world of intelligence and of self-conscious willing is not abandoned to mere chance, but must manifest itself in the light of the rational Idea" (p. 12 [*S.W.* XI: 36]). (4) It is impermissible to have recourse to the "mystery" of God to explain the appearance of evil in the world; God's will is knowable, the principles of divine activity are revealed in and through the human spirit (p. 16 [*S.W.* XI: 41]). (5) History must therefore take the form of rational theodicy, the demonstration that apparent evil is necessary through the "recognition of the positive elements in which that negative element

* "Idea," p. 25 (VIII: 30). See the remarks in Kelly, 1969, pp. 177-78, on the respects in which the final chapter of *Pure Reason* proposes the same task in the realm of metaphysics.

† The general relation between Kantian and Hegelian historical thought is clearly recognized by Goldmann, 1971, p. 206. See also pp. 218-19, and Delbos, 1926, pp. 270, 272.

disappears as something subordinate and vanquished" (p. 18
[*S.W.* XI: 42]). (6) Like Kant, Hegel compares the philosopher of
history to Kepler, and he makes manifest an implication that Kant
had merely suggested: just as Kepler's knowledge of mathematical
forms preceded and made possible his discovery of concrete
regularities of celestial motion, so the knowledge of the Idea of
history is the basis for the discovery of lawful regularities in human
affairs. Rational history is essentially constitutive, projective, a
priori (p. 79 [*S.W.* XI: 102]). (7) Although both lower organisms
and human life are purposive (teleological), there is an essential
distinction. Organic purposiveness is direct and unhindered, each
member of the species (with the exception of a few freaks of nature)
reaching its end. Human purposiveness is an extended process of
struggle through time, i.e., mediated or dialectical (p. 69 [*S.W.*
XI: 90]). (8) The purpose or essence of humanity is freedom, of
which history is therefore the progressive realization (pp. 22–24
[*S.W.* XI: 44–46]). (9) History moves forward, not through plan or
moral intention but through the antagonism and struggle engendered by selfishness: the "need, the instinct, the inclination, and
passion of man . . . *nothing great in the world* has been accomplished without passion" (pp. 28–29 [*S.W.* XI: 51–52]). (10) Accordingly, even the most important actors on the world-historical
stage are unconscious of the final purpose to which their actions are
directed (p. 40 [*S.W.* XI: 60]). (11) The purpose of history is not
directly connected with human happiness. Happiness is particular
and variable; it pertains only to the lowest (i.e., animal) desires and
individuals. Reason or freedom is "abstract" and universal; there is
a sort of self-satisfaction in the self-subsisting grandeur of freedom,
but it is not directed toward happiness.* (12) Therefore, Rousseau's
ascription of freedom to savages must be rejected. Freedom (= morality) is fundamentally universal or lawful, a product of human
development that must be won through struggle (p. 54 [*S.W.* XI:
73]). (13) Moreover, genuine freedom is to be distinguished from
the merely negative freedom, the "common limitation" or "mutual constraint of all" that secures a "small space of liberty for
each" and is characteristic of liberal or bourgeois society. "The

*Pp. 33–34. See also pp. 36, 41ff., 54ff., 78ff., 91 (*L.* VIII: 71; *S.W.* XI: 58,
61ff., 72ff., 95ff., 115–16).

caprice of the individual is not freedom" (p. 50 [S.W. XI: 70]).
(14) Rather, freedom is obedience to self-made laws. "Law is the
objectivity of Spirit; it is will in its true form. Only the will that
obeys the law is free, for it obeys itself and, being in itself, is free"
(p. 53 [S.W. XI: 71]). (15) Although freedom, being universal, is
rational, it is fundamentally distinguished from enlightenment or
from the "positive sciences." Freedom is equally characteristic of
all men, even the most simple and innocent. "The religiousness,
the morality of a limited life—of a shepherd, a peasant—in their
concentrated inward limitation to a few and quite simple circumstances of life, has infinite value. It has the same value as the
religiousness and morality of a trained intellect and of an existence
rich in scope of relations and activities" (p. 48 [S.W. XI: 68]).
(16) As moral beings, men cannot be regarded only as means;
participating through morality in reason and freedom, they are
"ends in themselves" (pp. 44-45 [S.W. XI: 64]).

Beyond this large area of agreement, Hegel takes a series of steps
against which Kant was enjoined by his most basic moral and
theoretical principles. As we have seen, Kant's hesitation concerning the status of history can be largely traced to a moral
alternative—otherworldly transcendence through immortality of
the soul—and to theoretical uncertainties—the shortness of human
life, the possibility of cataclysm destroying the human race or even
the earth itself. Hegel flatly rejects the possibility of transcendence: "One may have all sorts of ideas about the Kingdom of
God, but it is always a realm of Spirit to be realized and brought
about in man" (p. 20 [L. VIII: 27-28]). And he silently ignores
the problems posed by the particularity and natural existence of
humanity; or, rather, he claims to be able to deduce this apparent
particularity from the character of reason itself and to show
therefore that man must be what he in fact is and must continue to
exist eternally.

Moreover, Kant's moral dilemma was occasioned by the fact that
history appears to require (indeed, to consist in) immoral acts.
Hegel recognizes the conflict but resolves it by asserting that the
end justifies the means, i.e., by denying that morality is the
highest thing.

The history of the world moves on a higher level than that proper to morality. . . . The demands and accomplishments of the absolute and final aim of Spirit, the working of Providence, lie above the obligations, responsibilities, and liabilities which are incumbent on the individuals in regard to their morality. . . . The deeds of the great men who are the individuals of world history thus appear justified not only in their intrinsic, unconscious significance but also from the point of view of world history. It is irrelevant and inappropriate from that point of view to raise moral claims against world historical acts and agents. They stand outside of morality. . . . World history . . . could in principle altogether ignore the sphere of morality and its often mentioned difference with politics. It could not only refrain from moral judgments . . . but leave individuals entirely out of view and unmentioned (pp. 82-83 [*S.W*. XI: 105-6]).

This position is grounded in Hegel's rejection of formal (Kantian) morality as existing outside of history and constituting an eternally valid standard for its judgment.

To be sure, morality participates in the universality of Reason, but Reason progresses. The content of morality is therefore everchanging. Moreover, this change corresponds to the actuality of history, for the universality of Reason manifests itself in concrete human affairs: "The universal must be not only something which the individual merely intends, but which is in existence" (p. 51 [*L*. VIII: 92]). Hence, "each individual is also the child of a people at a definite stage of its development . . . he must bring the will demanded by his people to his own consciousness, to articulation. The individual does not invent his own content; he is what he is by acting out the universal as his own content." This process is "the whole of ethical life" (pp. 37-38 [*L*. VIII: 73-74]). But the universality of each people is expressed in its political organization, the State, in which "freedom achieves its objectivity" (p. 53 [*S.W*. XI: 71]). It follows that the universality of moral law cannot be distinguished from that of political law. From this perspective, the Kantian distinction between moral and institutional progress disappears.

All the difficulties that Kant encounters in attempting to formulate a consistent philosophy of history may be traced back to his most fundamental theoretical premise: the heterogeneity of nature, viewed as lifeless matter in motion according to fixed laws, and freedom, manifesting itself in purely inward moral intention. On this basis it becomes almost impossible to account for the peculiar nature of man, the only being in which the two realms are conjoined. In particular, the means whereby inward intention can manifest itself as human action—labor, political life, antagonism, and striving—remains mysterious. The entire world of human affairs with which history must deal becomes a sort of twilight zone, a battleground of two contending forces that in principle cannot touch or affect one another.*

Hegel restores, or more than restores, the integrity and significance of this world; in making it possible to speak once again of action as the actualization of human purpose and to assign worth or dignity to striving and passion (i.e., to "character"), in a way he makes possible the return to the commonsense world as it is perceived by men who must act in the world and take their actions seriously. But this could be achieved only by denying the validity of the basic Kantian distinction. For Hegel, reason is the material of nature as well as of freedom. As such, it is no longer *opposed* by nature. It is then infinite power, "for Reason is not so impotent as to bring about only the ideal, and to remain in an existence outside of reality . . ." (*Reason in History*, p. 11 [*S.W.* XI: 35]). It is only on this basis that Hegel can conclude that "the actual world is as it ought to be, that the truly good, the universal divine Reason is the power capable of actualizing itself."†

In short, the Hegelian doctrines of labor and struggle, of concrete, historically contingent morality, of the moral significance of concrete political life, and of history itself, all rest on the

---

*See Kelly, 1969, pp. 106-13. Kelly's assertion that according to Kant "free causality is not simply restricted to a neverland of *ought* or of motive which cannot appear, but . . . makes itself the source of new sequences of phenomenal causality" (p. 110) goes considerably beyond the conclusion that Kant himself was willing to endorse unequivocally. Compare *Pure Reason*, p. 479 (A 558, B 586). See also Kroner, 1956, p. 54.

†P. 47 (*S.W.* XI: 67). Goldmann, 1971, p. 226, correctly argues that Hegel's philosophy of history rests on the overcoming of Kant's "rigid separation between philosophy and empirical anthropology." But one must inquire into the *grounds* of this separation; Kant believed it to be both morally and theoretically necessary. It might be argued that the Hegelian synthesis does violence to both morality and theoretical science. At any rate, the controversy between Kant and Hegel on this point cannot be settled within the domain of the sociology of knowledge, as Goldmann seems to think (see pp. 199, 206). See also Kroner, 1956, p. 110.

possibility of interpreting the natural world according to reason, i.e., dialectically, of abolishing the dualism of the human and the natural and replacing it with a dialectical monism in which nature as a fundamentally deficient mode of being that "has its substance outside of itself" is strictly subordinated to human freedom (*Reason in History*, p. 23 [*S.W.* XI: 44]). We cannot enter into this question, but we note that a profound (and sympathetic) modern interpreter of Hegel has felt compelled to admit that the Hegelian philosophy of nature consists in an illegitimate transposition of categories derived from and applicable to human existence alone.* (This is also the judgment of "History.") If, as seems reasonable, we must say that the nondialectical, materialistic natural science that deals with the natural world as lifeless substance reducible to mathematical determination in principle is capable of giving an adequate account of nature, then precisely the Kantian dilemmas return in full force. If dualistic ontology is "the principal philosophic task of the future" (Kojève, 1969, p. 215 n.), then we are compelled to take the difficulties of the Kantian analysis of human action, morality, and history seriously, for his perplexities are ours as well. We must ask, with Kant, "How can man be human in the midst of, and as partially

---

*Kojève, 1969, p. 212 n. Marx states this critique of Hegel in classic form in "Economic and Philosophical Manuscripts of 1844" (Marx, 1972, pp. 83-103). See especially pp. 91-93, 102-3. For an opposing view see Fackenheim, 1967, pp. 75-115. Fackenheim argues that Hegel propounds a threefold "mediation" of Nature, Spirit, and Idea that, among other results, "supersedes natural science but unequivocally grants this latter independent status" (p. 112)—i.e., allows for the incorporation of the realm of nature into a monistic synthesis without the need to ignore or contradict empirical scientific categories and conclusions. Yet, according to Fackenheim, this threefold mediation, the "Hegelian middle," presupposes that "the dualism between non-philosophic life and philosophic thought is . . . false," that the unity of these two is "a reality already *present in life* before philosophy comes upon the scene to *convert it into thought*. . . . The problem of the Hegelian middle thus turns into the problem of the relation between religious life and philosophic thought" (pp. 110-11). Fackenheim devotes the last chapter of his book to "The Crisis of the Hegelian Middle," the breakdown of the bourgeois Protestant world the assumed permanence of which had provided the necessary ground for Hegel's claim that the opposition between philosophy and life, thought and existence, had finally been overcome. Remarkably, Fackenheim does not elucidate the consequences of this *political* disintegration for the *theoretical* overcoming of dualism that Hegel attempts, but the strict logic of Fackenheim's argument requires the conclusion that the "Hegelian middle" collapses back into the Kantian dualism of nature and freedom, empirical existence and inward thought or intention.

belonging to, the nonhuman natural world?'' before proceeding
to a phenomenology of political life; and, like Kant, we must be
prepared to follow the inquiry wherever it leads, no matter how
strange the path or our final resting place might appear.*

*Thus one must endorse the conclusion of Hassner, 1972, pp. 592-93: "Even
if it be admitted . . . that Kant fails to reconcile the external and the internal,
necessity and freedom, nature and morality, the evidence of physics and the
testimony of conscience, it must nevertheless be considered whether there is not
in each of these terms something irreducible which Kant alone has caused to
emerge in all its power. The critic of Kant's political philosophy can doubtless win
victories either on the field of the concrete political phenomena examined on the
level appropriate to them, or by challenging the coherence of the system as a
whole; but if the victories are to be decisive the criticism should deal with the
foundations of Kant's thought." It has been the burden of this essay to argue
that the foundations of Kant's thought are the foundations of our thought as well
but that this becomes apparent only when we attempt to grasp our present
situation as a whole.

6   Conclusion

Throughout this study the investigation of the concept of history has proceeded on two planes, the analytic and the descriptive. Analysis of Kant's argument has shown that the concept of history is incapable of performing the task for which it was designed: the theoretical mediation between a natural world indifferent to human will and human will impotent to transform that world in accordance with its moral intention. Moreover, the concept of history could not be shown to flow deductively from the basic premises of Kant's thought. Yet it is not difficult to understand why the concept of history suggested itself to him. Dualism, which seemed unavoidable, produced the theoretical dilemma of mind-body interaction and the moral impasse of fatalism or despair; and existing philosophical solutions were either unintelligible or unacceptable.*

On the descriptive plane Kant's argument has fared better. His emphasis on the growing unification and "europeanization" of world politics, the increasing cost and technological complexity of warfare, the interaction between war and domestic policy, and the heightened importance of economic interdependence among nations is clearly of continuing significance. Yet, as we have seen, there is in Kant's historical thought a sharp distinction between institutional and moral change. He holds out to us the possibility

*The most prominent solution was Leibniz' argument in the *Monadology* for "pre-established harmony" between the body as the realm of material cause and soul as the realm of final cause, an argument that from Kant's point of view was both ungrounded and "transcendent"—outside the purview of theoretical reason. See Leibniz, 1962, pp. 268-69.

that institutional progress will lay the foundation for a sweeping moral reformation without really describing concretely the link between the former and the latter (indeed, while appearing to deny on theoretical grounds that any such link is possible). The two centuries of political practice since Kant wrote have sadly mirrored this theoretical hiatus without wholly undermining the moral expectations that he was so instrumental in evoking.

The gap between the descriptive suggestiveness of Kant's argument and its theoretical inadequacy would seem to imply the need for a new theoretical analysis of the phenomena to which he called attention. The fundamental question is: What sense can be made of the Kantian concept of history as a constraint on individual human action that (i) arises neither from physical obstacles in the external world nor from the decisions of other individuals and (ii) induces important changes in the modes of existence of political communities, perhaps of all mankind, as aggregates or totalities? The following hypothesis suggests itself.

To speak of "human nature" is to speak of a constraint on human action that is neither external to man nor chosen by him. Let us suppose that human nature consists in a complex of needs and desires and that human actions consist in the employment of means directed toward their satisfaction. Even if a chosen act is conducive to a desired end, it almost invariably has unintended consequences, consequences that may be irreversible. The accumulation of unintended consequences thus can alter radically the context within which future decisions must be made. Human action transforms the natural world, but in the process its products become part of the new environing world in response to which subsequent action occurs.* If it is the case that human needs and desires are changed when surrounding circumstances are altered, then the unintended consequences of action might include not only new *situations* within which choice occurs but also new *objects* of choice. The question inevitably arises whether any general theoretical propositions can be advanced to characterize this dialectical sequence of change.

In reconstructing the Kantian idea of history, one need not focus

---

*For discussions of this process from the standpoint of economics see Kahn, 1968, and Schelling, 1971.

solely on the unintended consequences of individual decisions; complementary conclusions may be reached through an analysis of the intended consequences of collective decisions. Political life consists in part in a succession of agreements or conventions adopted as guides for action. These conventions are intended not only to reflect and gratify but also to channel and transform desires. But there may be limits to the alteration of desire. If conventions come to leave desires unsatisfied or to demand impossible changes in them, a chain of events will be set in motion that will eventuate in altered conventions. Every political founding is a laying-down or "hypothesis" that creates a dialectic between itself and the desires of the human beings it regulates. Given a sufficiently acute knowledge of human nature, the fate of any particular set of conventions can be foreseen, at least in general terms. In short, the act of conventional agreement creates a limited realm within which actions can be understood as ordered and unified.

But this leaves open the possibility that human events are a combination of local intelligibility and general randomness—that each community transforms itself in ways unrelated either to other communities or to its own past through a series of more or less arbitrary systems of conventions. The overall intelligibility of human events depends on establishing some relations within sequences of such systems.

In chapter 1 "modernity" was characterized as the first epoch of human existence in which the political consequences of theoretical inquiry or science were widely viewed as salutary and in which the technological products of science were deliberately employed in public policy on a significant scale. If it were the case that the political acceptance of science is incompatible with the maintenance of certain types of political beliefs, actions, and modes of organization, then sequences of conventions might be viewed as progressively working out the consequences immanent in the original act of acceptance. The history of modernity would then emerge as the vector-sum of two rationally comprehensible forces —the development of political communities guided by the immanent logic of science, and the needs and desires of the human beings who constitute these communities.

This formulation suggests a tension or lack of total congruence between human desire and the consequences of science. One might reasonably object to this on the ground that the political acceptance of science was predicated from the beginning upon the promise that the fruits of science would gratify desire and would have been repudiated if that promise had ever come to seem implausible. In fact it *was* claimed by the original proponents of political technology that the fruits of science would gratify desire; but the ends of desire were explicitly defined as peace, prosperity, and power. Modern history might then be viewed as the actions produced by the tension between the *totality* of human desire and the limited conception of desire underlying the treaty of peace between science and politics, that conception containing enough of the whole to preponderate over the excluded elements. Our future will be determined by the answers to two questions: whether the unintended consequences of political technology at length will restrict the ability of that technology to fulfill its lavish promises; and whether the present dissatisfaction with the kinds of desires that technology gratifies, the kinds of human beings and political life with which it is compatible and tends to foster, is a restricted and transitory phenomenon or rather the expression of widespread and ineradicable human desires the repression of which is the precondition of the gratifications we now enjoy.

Bibliography

This bibliography does not purport to be comprehensive. It is a list of those books and articles that have materially contributed to the manner in which questions have been posed and examined in this study. For the best modern bibliography of the period from Rousseau to Hegel see George A. Kelly, *Idealism, Politics and History*. Klaus Weyand's study, *Kants Geschichtsphilosophie*, contains an exhaustive bibliography of works dealing with Kant's philosophy of history. Lewis White Beck's *A Commentary on Kant's Critique of Practical Reason* has an excellent bibliography of works focusing on Kantian moral philosophy. (Complete bibliographical information for these three books is furnished below.)

Primary Works

Alfarabi. *Philosophy of Plato and Aristotle.* Translated and with an introduction by Muhsin Mahdi. Ithaca: Cornell University Press, 1962.

Aquinas, Saint Thomas. *Commentary on the De Anima.* Translated by Kenelm Foster and Sylvester Humphries. New Haven and London: Yale University Press, 1965.

———. *Commentary on the Metaphysics.* 2 vols. Translated by John P. Rowan. Chicago: Regnery, 1961.

———. *Commentary on the Nicomachean Ethics.* 2 vols. Translated by C. I. Litzinger. Chicago: Regnery, 1964.

Aristotle. *Metaphysics.* Translated by Hippocrates G. Apostle. Bloomington and London: Indiana University Press, 1966.

———. *Nichomachean Ethics.* Translated by H. Rackham. Loeb Classical Library No. 73. London: William Heinemann, Ltd., 1962.

———. *On the Soul.* Translated by W. S. Hett. Loeb Classical Library. London: William Heinemann, Ltd., 1935.

———. *Physics.* 2 vols. Translated by Philip H. Wicksteed and Francis M. Cornford. Loeb Classical Library. London: William Heinemann, Ltd., 1929.

————. *Poetics*. Translated by W. Hamilton Fyfe. Loeb Classical Library. London: William Heinemann, Ltd., 1965.

————. *Politics*. Translated by Ernest Barker. New York and London: Oxford University Press, 1958.

Bacon, Francis. *The New Organon*. Library of Liberal Arts No. 97. Indianapolis and New York: Bobbs-Merrill, 1960.

Descartes, René. *Philosophical Works*. 2 vols. Translated by Elizabeth S. Haldane and G. R. T. Ross. New York: Dover, 1955.

Galilei, Galileo. *Discoveries and Opinions of Galileo*. Edited and translated by Stillman Drake. Garden City: Doubleday, 1957.

Hegel, Georg Wilhelm Friedrich. *Sämtliche Werke*. 26 vols. Edited by Hermann Glockner. Stuttgart: Frommann, 1927–40.

————. *Hegel Als Geschichtsphilosoph. Sämtliche Werke*. Edited by Georg Lasson. Leipzig: Meiner, 1920. Volume 8.

————. *Encyclopedia of the Philosophical Sciences*. Vol. 1: *Logic*. Translated by William Wallace. Oxford: Clarendon Press, 1892. Vol. 2: *Philosophy of Nature*. Translated by A. V. Miller. Oxford: Clarendon Press, 1970. Vol. 3: *Philosophy of Mind*. Translated by A. V. Miller and William Wallace. Oxford: Clarendon Press, 1971.

————. *Lectures on the History of Philosophy*. 3 vols. Edited and translated by E. S. Haldane and Frances H. Simson. London: Routledge and Kegan Paul, 1968.

————. *Phenomenology of Mind*. Translated by J. B. Baillie. New York: Harper and Row, 1967.

————. *Philosophy of History*. Translated by J. Sibree. New York: Dover, 1956. "Introduction" translated by Robert S. Hartman under the title *Reason in History*. Indianapolis and New York: Bobbs-Merrill, 1953.

Hobbes, Thomas. *Leviathan*. Edited by Michael Oakeshott. Blackwell: Oxford, 1957.

Kant, Immanuel. *Gesammelte Schriften*. 24 vols. Berlin: Reimer, 1902–64.

————. *Critique of Judgment*. Translated by J. H. Bernard. Hafner Library of Classics No. 14. New York: Hafner, 1964.

————. *Critique of Practical Reason*. Translated by Lewis White Beck. Library of Liberal Arts No. 52. Indianapolis: Bobbs-Merrill, 1956.

————. *Critique of Pure Reason*. Translated by Norman Kemp Smith. London: Macmillan, Ltd., 1963.

————. *Education*. Translated by Annette Churton. Ann Arbor: University of Michigan Press, 1960.

————. *Foundations of the Metaphysics of Morals*. Translated by Lewis White Beck. Library of Liberal Arts No. 113. Indianapolis and New York: Bobbs-Merrill, 1959.

————. *Lectures on Ethics*. Translated by Louis Infield. New York: Harper and Row, 1963.

————. *Metaphysical Foundations of Natural Science*. Translated by

James Ellington. Library of Liberal Arts No. 108. Indianapolis and
New York: Bobbs-Merrill, 1970.

———. *Metaphysics of Morals.* Part 1: *The Metaphysical Elements of
Justice.* Translated by John Ladd. Library of Liberal Arts No. 72.
Indianapolis and New York: Bobbs-Merrill, 1965. Part 2: *The
Doctrine of Virtue.* Translated by Mary J. Gregor. New York and
Evanston: Harper and Row, 1964.

———. *Observations on the Feeling of the Beautiful and Sublime.* Translated by John T. Goldthwait. Berkeley and Los Angeles: University
of California Press, 1965.

———. *On History.* Edited by Lewis White Beck. Translated by Lewis
White Beck, Robert E. Anchor, and Emil L. Fackenheim. Library of
Liberal Arts No. 162. Indianapolis and New York: Bobbs-Merrill,
1963.

———. *Kant's Political Writings.* Edited by Hans Reiss. Translated by H.
B. Nisbet. Cambridge: Cambridge University Press, 1971.

———. *Religion within the Limits of Reason Alone.* Translated by
Theodore M. Greene and Hoyt H. Hudson. New York and
Evanston: Harper and Row, 1960.

———. *Universal Natural History and Theory of the Heavens.* Translated
by W. Hastie. Ann Arbor: University of Michigan Press, 1969.

Leibniz, Gottfried Wilhelm. *Basic Writings.* Translated by George R.
Montgomery. La Salle: Open Court, 1962.

Lucretius. *The Nature of the Universe.* Translated by Ronald Latham. Bal-
timore: Penguin, 1964.

Marx, Karl, and Frederick Engels. *The Marx-Engels Reader.* Edited by
Robert C. Tucker. New York: Norton, 1972.

Newton, Isaac. *Newton's Philosophy of Nature.* Edited by H. S. Thayer.
Hafner Library of Classics No. 16. New York: Hafner, 1953.

Nietzsche, Friedrich. *Joyful Wisdom.* Translated by Thomas Common.
New York: Ungar, 1964.

———. *Use and Abuse of History.* Translated by Adrian Collins. Library
of Liberal Arts No. 11. Indianapolis and New York: Bobbs-Merrill,
1957.

Plato. *Gorgias.* Translated by W. C. Helmbold. Indianapolis and New
York: Bobbs-Merrill, 1952.

———. *Laws.* 2 vols. Translated by R. G. Bury. Loeb Classical Library.
London: William Heinemann. Ltd. 1961.

———. *Republic.* Translated by Allan Bloom. New York and London:
Basic Books, 1968.

Rousseau, Jean-Jacques. *Du Contrat Social.* Paris: Garnier, 1962.

———. *Oeuvres complètes.* 3 vols. Edited by Bernard Gagnebin and Mar-
cel Raymond. Paris: Gallimard, 1959-64.

———. *First and Second Discourses.* Translated by Roger D. and Judith R.
Masters. New York: Saint Martin's Press, 1964.

Schopenhauer, Arthur. *Essay on the Freedom of the Will.* Translated by

Konstantin Kolenda. Library of Liberal Arts No. 70. New York: Liberal Arts Press, 1960.

Smith, Adam. *The Wealth of Nations.* New York: Modern Library, 1937.

Spinoza, Benedict de. *Works.* 2 vols. Translated by R. H. M. Elwes. New York: Dover, 1951.

Tocqueville, Alexis de. *Democracy in America.* Edited by J. P. Mayer. Translated by George Lawrence. Garden City: Doubleday, 1969.

Vico, Giambattista. *The New Science.* Edited and translated by Thomas Goddard Bergin and Max Harold Fisch. Ithaca and London: Cornell University Press, 1970.

Twentieth-Century Works

Ando, Takatsura. *Aristotle's Theory of Practical Cognition.* The Hague: Nijhoff, 1965.

Arendt, Hannah. *Between Past and Future.* New York: Viking, 1968.

Aron, Raymond. *Introduction to the Philosophy of History.* London: Weidenfeld and Nicolson, 1961.

Aubenque, Pierre. *La Prudence Chez Aristote.* Paris: Presses Universitaires de France, 1963.

Beck, Lewis White. *A Commentary on Kant's Critique of Practical Reason.* Chicago: University of Chicago Press, 1960.

———. *Studies in the Philosophy of Kant.* Indianapolis: Bobbs-Merrill, 1965.

Burtt, Edwin Arthur. *The Metaphysical Foundations of Modern Science.* Garden City: Doubleday, 1932.

Bury, J. B. *The Idea of Progress.* New York: Macmillan, 1932.

Cassirer, Ernst. *The Philosophy of the Enlightenment.* Boston: Beacon Press, 1960.

———. *Rousseau, Kant, Goethe.* New York: Harper and Row, 1963.

Cohen, Morris R. *The Meaning of Human History.* La Salle: Open Court, 1961.

Collingwood, R. G. *Essays in the Philosophy of History.* Edited by W. Debbins. New York: McGraw-Hill, 1966.

———. *The Idea of History.* Oxford and New York: Oxford University Press, 1967.

———. *The Idea of Nature.* Oxford and New York: Oxford University Press, 1965.

Cranston, Maurice, and Richard S. Peters, eds. *Hobbes and Rousseau.* Garden City: Doubleday, 1972.

Delbos, Victor. *La Philosophie Pratique de Kant.* Paris: Alcan, 1926.

Dray, William H. *Laws and Explanation in History.* Oxford: Oxford University Press, 1964.

———. *Philosophy of History.* Englewood Cliffs: Prentice-Hall, 1964.

Fackenheim, Emil L. "Kant and Radical Evil." *University of Toronto Quarterly* 23 (1954): 339-53.

———. "Kant's Concept of History." *Kant-studien* 48 (1957): 381-98.

———. *Metaphysics and Historicity*. Milwaukee: Marquette University Press, 1961.

———. *The Religious Dimension in Hegel's Thought*. Bloomington and London: Indiana University Press, 1967.

Fetscher, Iring. "Rousseau's Concepts of Freedom in the Light of His Philosophy of History." *Nomos IV: Liberty*. Edited by Carl J. Friedrich. New York: Atherton, 1962, pp. 29-56.

Forkosch, Morris D., ed. *The Political Philosophy of Arnold Brecht*. New York: Exposition Press, 1954.

Gauthier, René Antonin. *La Morale d'Aristote*. Paris: Presses Universitaires de France, 1958.

Goldmann, Lucien. *Immanuel Kant*. Translated by Robert Black. London: NLB, 1971.

Hassner, Pierre. "Les concepts de guerre et de paix chez Kant." *Revue française de science politique* 11 (1969): 642-70.

———. "Immanuel Kant." *History of Political Philosophy*, 2d ed. Edited by Leo Strauss and Joseph Cropsey. Chicago: Rand McNally, 1972, pp. 554-93.

———. "Situation de la philosophie politique chez Kant." *Annales de philosophie politique* 4 (1962): 77-103.

Heidegger, Martin. *Being and Time*. Translated by John Macquarrie and Edward Robinson. New York and Evanston: Harper and Row, 1962.

———. *The Essence of Reasons*. Translated by Terrence Malick. Evanston: Northwestern University Press, 1969.

———. *An Introduction to Metaphysics*. Translated by Ralph Manheim. Garden City: Doubleday, 1961.

———. *What is Philosophy?* Translated by William Kluback and Jean T. Wilde. New Haven: College and University Press Publishers, 1958.

———. *What Is a Thing?* Translated by W. B. Barton, Jr., and Vera Deutsch. Chicago: Regnery, 1967.

Heisenberg, Werner. *Physics and Philosophy*. New York: Harper and Row, 1962.

Hook, Sidney, ed. *Determinism and Freedom in the Age of Modern Science*. New York: Collier, 1968.

———., ed. *Philosophy and History*. New York: New York University Press, 1963.

Husserl, Edmund. *Phenomenology and the Crisis of Philosophy*. Translated by Quentin Lauer. New York: Harper and Row, 1965.

Hyppolite, Jean. *Studies in Marx and Hegel*. Translated by John O'Neill. New York and London: Basic Books, 1969.

Jaffa, Harry. *Thomism and Aristotelianism*. Chicago: University of Chicago Press, 1952.

Jonas, Hans. *The Phenomenon of Life*. New York: Dell, 1966.

Kahn, Alfred E. "The Tyranny of Small Decisions: Market Failures, Imperfections, and the Limits of Econometrics." *Economic Theories of International Politics*. Edited by Bruce M. Russett. Chicago: Markham, 1968, pp. 522-37.

Kelly, George A. *Idealism, Politics and History: Sources of Hegelian Thought*. Cambridge: Cambridge University Press, 1969.

Klein, Jacob. "Phenomenology and the History of Science." *Philosophical Essays in Memory of Edmund Husserl*. Edited by Marvin Farber. Cambridge, Mass.: Harvard University Press, 1940, pp. 143-63.

Kojève, Alexandre. "Hegel, Marx and Christianity." Translated by Hilail Gildin. *Interpretation* 1 (Summer, 1971): 21-42.

———. *Introduction to the Reading of Hegel*. Edited by Allan Bloom. Translated by James H. Nichols, Jr. New York and London: Basic Books, 1969.

Kroner, Richard. *Kant's Weltanschauung*. Translated by John E. Smith. Chicago: University of Chicago Press, 1956.

Krüger, Gerhard. *Critique et Morale Chez Kant*. Paris: Beauchesne, 1961.

Kuhn, Thomas S. *The Structure of Scientific Revolutions*. Chicago and London: University of Chicago Press, 1969.

Lakatos, Imre, and Alan Musgrave, eds. *Criticism and the Growth of Knowledge*. Cambridge: Cambridge University Press, 1970.

Löwith, Karl. *Meaning in History*. Chicago and London: University of Chicago Press, 1962.

———. *Nature, History, and Existentialism*. Edited by Arnold Levison. Evanston: Northwestern University Press, 1966.

Mahdi, Muhsin. *Ibn Khaldun's Philosophy of History*. Chicago: University of Chicago Press, 1964.

McFarland, John D. *Kant's Concept of Teleology*. Edinburgh: Edinburgh University Press, 1970.

Michelakis, Emmanuel M. *Aristotle's Theory of Practical Principles*. Athens: Cleisiounis Press, 1961.

Milo, Ronald D. *Aristotle on Practical Knowledge and Weakness of Will*. The Hague: Mouton, 1966.

Oates, Whitney Jennings. *Aristotle and the Problem of Value*. Princeton: Princeton University Press, 1963.

Rawls, John. *A Theory of Justice*. Cambridge, Mass.: Harvard University Press, Belknap Press, 1971.

Rosen, Stanley. *Nihilism: A Philosophical Essay*. New Haven and London: Yale University Press, 1969.

Ross, W. D. *Aristotle*. London: Methuen, 1923.

Sartre, Jean-Paul. *Existentialism and Human Emotions*. New York: Philosophical Library, 1957.

Schelling Thomas C. "On the Ecology of Micromotives." *The Public Interest* 25 (Fall, 1971): 61-98.

Strauss, Leo. *The City and Man*. Chicago: Rand McNally, 1964.

―――. *Natural Right and History*. Chicago and London: University of Chicago Press, 1965a.

―――. "Jerusalem and Athens: Some Preliminary Reflections." *City College Papers* No. 6. New York; The City College, 1967.

―――. *On Tyranny*. Ithaca: Cornell University Press, 1968.

―――. "Philosophy as Rigorous Science and Political Philosophy." *Interpretation* 2 (Summer, 1972): 1-9.

―――. *The Political Philosophy of Hobbes: Its Basis and Its Genesis*. Translated by Elsa M. Sinclair. Chicago and London: University of Chicago Press, 1963.

―――. *Spinoza's Critique of Religion*. New York: Schocken Books, 1965b.

―――. *Thoughts on Machiavelli*. Seattle and London: University of Washington Press, 1969.

―――. *What is Political Philosophy?* New York: Free Press, 1959.

Vlachos, Georges. *La Pensée politique de Kant: Metaphysique de l'ordre et dialectique de progrès*. Paris: Presses Universitaires de France, 1962.

Walsh, James J. *Aristotle's Conception of Moral Weakness*. New York: Columbia University Press, 1963.

Walsh, W. H. *Philosophy of History: An Introduction*. New York: Harper and Row, 1966.

Weyand, Klaus. *Kants Geschichtsphilosophie: Ihre Entwicklung und ihr Verhältnis zur Aufklärüng. Kant-studien,* Ergänzungshefte No. 85. Cologne: Kolner-Universitäts-Verlag, 1963.

Winner, Langdon. "Autonomous Technology and Political Thought." Unpublished dissertation. University of California, Berkeley, 1973.

Note. After this study was completed and as it was going to press, I received Michel Despland's *Kant on History and Religion* (Montreal and London: McGill-Queen's University Press, 1973). Though primarily concerned with the philosophy of religion, Despland's book contains a useful general treatment of the problem of history in Kant's thought as well as the first English translation of Kant's essay "On the failure of all attempted philosophical theodicies." The bibliography adds some items not contained in those referred to above. I regret that Despland's book was not available during the writing of this study, although I believe that Despland's emphasis on possible continuities between Kant's early and mature periods leads to a blurring of the rigor of Kant's mature thought at several important points.

Index of Passages Cited from Kant's Works

(For complete information on German editions, English translations, and abbreviations, see the "Note on Citations," pp. xi–xiv.)

German edition	English translation	Text
"An Old Question"		
VII:82	141	250
VII:84	142f.	38
VII:85	143	29
VII:87 n.	146 n.	29
VII:89	148	248, 249
VII:91f.	151	246, 249
"Conjectural Beginning"		
VIII:109	53	65, 76
VIII:110	54	77
VIII:111	55f.	78, 79
VIII:112	56	79
VIII:113	57f.	79, 80
VIII:114	58f.	80, 81, 96
VIII:115	59f.	70, 81, 82, 89, 100
VIII:116	60ff.	82, 83, 94
VIII:116 n.	61 n.	83
VIII:117f.	62f.	70, 83
VIII:117f.n.	61 f. n.	83, 84, 85, 92
VIII:118ff.	63ff.	87
VIII:119	63	89
VIII:120f.	65f.	71, 74, 90, 92
VIII:121	67	72, 73
VIII:122	67f.	72, 73
VIII:123	68	73, 74, 93

Index of Names
and Subjects